citizenship today

Approved publication

OCR
RECOGNISING ACHIEVEMENT

Jenny Wales

Contents

Unit 1:

Rights and

responsibilities

getting started as an active citizen

Rights with responsibilities

Getting you thinking

In 2005, more than 980 people were injured by fireworks. Some were seriously hurt

1 Where do most firework accidents happen?
2 Make lists of the rights and responsibilities of parents and children at private firework displays.
3 You must be over 18 to buy fireworks, and yet 50 per cent of all injuries were to children under 18. Who do you think is to blame for these accidents:

- companies that make fireworks
- shops that sell fireworks
- parents
- people who organise public displays
- the police
- the children themselves?

Give reasons for your answer.

4 What would you do to reduce the number of accidents with fireworks?
5 Turn your suggestions for question 4 into a firework safety code.

Firework injuries in the UK

Age groups of young people injured

- Under 13: 281
- Over 20: 422
- 13–17: 213
- 18–20: 69

Place where accident occurred

- Indoors 25
- Other 6
- Street or other public place 247
- Family or private party 475
- Large public display 121
- Semi-public party (e.g. scouts, club) 38

Source: Firework injury statistics 2005, BERR

Rights and responsibilities

Everyone over 18 has a right to buy fireworks. This right, like many others, brings with it certain responsibilities. You must follow the firework code: never throw a lighted firework at anyone, and never set them off in the street where they might alarm pets, or disturb elderly neighbours who have a right to peace and quiet. The age limit for buying fireworks is set by law at 18 because this is the age at which the law expects people to be responsible enough to handle fireworks.

Rights and responsibilities are best thought of as two sides of the same coin. You have a right to own a bike and ride it down your street, but you also have a **responsibility** to ride it carefully so you don't endanger pedestrians or other road users. For example, if you ride without lights in the dark, you could cause a motorist to swerve and crash while trying to avoid you. Even if no one was hurt in the accident, it could cause problems for the driver if they need their car to do their job.

You will find out about the link between rights and responsibilities.

Rights at home

Being a member of a family can be complicated. We have to share and work together but it is not always easy. Families often make rules about bedtimes, when to be home and dividing up the chores. These are the responsibilities we have to each other. If people **respect** each other, life goes more smoothly because everyone recognises the needs of others.

Rights and age limits

As we grow up, we become increasingly able to make decisions about the difference between right and wrong, and how we should behave. This has been taken into account in the laws that tell us what we can do at different ages.

1 Why does the law impose age limits like these?

2 Which of these age limits would you change? Explain why.

3 Who is being protected by each of these age limits?

Some of your legal rights in the UK

Age	10	13	16	17	18
	Criminal responsibility	Buy a pet on your own Get a part-time job	Get married Leave school Work full time Buy a lottery ticket Ride a moped	Drive a car Pilot a plane	Vote in an election Make a will Buy fireworks

Action

Research at what age and under what conditions young people have a legal right to drink alcohol. Carry out a survey to find out what your group thinks about these rights and age limits. How easy is it to police these laws?

Check your understanding

1 List some responsibilities that go with the following rights: the right to an education; the right to drink alcohol; the right to own and drive a car.

2 What rights and responsibilities do you have at home? Are there any you would like to change? If so, explain why. What effect would the changes have on other people?

... another point of view?

'People should never have rights without responsibilities.'

Do you agree with this statement? Give reasons for your opinion, showing you have considered another point of view.

Key Terms

respect: to have a good opinion of someone

responsibility: something it is your duty to do or to look after

What are human rights?

Getting you thinking

1 What are these children deprived of?
2 Make a list of the things you think every child should have.
3 Use your list to write a statement of children's rights.

Human rights

People all over the world suffer because their basic needs are not met. Some people's freedoms are limited by the country in which they live. Nobody should live without these basic **human rights**:

- the right to education
- the right to work
- the right to fair conditions at work
- the right to travel
- the right to food and clothes
- the right to healthcare
- the right to meet with friends
- the right to own property
- the right to follow your religion
- the right to marry and have children
- the rights of minorities to be treated the same as the majority.

1 Which of the rights listed above are the most important to you? Why?
2 Can you think of some situations where any of your rights might be threatened?
3 What examples are there in the news of people's human rights being threatened?

The case of A versus the United Kingdom

A nine-year-old boy was beaten with a cane by his stepfather. When taken to court, his stepfather claimed that his actions were within English law, which allows parents to use 'reasonable force' to punish a child. He was found not guilty. The boy's lawyers took the case to the European Court of Human Rights, which decided that the boy had suffered 'cruel, inhuman and degrading punishment'.

The boy was awarded £10,000 damages and the UK government agreed to change the law to give better protection in future.

There has still been no change in the law. Parents can still use 'reasonable force'.

You will find out about human rights and how they affect us.

The United Nations and human rights

The United Nations is an international organisation. It was set up in 1945 and most countries in the world now belong. Together, these members have developed two important statements of human rights. The Universal **Declaration** of Human Rights was created in 1948 and the **Convention** on the Rights of the Child was agreed in 1981.

The Convention on the Rights of the Child (CRC)

This **convention** requires governments all around the world to think about the needs of young people, and to consult them about matters that affect them, such as education, family life, law and order. Millions of young people do not have relatives to look after them; those caught up in civil wars in Africa, for instance. The CRC recognises this and says that young people must have rights of their own; rights that don't depend on parents or other adults.

There are still 250,000 children serving as soldiers around the world. The CRC states that 'Governments should not allow children under 15 to join the army.'

Action

Gathering samples of everyone's DNA might help to catch criminals. Look at the UDHR and decide whether this action would contradict any of its articles.

Can you think of any other situations in which different human rights would come into conflict with one another?

Check your understanding

1 Why was the Universal Declaration of Human Rights written?
2 What is the main difference between the scope of the Universal Declaration of Human Rights and that of the European Convention on Human Rights?
3 What can European citizens do if they feel their human rights are being denied?
4 Does everyone have the rights that are set out in the UDHR and the ECHR? Give examples.

These statements set out standards for everyone, everywhere; but in many parts of the world people's human rights are still abused. The Declaration offers guidance for countries but cannot be enforced legally if a country's laws do not take it up. The UK, for example, has its own Human Rights **Act** which sets out how the rights will be applied.

Universal Declaration of Human Rights (UDHR)

The UDHR was drawn up by world leaders after the Second World War. They wanted to prevent such terrible things happening again. It states that everyone has a right to life and liberty, freedom of speech and movement, a fair wage, a fair trial, education and many other basic human rights.

Huang Qi was arrested. He had been involved in assisting families to bring a legal case against the local authorities. Their children had died when school buildings collapsed in the earthquake

The European Union and Human Rights

The European Convention on Human Rights (ECHR) was created in 1950. It sets the framework for European countries. If the residents of one country don't think they have had a fair response from the courts, they can take their case to the European Court of Human Rights.

Key Terms

Act: a law passed by Parliament

convention: an agreement (often between governments)

declaration: a document setting down aims and intentions

human rights: things that people are morally or legally allowed to do or have

Taking part

Getting you thinking

1 How are these young people participating in school life?

2 Do you take part in school life in other ways?

3 One of them has a complaint. What could they do about it?

4 Do you think participating in school life affects how students think about the school?

> We've got to do something about the parents who park on the zig zag lines. One Year 7 nearly got knocked over yesterday.

> I'm so fed up! I want to do Business Studies next year but it doesn't fit with Spanish.

> Must go – I've got to pay my deposit for the trip to the First World War sites.

> There's a governors' meeting tonight. We're discussing the plans for the new building.

> I'm off to the school council meeting. We're making plans for the new minibus.

> What are you doing in Community Week? We're running a Sports Special at the primary school.

BUDDY

Joining in

All schools have different ways in which students can join in. For example, there are stories of students painting the social areas of their school or making an environmental garden, and many schools run projects where students work together to combat problems such as bullying.

All these ways of joining in help people to have more respect for the school and their fellow students. If you have created and looked after something, or have worked hard to make the school a better place, you want it to stay like that. If you see others spoiling it in some way, you will probably want to stop them.

A school where there is lots of participation is likely to have many students who have a sense of belonging and, therefore, respect its way of life.

Students and staff during a school council meeting

You will investigate how you can take responsible action to develop the school community.

Having a voice

There are other ways in which students can help to run the school. Do you have a **school council**? In most schools where they operate, every class and year group has a representative on the council. Sometimes there may be year-group councils, because younger students can find it hard to be heard when in meetings with older students. The school council will discuss things that they want changing, or comment on proposals from the staff.

When all students in school feel that they have a voice, they are likely to be happier about the decisions that are made. When people have listened to the arguments, they are more likely to respect the decisions that have been made, even if they do not agree with them.

What decisions?

The level of involvement of the council can vary, but many are consulted when important decisions, such as teacher appointments, are made. One newly appointed deputy headteacher said, 'The toughest part of the whole interview was the one with the students.' It was tough because he respected the students' views and knew that these were the people he had to be able to influence if he was to have a successful future. It's much easier to work with people if they respect you.

City Challenge

Having seen the benefits that a genuine, whole-school student voice can have in turning around struggling schools, the government, through the City Challenge, is subsidising local authority advisers to enable them to become school council experts.

The subsidy is part of a government initiative to stop the cycle of under-achievement among disadvantaged children in primary and secondary schools in Greater London, Greater Manchester and The Black Country. This programme aims to produce more outstanding schools, to help schools to increase performance in key subjects, and to significantly improve student achievement.

- Why do you think an effective school council might help schools to raise achievement?

Action

1. Does your school have a school council? If it does, what has it discussed recently? If it doesn't have a council, do you think it should? Why?
2. What issues would you like to raise through the school council?
3. Do you think your school council is effective? Explain your answer.
4. What could you do to make it more effective?

Check your understanding

1. In what ways can you join in as part of the school community?
2. In your own words, say why it can be useful to have a school council.
3. How does it benefit:
   a you
   b others?

... another point of view?

'It's easier to work with people if they respect you.'

Do you agree with this statement? Give reasons for your opinion, showing you have considered another point of view. Think of examples where working together could be made easier if those taking part had more respect for each other.

Key Terms

school council: a group of people who represent the classes and year groups of the school. They give students the opportunity to participate in decision making

What is an economy?

Getting you thinking

1 How many of these people provide a product or service that we might buy or use?

2 List those products or services that you think are supplied by the council or government.

3 Do any of the people provide goods or services without getting paid?

4 How many are consumers of goods and services?

5 Make as many links as you can between these people.

6 Which of the people or services do you think might need more financial support?

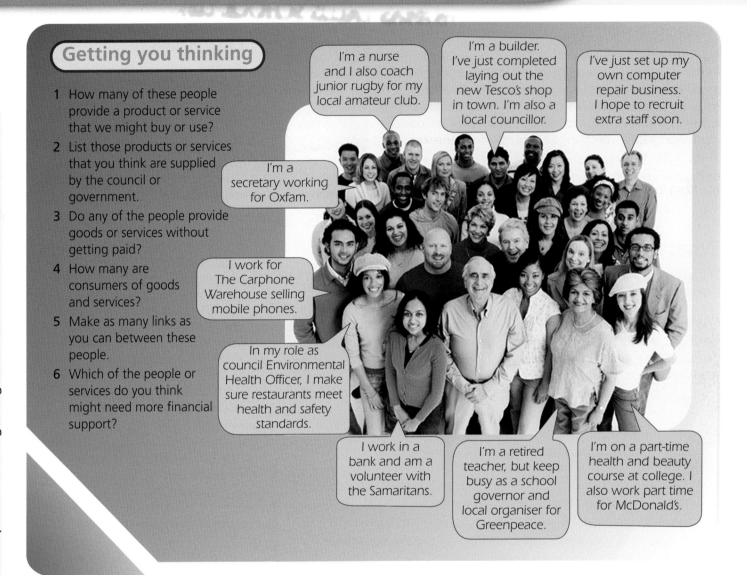

I'm a nurse and I also coach junior rugby for my local amateur club.

I'm a builder. I've just completed laying out the new Tesco's shop in town. I'm also a local councillor.

I've just set up my own computer repair business. I hope to recruit extra staff soon.

I'm a secretary working for Oxfam.

I work for The Carphone Warehouse selling mobile phones.

In my role as council Environmental Health Officer, I make sure restaurants meet health and safety standards.

I work in a bank and am a volunteer with the Samaritans.

I'm a retired teacher, but keep busy as a school governor and local organiser for Greenpeace.

I'm on a part-time health and beauty course at college. I also work part time for McDonald's.

What is an economy?

Everyone in the United Kingdom is part of the **economy** as a consumer, producer or citizen.

We are all consumers: whatever our age, we buy the products of business.

Some of us are producers who help make products or provide services. That includes the part-time employee for McDonald's, as well as the secretary working for Oxfam.

Private and public sector

Most of the things we buy are made by businesses in the **private sector**. These businesses are run by individuals or **shareholders**. A shareholder owns part of the company but leaves the organisation to its managers.

The main objective of businesses in the private sector is to make a **profit** for their owners, but the private sector also includes charities that raise money for good causes.

The rest of the economy is owned or run by the government and local councils. This is called the **public sector**. It includes social services, fire and police, education, defence, law, community and sports centres, housing and transport. A key objective for the public sector is to satisfy local residents. If it fails to do so, the political party that controls the council may not be re-elected at the next election.

You will find out what we mean by the economy and how you fit into it.

The power of competition

The economy is fired by people wanting to buy things. Businesses will provide these things if there is a profit to be made. If consumers buy less of a product, less will be produced. The resources that were used to make it may be used by another business for another purpose. Many food shops in town centres have closed because people use out-of-town supermarkets. The empty shops, the resources, are now used by other businesses, such as mobile phone shops. Food shops are also coming back into town as small convenience stores. Businesses want to make a profit and will look for new opportunities.

What would happen if everyone had to pay for healthcare?

Is it fair?

People who don't have enough money to pay for things they need and want aren't able to have them.

If everything was provided by the private sector, many people would suffer. If you can't afford education and are in poor health, it can be difficult to find a job and do the things other people do.

As a result, the government provides public sector services and other social benefits. Some are free for all, whilst others are provided according to need. We pay taxes to cover the costs of these and other services.

What effect does competition have on business?

1.2 Our rights and responsibilities as citizens within the economy and welfare systems

Action

Do a survey of ten people you know to find out how they contribute to our economy. You could ask whether they produce goods or services. Do they work in the private or public sector? What have been their major purchases over the past year?

Check your understanding

1 What makes up the economy?
2 What is the difference between the private sector and the public sector?
3 Why do we need the public sector?
4 Why do the government and local councils collect taxes?
5 What effect does it have when supermarkets move back into the high street?

... another point of view?

'Taxes are just a burden. I don't want to pay them.'
Do you agree with this statement? Give reasons for your opinion, showing you have considered another point of view.

Key Terms

consumer: a person who buys goods or services for their own needs

economy: this is made up of all the organisations that provide goods and services, and all the individuals and organisations that buy them

private sector: this section of the economy is made up of businesses or organisations that are owned by individuals or by shareholders

profit: the money that you gain when you sell something for more than you paid for it or than it cost to make

public sector: this is made up of organisations owned or run by the government and local councils

shareholder: someone who owns part of a business by owning shares in a company

Your role in the economy

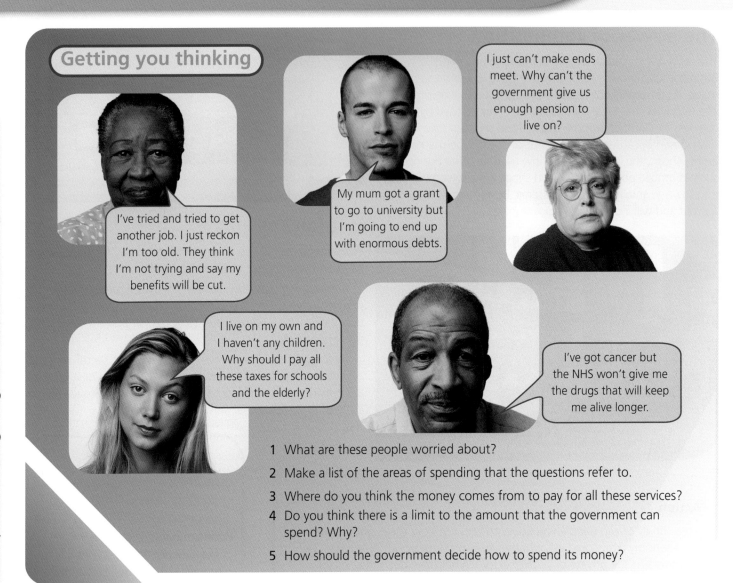

Getting you thinking

I've tried and tried to get another job. I just reckon I'm too old. They think I'm not trying and say my benefits will be cut.

My mum got a grant to go to university but I'm going to end up with enormous debts.

I just can't make ends meet. Why can't the government give us enough pension to live on?

I live on my own and I haven't any children. Why should I pay all these taxes for schools and the elderly?

I've got cancer but the NHS won't give me the drugs that will keep me alive longer.

1 What are these people worried about?

2 Make a list of the areas of spending that the questions refer to.

3 Where do you think the money comes from to pay for all these services?

4 Do you think there is a limit to the amount that the government can spend? Why?

5 How should the government decide how to spend its money?

What's your responsibility?

Most people in the country are employed unless they are too young or old. People in employment usually have higher self esteem because they can look after themselves. Places where many people are unemployed tend to be poorer because there is less money to spend on looking after the community as a whole. Whenever you spend or earn money, you pay tax – so you help to pay for the services you receive. You also help to pay for services that you don't receive at the moment but which you might receive in the future.

What does the government spend?

The government spends its money on a wide range of services. Over the years, there has been a steady increase in the amount that governments spend. At the moment, it amounts to about £10,000 per person, per year. People's voting decisions often depend on what the political parties say they will do about taxes and spending if they win the election.

The first pie chart on page 15 shows the main areas of spending and the proportion spent on each area. The way it is divided up varies a little from year to year but the overall picture stays much the same.

Where does the money come from?

If the government is to provide these services, it needs to raise money to pay for them. The money, or **government revenue**, comes from taxation or borrowing, as the second pie chart shows.

You will find out how people participate in the economy and how and why taxes are raised.

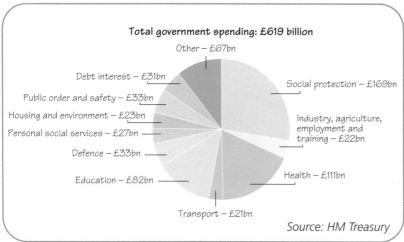

Total government spending: £619 billion

- Other – £67bn
- Debt interest – £31bn
- Public order and safety – £33bn
- Housing and environment – £23bn
- Personal social services – £27bn
- Defence – £33bn
- Education – £82bn
- Transport – £21bn
- Health – £111bn
- Industry, agriculture, employment and training – £22bn
- Social protection – £169bn

Source: HM Treasury

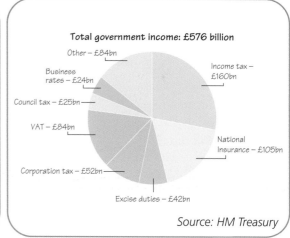

Total government income: £576 billion

- Other – £84bn
- Business rates – £24bn
- Council tax – £25bn
- VAT – £84bn
- Corporation tax – £52bn
- Excise duties – £42bn
- Income tax – £160bn
- National Insurance – £105bn

Source: HM Treasury

Corporation tax is paid on the profits of all businesses.

National Insurance is a tax on income. People often think it pays for pensions and benefits but it just goes into the pot with the other taxes.

Excise duties are charged on a range of items, many of which are not very good for you if you have too much of them. These include alcohol and cigarettes.

Income tax is not paid by people who earn very little, but as your income rises you pay more tax. It is worked out as a percentage of your earnings. People on high incomes pay a higher percentage of their earnings in income tax.

Value added tax (VAT) is paid on almost everything we buy apart from food, children's clothes, books and newspapers. The amount paid is a percentage of the total value of the products.

Other taxes include those on cars and petrol. These allow governments to tax particular items to raise money or to try to reduce the amount we buy. Some taxes are raised in local areas. These include council tax and business rates.

What taxes?

Action

The Treasury is the government department responsible for the **Budget**.

Look at its website at www.treasury.gov.uk to find out how the government raises and spends its money. Click on the 'Budget' heading on the site. You will find a summary document that explains the government's spending decisions.

... another point of view?

'If the NHS wants more money, it should get it.'

Do you agree with this statement? Give reasons for your opinion, showing you have considered another point of view.

Check your understanding

1 How does the government raise the money to cover its spending?
2 Explain the different types of taxation that the government uses to raise money.
3 What has been happening to the amount of government spending over the years?
4 Why might government spending influence the way people vote?

Key Terms

Budget: the process each year when the Chancellor of the Exchequer explains how the government will raise and spend its money

government revenue: the money raised by the government

Local services – local spending

What does the council do?

Your local council is responsible for a range of services for your community, including education, social services, leisure, planning, transport, housing, fire and the police.

The amount of spending will depend on many different things. Here are some examples:

- If the population of the area is very young, they will need lots of schools.
- If there are many old people, they may need help from social services.
- If there are lots of people, there will be lots of refuse to collect.

A brand new sports centre, for example, is a very expensive item that has to be paid for. The council will work out how much it needs to spend in the coming year and then calculate how much money it must raise.

The council funds schools, which are free. It runs sports centres that are usually cheaper than private clubs. The council provides these services because many people would not be able to afford to pay for them otherwise.

Sometimes councils work together with private businesses to run their services. Council houses can be sold to private housing associations, and councils can use the money to repair remaining council property or to build new council housing. Councils often pay businesses to run leisure facilities for them.

Central government sets a limit on how much money each council can spend, so the council has to work out its priorities. It never has the money to provide everything it would like to. When you vote in local elections, you are helping to decide what happens where you live.

You will discover which services are provided by local government and how the money is raised to provide them.

A local council's income and expenditure (in £ million)

Expenditure

Social services £37.4

Fire and police £8.6

Planning and transport £12.8

Leisure £8.8

Housing £4.5

Other £6.7

Education £62.3

Income

Business rates £45.3

General government grant £26.1

Council tax £68

Tax surplus from last year £1.8

1 Make a list of services provided by this council. Put them in order according to how much they cost.
2 Why does the council spend money on these services?
3 If the council decided to spend more on leisure, where might the money come from?

Action

How does your local council raise and spend its money? You can find out from the town hall, council offices or the library. The council might also have a website with the information.

Check your understanding

1 What sorts of services do local councils provide?
2 Where do local councils get their money from?
3 Why does central government give more money to some councils than others?
4 Why is it important to vote in local elections?

... another point of view?

'Local taxation should be based on how much you earn instead of the value of your house.'

Do you agree with this statement? Give reasons for your opinion, showing you have considered another point of view.

Where does the money come from?

In order to pay for these services, the local council raises money from residents and businesses in the area. A large part of its spending comes from central government.

Council tax is paid by all the residents of the area. The amount that each person pays will depend on the value of the house they live in. People who live in bigger houses will pay more than those who live in smaller houses.

Business rates are paid by all the local businesses. The amount that is paid depends on the rent that could be charged for the office, shop or factory that the business uses.

Central government contributes a major part. The amount it contributes depends on the needs of the specific area and how much can be raised locally. Poorer areas tend to receive more from central government than richer parts of the country.

Central government helps poorer areas more because it is harder for them to raise money locally. If many people are unemployed, houses will tend to have a lower value, so the council tax will only bring in a relatively small amount of money. Spending in these areas often needs to be greater because people who live there need a lot of help from social services.

Key Terms

business rates: a form of tax paid by all the businesses in an area. The amount a business pays depends on the rent that could be charged for their premises

council tax: a tax paid by everyone who lives in an area. It is based on the value of their house

Protecting the customer

Getting you thinking

A new head of hair in two weeks

1 Match these questions to the situations above: Can I get my money back? Can I get compensation? Can that be true?

2 Who do you think is at fault in each of the examples: the retailer, manufacturer or consumer? Explain why.

3 Have you ever had to complain about something you have bought? How did you go about it? What was the result?

What are my rights?

When you buy something from a shop, by mail order or over the internet, you are called a **consumer** and, as a consumer, you have certain rights. You are also a consumer when you pay someone, such as a hairdresser, a photographer or an accountant, to provide a service.

Some of the most important laws protecting consumers' rights include:

- the *Trade Descriptions Act*, which makes it a criminal offence to make misleading claims about goods or services. For example, 'Was £200. Now £149.99' is misleading if the goods have never been sold at the higher price. If a film processor offers a one-hour service, this must be true.

- the *Sale and Supply of Goods Act*, which is concerned that goods sold must be of satisfactory quality and fit for the purpose they are sold and advertised for.

- the *Food Safety Act*, which covers the preparation and selling of food and drink in both shops and restaurants. The Act makes it an offence to sell or serve food or drink that is unsafe.

- the *Consumer Protection Act*, which means that consumers can claim for damages if they are injured as a result of using faulty goods. If a child is hurt by an unsafe toy, the manufacturers could be prosecuted.

Is it safe?

You will find out how the rights of consumers and businesses can conflict and how issues can be resolved.

How can you enforce your rights?

If you have bought goods or services and you are dissatisfied with them, you have a right to claim your money back, to an exchange or to a repeat of the service.

1 Contact the trader with details of your complaint, say what you want done and give them a chance to put the matter right.

2 If you are not happy with the outcome, you can seek advice from the **Citizens Advice Bureau** (CAB). They can help with a wide variety of problems, including shopping complaints.

3 The Citizens Advice Bureau may recommend you go to a **Trading Standards Department**. They can investigate complaints about misleading descriptions or prices, and the safety of consumer goods. They can take action against people who break the law.

4 The **Office of Fair Trading**, a government office, can also take action against traders who break consumer laws.

Action

Working in pairs, think about why traders and businesses prefer to sort out complaints themselves.

Check your understanding

1 If you bought a CD at a reduced price because the CD cover was damaged, would you be able to take it back to the shop and claim a refund? Give reasons for your answer.
2 If you bought something from a shop and it was faulty, but the shop refused to refund your money, what could you do?

... another point of view?

'Consumers should look after themselves.'
Do you agree with this statement? Give reasons for your opinion, showing you have considered another point of view.

Sellers have rights too

In certain situations consumers cannot claim refunds or demand exchanges. If you bought a shirt in a sale and you knew it had a defect, you would not be able to claim your money back, because the seller didn't hide the problem from you when you bought it.

Sellers do not have to exchange goods, but most will do so as long as the goods have not been used. So, if you have bought some clothes and you change your mind about them later, you will find most shops are happy to exchange them, even though they don't have to by law.

Home shopping and the internet

When you buy on the internet from a company trading in the UK, you are covered by more or less the same legislation as that which covers shop purchases:

- the goods you've bought should be of satisfactory quality
- they should be fit for the purpose they are sold for
- they should be as described by the seller.

Key Terms

Citizens Advice Bureau (CAB): an organisation that offers free advice on consumer and other legal matters

Office of Fair Trading: a government office that can take action against traders who break the law

Trading Standards Department: an official body that enforces consumer-based law

Responsibilities in the workplace

Getting you thinking

1 Explain each of ASDA's rules.

2 Why does ASDA expect its staff to have a responsible attitude to their work?

3 ASDA expects its staff to be responsible. What should the staff expect from ASDA?

4 Can you think of any ways in which an employee's responsibilities might conflict with their rights?

What ASDA expects from you

Attendance

If you don't come to work, your work has to be done by your colleagues and it reduces our opportunity to offer good customer service. However, sometimes absence from work is unavoidable. If you can't come to work, please contact the store no later than two hours before the start of your shift.

Punctuality

Customers expect us to be available to give them the service they want, so all colleagues must avoid lateness.

Appearance

Colleagues must wear the uniform provided by the Company and adhere to the dress standards.

Friends and relatives

Colleagues must not serve relatives or friends at either counters or checkouts.

Mobile phones

Colleagues are allowed to make personal calls during their break times from pay phones provided in store. Colleagues may not carry or use personal mobile phones whilst working.

Your responsibilities as an employee

Just as employers have responsibilities towards their employees, so the employees have responsibilities towards their employer.

Employees must carry out their responsibilities as set out in the **contract of employment**. Employees should receive this within eight weeks of starting a new job. This contract sets out what the employer and the employee are expected to do. This is important: there are two sides to the contract and both the employer and employee must do what they have agreed to. If the employee fails to do this, they can be dismissed. If the employer doesn't keep their side of the contract, the employee can take them to an **employment tribunal**.

A contract should include the following:

- names of employer and employee
- entitlement to sick pay
- date of starting
- pension details (if any)
- rate of pay and working hours
- complaints and disciplinary procedures
- place of work
- conditions for ending the employment contract
- holiday entitlement.

You will understand that both employers and employees have responsibilities that might conflict with one another.

What if it goes wrong?

People can be dismissed if they are unable to do the job properly or have been involved in any misconduct, such as fighting, discrimination, deliberate damage or theft. A minor misconduct, such as bad timekeeping, usually results in a verbal **warning**. If this continues, there will be a written warning and, if there is no further improvement, it can end in **dismissal**. A major misconduct, like theft, can lead to instant dismissal.

Dismissal is different from **redundancy**. Redundancy occurs when the job has ended and no one is being taken on to replace you. It is the employer's responsibility, and the employee will receive a payment at least equivalent to one month's pay for every year employed by the business.

Disagreements over dismissal

There might be a disagreement between the employer and the employee over a dismissal. If it can't be sorted out, the case can be taken to an employment tribunal. This is a type of court of law that has the power to fine the business and make it pay damages to the employee if it finds that the employee was not to blame. If the dismissed person belongs to a union, they can seek advice from it and the union can represent them at the tribunal. Sometimes tribunals come out in favour of the employer and sometimes in favour of the employee.

An industrial tribunal: a more informal court of law

Action

Look in a local or national paper to see if there are any reports of an industrial tribunal. What was the issue? Who won? Why? Had one side acted irresponsibly? If so, explain how.

Check your understanding

1 What is the contract of employment for?
2 What reasons can be given for dismissal?
3 What is the difference between dismissal and redundancy?
4 What can an employee do if they feel they have been mistreated?

... another point of view?

'Rights at work are more important than responsibilities.'
Do you agree with this statement? Give reasons for your opinion, showing you have considered another point of view.

Key Terms

contract of employment: a document that details an employee's and employer's responsibilities for a particular job

dismissal: when employers end an employee's contract of employment (sometimes called 'sacking')

employment tribunal: a type of court dealing only with disagreements over employment laws

redundancy: when a person loses their job because the job doesn't need to be done anymore

warning: written or spoken warning given by an employer to an employee if the employer thinks the employee has been breaking the contract of employment

Fair play at work

Getting you thinking

1 What sorts of problems do you think people might face when at work?
2 How do you think an employer might make their staff's working life better?
3 What effect do you think a happy workforce has on a business?
4 What do you think the law should have to say about working conditions?

Why do we need employment laws?

Employment laws exist to protect employees and make sure businesses carry out their responsibilities towards their staff. Without these laws, people's human right to fair conditions at work could be harder to protect.

Exploiting people

Before laws were introduced to protect people, some employers treated their staff unfairly. Employees suffered through:

- long hours
- dangerous and unhealthy working conditions
- poor pay
- not being treated as individuals, with individual needs.

There was no government support in terms of unemployment benefit or sickness pay, so employees could not afford to argue with their employers, nor could they afford to be ill.

Unions

Employees began to form **trade unions**. They negotiated with employers to reach fairer agreements on pay and working conditions. Over the years, these agreements have led to huge improvements in the rights of employees.

By trying to persuade employers and Parliament to adopt fairer and safer working practices, the unions proved to be effective pressure groups in looking after the interests of their members. A group of people bargaining together is more powerful than individuals working alone.

Unions protect the rights of their members

You will find out about ways in which employees can be protected.

How does the law protect?

The **Equal Pay Act** means that men and women in jobs that require the same effort, skills or responsibility should be paid the same amount.

The **contract of employment** is an agreement between employer and employee setting out the pay and conditions, including holiday entitlements.

The **Sex Discrimination Act** and the **Race Relations Act** protect individuals from being treated differently because of their sex, nationality or ethnicity.

The government also sets a **minimum wage** in order to protect people from exploitation. It is changed to meet rises in prices.

The **Employment Equality Regulations** protect people from discrimination on the basis of age, religion and sexual orientation.

The **Disability Discrimination Act** means that people who are disabled must be given equal opportunities.

Health and safety laws are designed to reduce accidents. Employers must provide a safe working environment and train employees to work safely.

European regulations

Some **European Union** members have signed up to a Social Chapter. The Chapter sets employment rights, such as maternity and paternity leave, so that everyone has guaranteed working conditions.

The UK has not signed the Chapter because higher wages and better conditions would push up the business costs. UK businesses would therefore become less competitive as prices would rise and it would be harder to sell their products. This might mean that the number of jobs in the UK would fall.

Action

1. Find out what unions provide for their members.
2. Produce a union recruitment poster giving reasons why employees should join. You can get ideas from www.tuc.org.uk or www.unison.org.uk.

Check your understanding

1. Who do unions represent and what are they trying to do?
2. What areas do the main employment laws cover?

... another point of view?

'The UK should sign the EU's Social Chapter.'

Do you agree with this statement? Give reasons for your opinion, showing you have considered another point of view

Key Terms

employment laws: laws passed by Parliament and by the European Union law-making bodies that set out the rights and responsibilities of employers and employees

European Union: a group of 25 countries that works together in fields such as the environment, social issues, the economy and trade

trade unions: organisations that look after the interests of a group of employees

Protecting the roof over your head

Getting you thinking

The tenant had smashed windows, stuffed the kitchen sink with food waste, ruined some of the carpets, scribbled graffiti on walls, cut some of the electrical wires, including those to the boiler, and made holes in the ceiling where plugs and cords hung down from the loft.

'My landlord withheld around 90 per cent of my deposit. He said the wooden floor was scuffed and needed relaying but I've been to the flat since and no work has been done to the floor at all, so we each lost £350 for nothing.'

1 How has the landlord or tenant failed to be responsible in each of these cases?
2 What do you think the landlord and tenant have the right to expect from each other?

Fair housing

Housing is always a sensitive issue because people feel insecure if their home is under threat. There are rules, laws and organisations to help both landlords and tenants to make everything work more smoothly. Both sides have rights and responsibilities to each other.

A tenant has the right to:
- know the terms of the tenancy (it is important to study the terms carefully before signing)
- know the name and address of the landlord
- accommodation in a good state of repair
- reasonably quick and effective repairs
- safe accommodation (all electrical, gas and other systems and appliances should meet modern safety standards and are subject to regular checks)
- peaceable and quiet enjoyment of the accommodation
- a reasonable period of notice if the landlord wants the tenant to leave
- the return of the security deposit within a reasonable period of time, subject to the property being clean and damage free and there being no outstanding accounts.

A tenant has a responsibility to:
- give honest and truthful statements about him/herself
- pay a reasonable rent
- pay the rent as and when it is due
- respect and care for the landlord's property, furniture and fittings
- pay the landlord for any damage, beyond normal wear and tear
- report defects to the landlord immediately as they become apparent
- only use the property as residential accommodation
- only keep pets if the landlord approves
- not do anything that would cause nuisance, damage or annoyance to the landlord or the neighbours
- not bring in other residents without informing the landlord
- give notice to quit in writing at least four weeks before leaving
- not use the security deposit in place of rent.

You will find out about the rights and responsibilities of landlords and tenants.

If things go wrong...

- **Where to get advice**

  When it comes to the law, people often need advice. Getting things wrong can be time consuming and expensive. You can get advice from a Law Centre, the Citizens Advice Bureau, a Housing Advice Centre or a solicitor.

- **Why can deposits be difficult?**

  Deposits are often an issue. When you rent a house or flat, you are asked to put down a deposit, which the landlord keeps in case you damage the property. Landlords have to keep this money safe and return it to you when you leave unless you have done any damage. Tenants and landlords often have different views about damage. Sometimes it is a genuine disagreement but on other occasions, such as in 'Getting you thinking', the landlord is taking advantage of the situation.

- **Solving the problems**

  Deposit disputes need to be resolved quickly and cheaply. Tenants usually need the money as a deposit on their next property, and landlords need to know how much will be available to spend on redecoration and repair. The Deposit Protection Service is a free service which offers a judgement as to who should pay what.

The local council can help. It can take legal action against a landlord if:

- the tenants are harassed or evicted
- the **tenancy agreement** is broken
- the utility services have been cut off.

Trade-offs

> Lots of landlords are selling up because the rules and regulations keep changing and are more and more onerous. Therefore there are fewer houses to rent and this decrease in supply has meant rent has risen, as the demand still exists.
>
> *Sandip*

Every tenant wants the rules to be as strict as possible and rents to be as low as possible but renting property is just like buying and selling anything else. People need houses and flats to rent but landlords sell off their properties when it all becomes too difficult.

Check your understanding

1 What is a tenancy agreement?
2 Why is it important for landlords and tenants to know where they stand?
3 Why is the deposit likely to cause difficulties?
4 How can disputes be resolved?

... another point of view?

'There should be no controls on rented accommodation.'
Do you agree with this statement? Give reasons for your opinion, showing you have considered another point of view.

Action

Have a look at a tenancy agreement. There are plenty on the internet. Work out why each item is included and explain why it is important.

Key Terms

tenancy agreement: a legal agreement between a landlord and tenant

Making a difference

Getting you thinking

SMASH stands for Swindon Mentoring And Self Help. It aims to support vulnerable young people who need help to achieve their full social, emotional, health and educational potential. The overall aim of the project is to increase their potential for achievement in the future.

The charity depends on **volunteers** who want to give something back to the community. SMASH matches a volunteer to an individual they get on with and who has similar interests. They commit to meeting once a week for a year. It works well because the mentors are not officials or family so it's often easier to talk.

All sorts of problems

Trouble with the police?

Problems at home?

Problems with friends?

Problems with confidence or anger management?

Trouble at school?

Just need someone to talk to?

1 What sort of organisation is SMASH?

2 Why might young people want help?

3 How are the mentors making a difference to their community?

4 Why is it important to help these young people?

5 Why do you think people become mentors?

6 Why do you think communities benefit from the help of volunteers?

Taking action

The people who set up SMASH were working together to offer a service to their local community. The mentors are taking individual action to help people in their local community. Each young person who is helped by SMASH knows that their mentor is giving up their own time and isn't being paid – so they must really care.

You will discover how individuals and groups can make an impact on their local community.

Why help your community?

People volunteer in the community for all sorts of reasons, as the chart below suggests. Most people get personal satisfaction from seeing the results of their contribution to the community. They really enjoy the activity too. Many feel that it helps them because they develop their skills as well as making a difference.

People in communities are always **interdependent**. Do people come into your school to help? Have you been a cub, a brownie or a member of an organisation that depends on people helping? Do you or your family support others in the community? Perhaps your community would be different without such help.

	%
I wanted to improve things/help people	53
Cause was important to me	41
I had time to spare	41
I wanted to meet people	30
Connected with needs/interests of family or friends	29
There was a need in the community	29
Friends/family did it	21
To learn new skills	19
Part of my religious belief	17
To help get on in my career	7
Had received voluntary help myself	4
Already involved in the organisation	2
Connected with my interests/hobbies	2
To give something back	1

Check your understanding

1 Do you belong to any organisation that people contribute to on a voluntary basis?
2 Who benefits from people's support in the community?
3 Why do people help others in the local community?
4 Why do some businesses encourage their staff to support organisations in the community?
5 What impact does this support have on communities?

... another point of view?

'I don't want to give up my time to help others.'

Do you agree with this statement? Give reasons for your opinion, showing you have considered another point of view.

Business volunteers

Volunteering can happen in all sorts of ways. Many businesses encourage their staff to get involved. There are benefits for both sides. When a business give its staff time off work to become involved with voluntary activities, they find that they learn all sorts of new skills because they learn to work with all sorts of different people.

Costain and Katesgrove Primary School

'Ours is a very old Victorian school and the playground was showing its age. The walls were last painted years ago and the old wooden equipment was suffering from rot.

'Costain came in and brightened it up using long-lasting paint, which the children love. One wall was decorated with the children's handprints. The team who did the work put their handprints on the wall too. The younger children were thrilled that their little playground had finally got some attention.

'The fact that Costain can offer its time and fund something that's going to impact on young people so positively is fantastic. And the team that came in really engaged with the children – they didn't cut themselves off. This project felt like a partnership from the beginning and we are very keen to keep that going.'

1 How did the school benefit?
2 How did Costain benefit from helping the school?

Action

Find out about the different ways in which people help others in your local area. Work out who benefits from the activities. Make a presentation to the class or a larger group about how the community works together.

Key Terms

interdependent: people and organisations working together to support each other

volunteer: someone who works for free for a community

Sweet shops and sweatshops

Getting you thinking

Drissa was sold to a plantation owner, taken to a remote plantation and forced to work from dawn until dusk with no pay. The work was exhausting but if Drissa showed signs of tiredness he was beaten. When Drissa was caught trying to escape, he was tied up and beaten until he couldn't walk. At night, along with 17 other young men, he was locked in a small room with only a tin can as a toilet.

The average UK consumer spends about £72 a year on chocolate. The total world market is worth £4 billion a year.

1 Why do cocoa producers use slave labour?

2 How does Fairtrade help?

3 Do customers have a responsibility?

4 When you buy your next bar of chocolate, will you think about how it has been produced?

Fairtrade is the only guarantee that products, such as chocolate, are 'slave free' and have not been made using forced labour. All Fairtrade products have to meet strict conditions, including ensuring that no forced or illegal child labour has been used. Fairtrade goods also give producers a fair price for their produce, thus helping to challenge the unfair trading systems that keep people in poverty.

FAIRTRADE

Source: Anti-slavery International

Trade, producers and customers

Trade is a very important way for any country to earn money and create jobs. People and countries have traded for thousands of years, but in today's global economy, information, goods and money can be moved around the world at an incredible speed. Companies aim to make the best product at the cheapest price.

In some countries there are no laws about conditions of employment. In others, the laws are not enforced. Many businesses choose to make their products in those countries where people work for very low wages. If the prices of the products are low, customers buy more of them – so it's a competitive circle.

Making trade fairer

The Fairtrade Foundation supports trade that is good for the producer – a **fair trade** system that ensures more of the price consumers pay goes to the producer. Fairtrade staff are paid a fair wage, have good working conditions and are allowed to form trade unions to defend their rights. The Fairtrade Foundation gives kite marks to products that meet the standards it sets. If you buy these products, you know that you are helping to improve people's lives.

You will discover how you can affect people's lives in the wider world.

Would you buy this dress for £12?

Can you make a difference?

How often have you heard people say 'I don't know how they do it for the money'? The truth is that we do know how they do it. The dress is made in China or another part of the world where labour is cheap and there are few controls over working conditions. Even when there are laws to protect workers, they are often ignored.

1 How are clothes made so cheaply in countries like China?
2 Do you buy clothes because they are cheap?
3 Do you think about why they are cheap?
4 Would you still buy them if you knew about the lives of the people who make the clothes?
5 Are there any arguments for continuing to buy very cheap clothes?

Interdependence across the world

Decisions we make affect people now and in the future. If cocoa producers earn a decent wage, they can afford to send their children to school and help them to develop skills that will be useful in the modern world.

It is important to think through your decisions. Most people dislike the idea of child labour but even Oxfam argues that we have to be careful. If child labour is banned, in some places families will starve. In others, children's jobs will disappear and they will end up working illegally in more unpleasant occupations. If we **boycott** some products, we can make people's lives worse.

Action

Find out more about Fairtrade and the range of products available. Organise a Fairtrade day or an assembly to persuade other students to support Fairtrade products.

Check your understanding

1 Why are people paid low wages and made to work in poor conditions in some countries?
2 Do customers have a responsibility for this? Explain your answer.
3 How does Fairtrade help workers in less economically developed countries (LEDCs)?
4 How can our decisions about buying things help people now and in the future?

... another point of view?

'People in the UK should boycott companies that sell "dirty" clothes and trainers.'

Do you agree with this statement? Give reasons for your opinion, showing you have considered another point of view.

Key Terms

boycott: to refuse to use or have anything to do with something

fair trade: a way of buying and selling products that aims to pay the producer a fair price

What is sustainable development?

Getting you thinking

Farmers need to fertilise fields to keep yields up. Fertilisers can damage the environment

1 What land, energy and resources are being used in each of these activities?

2 Look at each image and make a list of the environmental costs of each activity.

3 What will happen if we continue to increase the number of holidays we take by plane or the miles we drive?

4 Fertilising fields mean more can be produced – so food is cheaper. Make a list of the advantages and disadvantages of doing this.

5 Why is it important to think about the effect of our actions on the environment?

6 Why can it be difficult to decide how to limit environmental damage?

Hard choices

Imagine you live in a very poor country, in a small rural village. You need fuel to cook food for your family. You may also need fuel to boil your drinking water to stop your children getting sick. The only way to get this fuel is to cut down the trees near your village. But you know that if you do this, the precious topsoil will blow away and eventually the desert will swallow up your village.

The villagers have to make the hard choice between solving a problem they have now and not making problems for the future. This kind of choice has to be made by everybody, although the circumstances are different everywhere.

In the UK and other **MEDCs** where there is economic growth, people expect their standard of living to improve. People can buy all sorts of things to make life more comfortable. They usually work shorter hours than people in **LEDCs** and have better access to healthcare and education. These can all be good things but there are some drawbacks.

Growing food and building homes, roads, schools and hospitals uses land, energy and resources. The demand for products and services can mean pollution increases and natural resources are used up. In time, these factors could actually decrease the standard of living. So the choice is between having what we want now and making sure future generations don't suffer.

You will find out about sustainable development and consider ways in which it can be achieved.

Sustainable development

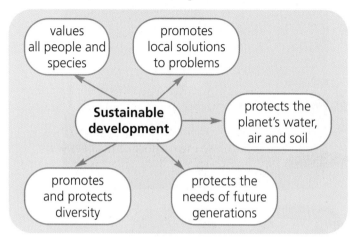

Sustainable development means we can improve the way people live today, without harming the prospects for the future. Different resources can be used so that scarce or dangerous materials are no longer needed. New materials can be designed to use less energy. Standards of living can be improved in ways that protect the environment, and harmful products can stop being made.

Sustainable solutions

There are many issues and many solutions in the search for sustainability. You will find more examples from a global perspective on pages 32–9.

Action

Organisations such as Comic Relief, Oxfam, Christian Aid and Action Aid sponsor sustainable development projects. Research the work of one or more of these organisations and identify two to three problems they have addressed, and the solutions that the organisations and their local partners employed.

Check your understanding

1 In your own words, explain what is meant by 'sustainable development'.
2 Give one reason why it will be important in future to find sustainable solutions to environmental problems.
3 Why are the following considered to be sustainable developments:
  • digging wells • building schools • planting trees?
4 Can wind power be described as a sustainable energy source? Give reasons.
5 Why has commercial fishing in the North Sea been restricted?

Energy

As supplies of coal, oil and natural gas are limited, they will only sustain our needs for so long before we will be forced to find alternative, sustainable sources of energy. One solution could be wind power. The UK already has many wind farms, mostly in Wales, Scotland and Cornwall. The amount of the world's electricity generated by wind power has grown five times in less than a decade. Offshore wind farms could, in theory, produce twice the UK's electricity requirements.

Food

For decades, large UK and European fishing fleets have fished in the North Sea. In recent years it has become clear that fish stocks there were so low that there was a real danger the North Sea would be fished out. Over-fishing had not allowed enough time for fish to breed and stocks to recover. Now fishing in the North Sea is strictly controlled. Stocks are starting to recover and are a sustainable resource for the future.

Resources

Similarly, if you cut down forests for timber and paper faster than nature can replace them, you will end up with no trees. However, trees are a **renewable** resource. Many countries now plant fast-growing trees to replace those chopped down. You will often see goods labelled: 'Made from timber from a sustainable forest'.

... another point of view?

'We should pay higher taxes on energy from non-sustainable sources.'

Do you agree with this statement? Give reasons for your opinion, showing you have considered another point of view.

Key Terms

LEDC: a less economically developed country

MEDC: a more economically developed country

renewable: able to be replaced or restored

sustainable development: living now in a way that doesn't damage the needs of future generations

Prices and the poor

Getting you thinking

1 Who will be affected by a rise in the price of petrol? Put the people in the photos in order from those who will be most affected to those who will be least affected.

2 Explain what the effect will be on each group of people.

Is oil running out?

There is a limited amount of oil and we have been using it up at a faster and faster rate. As the amount that is available falls and people want to buy more, the price rises. We may not run out – but it will just become so expensive that most people can't afford to use it.

How we use oil

How would a rise in the price of oil affect your lifestyle?

Who is affected by a rise in oil prices?

A rise in oil prices affects almost every aspect of our lives. It makes everything more expensive. The diagram showing the uses of oil demonstrates just a few examples of the ways that oil is used in our daily lives. Imagine how things would be without it.

- **How do rising resource prices affect people in MEDCs?**

  If oil prices rise, the price of almost everything rises. It costs more to grow food, to transport it to the supermarket and to take it home. Much public transport depends on oil – so it is not just the car driver who is hit. Everyone suffers, but people on low incomes are hit harder because the basics form a higher proportion of their income.

  If everything becomes more expensive, people can afford to buy less, so fewer people will be employed to make products or sell services. It can mean a rise in unemployment, which in turn makes everyone poorer.

You will find out about the impact of rising prices as natural resources grow scarce.

- **How do rising resource prices affect people in LEDCs?**

When the economy of a country grows, more resources are put to work. If the resources become more expensive, development is going to be slower. Slower growth means that more people are trapped in unemployment and poverty. If people have jobs they can buy better food and pay for education for their children.

The very poorest people, such as the woman gathering firewood in 'Getting you thinking', are probably least affected to begin with, but rising resource prices will mean that it will take longer for such people to move out of poverty.

Is it fair?

Different people are affected to a different degree by the rise in the price of oil. It certainly isn't fair but it is very difficult to come up with a solution. When there is a petrol strike, we face shortages. There are two solutions to this problem:

- People wait in long queues – first come first served.
- Supplies are rationed so people can only have a limited amount each.

The second solution is fairer but may not take people's different situations into account.

Is there a solution?

To overcome the problem of the scarcity of oil, electric cars and other solutions are being developed. When things become scarce, industry looks for alternatives. Electric cars have been a possibility for a long time but the motor industry has only recently started to work on them seriously. Hybrid cars, which run on LPG or petrol are now available as a greener alternative to the traditional version.

Will electric cars help keep petrol prices down?

Action

Imagine that petrol has become too expensive for most people to buy. Remember that people have very different needs for fuel according to where they live, the work they do and the people who depend on them.

Work out how you would set about allocating fuel to different groups of people. What criteria would you use to decide how much different people received?

Check your understanding

1 Why do prices go up when things become scarce?
2 Why is the world so dependent on oil?
3 How would your life be different if oil ran out?
4 Who, in MEDCs, is most affected by a rise in the price of oil? Explain why.
5 Who, in LEDCs, is most affected by a rise in the price of oil? Explain why.
6 Why is the development of an economy affected by a rise in the price of oil?
7 How can slow development affect people?

... another point of view?

'If resources become scarce, we should just let people buy what they can afford.'

Do you agree with this statement? Give reasons for your opinion, showing you have considered another point of view.

1.3 Our rights and responsibilities as global citizens

Transport crisis?

Getting you thinking

High-speed trains reduce journey times

If you are travelling a distance between 400 and 800 km, high-speed trains are the quickest way to travel – faster than flying.

Evidence from other countries suggests that high-speed rail links would reduce demand for domestic air services.

High-speed rail links would link the rest of the country to Europe.

1 What effect would high-speed rail links have on journey times?

2 What effect would they have on domestic flights?

3 What effect might they have on road traffic?

4 How would high-speed rail links help the environment?

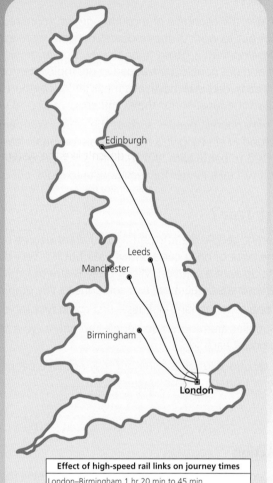

Effect of high-speed rail links on journey times
London–Birmingham 1 hr 20 min to 45 min
London–Manchester 2 hr 20 min to 1 hr 30 min
London–Leeds 2 hr 15 min to 1 hr 20 min
London–Edinburgh 4 hr 30 min to 2 hr 45 min

Traffic congestion reduces sustainability in two different ways:

- It increases pollution.
- It wastes time that businesses and people could use in other ways.

It is therefore important that schemes are developed to reduce congestion and its impact. Governments, businesses, groups and individuals can all play their part.

The real cost of motoring

A car gives you the freedom to go where you like, when you like. But what is the real cost of motoring?

Over 200 new cars are sold every hour in the UK, and though newer cars have 'greener' engines, they still emit greenhouse gases. Road traffic is now a major cause of air pollution. Traffic fumes not only pollute our cities, they affect rural areas too.

Government figures predict that road traffic will increase by 75 per cent in the next 30 years. As congestion nears gridlock in many towns and cities, the average UK motorist spends a total of five days a year just sitting in traffic jams. Many people say they would use public transport if it were cheaper, cleaner and safer.

You will investigate the challenges created by traffic, and consider some sustainable solutions.

Possible solutions

Road pricing

This involves road users paying to use roads. Cars can be fitted with electronic number plates that give signals to special computers. The computers work out when the car was on a particular road and the driver is charged. In Singapore, this system has reduced rush-hour traffic, pollution and damage to roads. In London, people pay the congestion charge to drive their cars into the central area. One problem with **road pricing** is that the population doesn't like the system very much. Another problem is that if the charges seem insignificant to richer people, but expensive to poorer people, the poorer people may be disadvantaged.

Improving public transport

Better public transport might encourage people to stop using their cars so much. Possible plans are to:

- improve bus reliability
- decrease bus journey times
- develop tram systems
- reduce car traffic.

This could be done by:

- creating bus lanes on important routes and making sure cars don't use them
- giving priority at traffic lights to buses, pedestrians and cyclists
- stopping cars parking on busy routes.

Ze vélorution – a French solution

Le vélo – 'the bicycle' – is a Parisian solution to city centre congestion. Rental bikes – 20,000 of them – are parked round the city. For 1€ you can use the bikes for the day, for 5€ they're yours for a week, and for just 29€ you can use the bikes as often as you like all year. The first half hour is free – and most people make use of this option. Every bike is rented out ten times a day. A total of 100,000 people have already signed up for a year's subscription. The scheme is run by a business that aims to make a profit.

Can Agenda 21 help?

At the United Nation's 'Earth Summit' in Rio de Janeiro in 1992, member countries agreed to work together to promote sustainable development around the world. Local Agenda 21 (LA21) sets out how this is to be done at a local level. Although LA21 is a 'global' plan, it stresses the importance of involving local people when planning projects.

Action

1 Research alternative forms of transport that might be used in towns and cities, such as electric-powered cars. Do they offer sustainable alternatives to petrol/diesel-driven vehicles?

2 How does road traffic affect the lives of people in your local area? What could be done to improve the situation?

Check your understanding

1 In what ways should public transport be improved to encourage more people to use it?

2 What are the advantages of the possible solutions to the car crisis? Are there disadvantages?

... another point of view?

'Building more roads is the only solution to the UK's traffic problems.'
Do you agree with this statement? Give reasons for your opinion, showing you have considered another point of view.

Key Terms

road pricing: a scheme that charges road users according to how much they use a road

Can Agenda 21 help?

Getting you thinking

Surrey County Council promotes walking buses

Schools in Surrey are encouraged to organise walking buses for children who live less than a mile from school. The walking buses

- improve the children's health through exercise
- make the children more alert in class
- increase the children's awareness of the local environment
- are a valuable social opportunity
- prepare the children for independence as they grow older
- reduce traffic outside the schools.

1 How do walking buses make a community more sustainable?

2 Is sustainability just about the environment? In what ways do walking buses contribute to community sustainability?

What is Agenda 21?

At the United Nation's 'Earth Summit' in Rio de Janeiro in 1992, member countries agreed to work together to promote sustainable development around the world. A total of 178 countries signed up to the agreement. The Commission on Sustainable Development was set up by the UN to monitor and report on implementation of the agreements at the local, national, regional and international levels.

What is Local Agenda 21?

Local Agenda 21 (LA21) sets out how sustainability is to be achieved at a local level. Although LA21 is a 'global' plan, it stresses the importance of involving local people when planning projects.

Two-thirds of the 2,500 action items of **Agenda 21** relate to local councils. Each local authority has had to draw up its own Local Agenda 21 (LA21) strategy, following discussion with its citizens about what they think is important for the area. Sustainable development must form a central part of the strategy.

Like Agenda 21, LA21 focuses on an economic, social and environmental agenda, and develops solutions to problems through encouraging better, more efficient practices. It realises that sustainable development is achievable, without sacrificing the quality of our lives.

How does LA21 work?

LA21 regards sustainable development as a community issue, involving all sections of society, including community groups, businesses and ethnic minorities. Involving the whole society will give everyone the opportunity to participate and will generate a resource of enthusiasm, talent and expertise.

Many local authorities have begun schemes of cooperation to allow them to exchange ideas about sustainable development. Groups of local authorities can join together to give themselves a louder voice to influence large companies.

LA21 in practice

Allerdale's first local producers' market was held in Cockermouth, and it was a fantastic success.

The event was organised by organisations that want to see local producers succeed. Thousands of people flocked to the market. A wide range of high-quality local produce was available on the day, including honey, mustard, cheeses, vegetables, organic meats, vegetables, Lakeland trout, pheasant and duck, spinning wool, ice cream, bread, cakes and preserves.

Cookery and woodturning displays proved to be very popular and entertainment was provided by a local jazz band.

This type of event is a perfect example of Local Agenda 21 in action and shows the links between the economy, the environment and local communities.

You will discover how Agenda 21 can help the world and local communities become more sustainable.

Drake Hall Prison wins sustainability award

The women's prison at Drake Hall, near Eccleshall, has been encouraging prisoners and staff to become more sustainable. A Green Week was held for staff and prisoners, and a series of initiatives are now being carried out to focus on waste and energy reduction, nature conservation and health improvement. These initiatives involve poster and sticker campaigns, the re-use of many items and the introduction of modern, clearly visible, recycling bins, a composting machine for kitchen food waste and their own biodiversity action plan. This has resulted in a review of their sustainability policy. They have won Stafford Council's Sustainable Development Charter Award.

Camden's Community Strategy

This strategy has targets for education, employment and the economy. The following is Target 52:

'We will work towards reducing unemployment in Camden to the average across London. We will particularly concentrate on those communities that experience higher unemployment rates than the borough average.'

Measuring success

Liverpool has set indicators to measure how successful the city is in achieving LA21 targets. Here are just a few of the indicators:

Some of Liverpool's LA21 indicators

- percentage of households served by a kerbside collection of recyclables
- percentage of council vehicle fleet using alternative or low-emission fuel
- percentage of pupils achieving Level 4 or above in the Key Stage 2 Mathematics test
- infant mortality rate per 1,000 live births
- re-offending rate by young offenders
- number of people sleeping rough on a single night
- percentage of children in secondary schools participating in the Youth Parliament

Check your understanding

1 What is Local Agenda 21?
2 What does sustainability in local communities mean?
3 Why is it important to work in local communities?
4 How do the examples above help communities to be sustainable?
5 How can the success of LA21 be measured?

... another point of view?

'Working at a local level alone can have little impact on the sustainability of the whole world.'

Do you agree with this statement? Give reasons for your opinion, showing you have considered another point of view.

Action

Find out about the LA21 plans in your area.

Key Terms

Agenda 21: a global plan set up by the United Nations to achieve sustainability

Local Agenda 21: a global plan to ask local people how they think their immediate environment could be improved

Can aid help?

Getting you thinking

UK and Niger – what's the difference?

1 What evidence is there to suggest that the UK is better off than Niger?

2 Do you think the cost of buying basic needs is the same?

3 What data might suggest the gap between the two countries is increasing?

4 Why does this data suggest that Niger will have difficulty catching up with more economically developed countries?

5 What help do you think would lift the people of Niger out of poverty?

	Niger	UK
How much the economy is worth per citizen	$244	$36,509
How fast the economy grew	–0.5%	2.5%
Doctors per 100,000 people	2	230
How long people live	54.5 years	79 years
Number of children dying before the age of 5 for every 1,000 people	256	7
Internet users per 1,000 people	2	473
Adults who can read	28.7%	100%
Children enrolled in secondary school	8%	99%
International aid	Receives aid	Gives aid
Free education, healthcare and state pensions	No	Yes

Source: Human Development Report 2007/8

Life in Niger

Niger is one of the world's poorest countries. As you can see from the data above, life there is very different from life in the UK. Not only is life difficult for many, but there are often disasters which mean that people need emergency help.

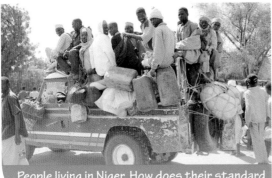

People living in Niger. How does their standard of living compare with yours?

Emergency aid

When disaster strikes, immediate help is needed. People are often very generous and give money to appeals that support countries where there have been earthquakes, hurricanes, floods and

Aid has begun reaching feeding centres for the 2.5m people facing starvation

Crops in Niger were badly hit this year by drought and a plague of locusts.

A cargo plane flying from Brindisi in southern Italy landed in the Niger capital, Niamey, on Friday, carrying 44 tons of high-energy biscuits. The biscuits are used in emergency situations to replace proper meals.

Doctors have warned that disease is now also a serious threat, particularly to undernourished children.

other types of disaster. In the UK, the Disasters Emergency Committee organises the work of charities and governments to prevent them duplicating activities. There is no point, for example, in sending lots of equipment to provide clean water and no tents. The Committee aims to support people in the short term.

You will consider different ways of giving aid to poor countries.

Aid to help development

If countries are going to develop from extreme levels of poverty, they are going to need help – but it has to be the right sort of help. There is no point in providing money to build big roads in countries where no one has cars. There is no point in providing computers that need to be plugged into power sockets when there is no electricity.

- Simple water pumps that can be maintained easily and do not require energy or complex spare parts are fine.
- Education works well. It helps people to get jobs and support their communities.
- Small loans help people get businesses going. Loans encourage people to support themselves.
- Immunisation programmes help people to stay healthy.

These are all examples of long-term support that help people to help themselves. Although **emergency aid** is necessary, it is **development aid** that makes a difference in the long run. Aid often involves sending people with expertise as well as money. If a well is installed in a village, it will need looking after. Pump Aid, a charity that helps to ensure people have a supply of fresh water, sends people to carry out the installation.

Girls' education

Members of the French and British governments visited Niger. They promised aid to support the development of education for girls in the country. The UK will give the country £7 million over three years, with the possibility of further help later.

Action

Work out the criteria you would use to decide whether to give aid to a country. Think about who it is for, how it will be used, whether it will reach them, and whether it will have an effect.

Once you have decided on your list, look at the website of one of the major charities, such as Oxfam, and decide whether their work meets your criteria.

Check your understanding

1. What is emergency aid and why is it important?
2. What is development aid and why is it important?
3. Which has more impact in the long run?
4. Why might governments give money to some countries rather than others?

... another point of view?

'Countries should look after themselves.'

Do you agree with this statement? Give reasons for your opinion, showing you have considered another point of view.

Who gives aid?

Governments, international organisations and charities all give aid.

Sometimes governments can be motivated by politics. They want to keep a country on their side. China, for example, has given a lot of money to some poor African countries in order to win their support on international issues. Many western European countries give money to countries they have had links with in the past.

In England, the Department for International Development organises the aid given by the government.

Key Terms

emergency aid: help given by one country to another when disasters occur

development aid: help given by one country to another to help the country to develop

Choosing your Campaign

Students at St Brendan's held a concert to campaign for Fairtrade. They wanted the college to change its policy on using Fairtrade products. They offered all sorts of Fairtrade goodies donated by local supermarkets. To get the message across, the bands had a backdrop that couldn't be ignored.

The slideshow promoted the Fairtrade message and celebrated the group's campaigning. This was just one of many activities they ran to promote their mission. Fairtrade roses sold like hot cakes on Valentine's Day.

1 Why do you think the students decided to campaign for Fairtrade?
2 Why do you think the students decided to hold a concert to campaign for Fairtrade?
3 What issues do you care about?
4 What campaigns have you seen to be successful?

Unit 1: Rights and responsibilities – getting started as an active citizen

Making your voice heard

Citizenship is all about advocacy. The Citizenship Campaign gives you the chance to make your voice heard by people in positions of power. There are lots of ways of participating. You might want to persuade fellow students to make your voice louder.

There are many questions to ask before you make a decision.

- Who needs helping?
- Is there an issue in your local area?
- Are there people whose voices aren't being heard?
- Is there something that needs changing?
- What's unfair?
- **What's the issue?**
- Is there an issue you care about?
- Are there people who aren't playing their part?
- Are there people who aren't listening?
- Do you need to spread the word?

How does it fit into Citizenship?

You have a wide choice of topics for your Campaign. The list on the opposite page covers the range of Citizenship activities in Unit 1 with examples of what you might do. If you really want to do something else, you will need to negotiate with your teacher.

Students plant windmills when signing up to their Go Green campaign

1 The legal rights or responsibilities of a young person

> Should the age of criminal responsibility be changed?

2 Awareness of fundamental human rights

> Does the school community need to know more about how young people's rights are infringed in a particular country?

3 Human rights in conflict

> Are people's rights to protest limited by anti-terrorism legislation?

4 Promoting greater student engagement in school or college

> How can we persuade more students to participate in the school or college council?

5 Our rights and responsibilities in the economy

> Should the local council provide more services for the young or the old?

6 Our rights and responsibilities as consumers

> Consumers have rights but many people know little about them. How can we help consumers to understand how they are protected?

7 Our rights and responsibilities in employment

> Should the minimum age at which young people can work be changed?

8 Our rights and responsibilities as tenants

> If young people can leave school at 16/17, should they be allowed to sign a tenancy agreement if they want to rent a flat?

9 Our responsibilities for the earth's resources

> Should we be using more recyclable materials in school or in our community?

10 Our responsibilities as global citizens

> Should we buy clothes from countries where people have very poor working conditions?

11 Our responsibilities to support the people of other nations

> Should our school community do more to support students in a school in a less economically developed country (LEDC)?

What's your Campaign all about?

There are all sorts of ways of campaigning. It's all about making your voice heard – or helping others to do so. School might be the right place to start.

- Is there something you really care about?
- Where do you want to be heard?
- Who do you want to listen?
- If you want other people to care about your particular issue, you might want to devise a campaign to persuade them.
- There may be others who care about the issue too. Get them together to organise the Campaign.
- What's the best way to persuade people to listen?

Perhaps there are issues outside school – is a new supermarket being built, is there a plan for a new runway, or are there environmental issues?

Perhaps the issues are further afield – fair trade or prisoners who have been locked up without a fair trial?

How are we going to make a difference?

What's your issue?
  What do you want to change?

What's your aim?
  How will you improve things?

What do you need to know?
  What information do you need to collect?

Who has the expertise?
  Do you have experts in your team? If not, ask others.

What's the threat?
  Who are your opponents? Can you persuade them?

What's the plan?
  Set a clear plan with a timeline. Stick to it!

Be realistic!

Which Campaign?

The Campaign is an important part of your course. You need to plan, collect evidence and keep a record of what happened at every stage as it is very important that you show what you and everyone else did. You will also need to work out how well it went. You may already be involved in suitable activities, but if not, you'll need to choose what to do. There are many possibilities for you to consider.

What's the issue?

- Do you care about human rights? Who is being treated badly?
- Do you care about democracy? Who isn't having a say?
- Do you care about things being fair? Who isn't being treated as you think they should?
- Do you care about the law? Does something need changing?
- Do you care about the choices the government is making? What can you do about it?
- Do you care about the environment? What can you change?
- Is something going wrong in your community? Can you change it?
- Are people ill informed about our role in the world? Can you help?

Your Campaign could be based on any of these ideas or many others. Remember that being involved in something that really interests you always makes the task easier. For example, does the environment concern you? Are you worried about drugs in your area? Or do you want more facilities for young people in the community?

Young people campaign for human rights

The right choice

The one really important thing to remember is that your Campaign must fit into the Citizenship Studies specification.

If you want:

- to set up a branch of Amnesty International and encourage other people to fight for the freedom of prisoners who have been imprisoned without a fair trial – then it's human rights.
- to campaign about knife crime in your local area – then it's responsibilities within the wider community.
- to persuade the council to spend more money on activities for young people – then it's the economy.
- your school to go green – then it's sustainability.
- the government to offer more support to people in a particular country – then it's being a global citizen.

There are endless possibilities.

Take action

Sit down with a blank sheet of paper and think about all the campaigns you might want to carry out.

1 Start by writing down all your ideas.

2 List all the advantages and disadvantages of each idea.

3 Put them in order from best to worst.

4 Is the one at the top the one you really want to carry out? If so, go ahead. If not, have another look at the list.

Although it's really part of planning, brainstorm how you might go about putting this Campaign into action. This will help you to decide whether your idea is realistic.

Check point

Before you make a final decision, check with your teacher that your Campaign is suitable for the course requirements.

You will need to explain how your plan addresses Citizenship issues, so it's a good idea to think about this right from the start of your activity.

Make sure you are clear about your objectives. You'll be asked what they were and whether you achieved them.

What do you need to know?

Before you begin, you will need to do some research about your Campaign so you know how to approach it. Are there a variety of views on the issue? Who thinks what? Can you persuade people to change their mind? Does your research change your views?

What's the objective?

You may want to save the world – but be realistic! It is much easier to be successful if you start small.

Be very clear and focus on your key message – don't include lots of issues at once.

Think about who you want to persuade:

- How do you want them to be different?
- Identify them clearly so you can work out whether you have been successful.

Students from St Richard's College and their publicity campaign to educate other students about waste issues

How does it link to Citizenship?

Work out which part of Unit 1 your issue fits into.

Is it:

- Our rights and responsibilities to each other within the family and the wider community?
- Our rights and responsibilities as citizens within the economy and welfare system?
- Our rights and responsibilities as global citizens?

Look carefully at the themes and work out exactly where it fits.

Developing your skills – spreading the message

1 How could a local radio station help with your Campaign?

2 What other media might you use?

3 What would you need to think about before talking to the media?

How to spread your message

What's your message?

What is the single most important point that you want your target audience to remember? This is your 'message'.

Your message should now be the focus for every conversation that your pressure group has with the public.

What's the evidence?

What facts support your argument?

You must give the target audience a reason to believe you.

Who is your target audience?

A target audience is the group of people you are trying to reach with your message. Who is most interested in your point of view? Why?

For example, if an issue will have an impact on the environment, you might choose young parents as a target audience. They may be concerned about how it affects their children's future.

Presenting your message

Present your message in an interesting and emotive way. What headline could you use to grab the attention of the reader?

What sort of words could you use to stir their emotions? Destroy, hopeless, saved, heroic and desolate are words often used for the impact they have on a reader.

How to persuade people

Put across your point of view

Ask some questions and use the answers as a starting point. You may even provide the answers yourself. This gets people interested in what you have to say, and helps them to agree with your point of view.

Try:

- Why should we be interested?
- Haven't we heard enough?
- Why do they oppose/propose this?
- What will we gain from this?

Make it easy for people to agree with you

If you want people to agree with your point of view, show them that you have lots in common with them. If you like the same things, you are more likely to get on!

You need to do this before starting to talk about the topic you want to discuss.

Try:

- As a member of this community for many years...
- We all want the best solution...

Think about the opposition?

Consider the opposition's point of view before you start. You'll be able to answer their questions if you are prepared. This shows everyone that you have a balanced point of view.

Always have a short, snappy ending

End your argument on a high note using a short, snappy sentence, such as 'We need the skateboard park NOW!'

How to approach the local media

The local media is very important to the success of a local campaign because:

- it affects the local community
- it provides a great way of getting free publicity and attracting support from other people.

Preparing a press release

A press release should tell the journalists who work at the local paper, radio or TV station all they need to know about your Campaign. It should outline:

- what the issue is
- why it is of interest to the local community
- contact details for you and your group
- suggestions of interesting pictures for newspaper and television.

It should be written in snappy language like a newspaper article, and be aimed at your target audience. Press releases are sometimes printed in a newspaper with very little editing, so try to use a catchy headline.

When your press release is ready, find out the address or email of a named contact at a local newspaper, or a radio or television station. Write a letter or send an email to that person. The letter or email should explain why you feel so strongly about the issue, and ask the journalist to contact you for any further information.

Take action

Work out:

- what your message is
- who your target audience is
- why your message will appeal to your target audience
- how you will sell it to them
- who you need to talk to in your local area. Remember that they are probably people of power and influence – so their evidence will be helpful.

Check point

Discuss making contact with the local media with your teacher first.

Ask for a copy of any interviews. It will all add to your evidence.

Developing your skills – planning a protest

SAVE LIVES – STOP KNIVES!

More than 1,000 people joined the families and friends of knife and gun crime victims in a protest march across London.

Vanessa Hyman and her daughter Cheyna protest over the murder of Anton, their son and brother

The idea for the People's March was started on Facebook by Sharon Singh and Gemma Olway from South West London. The march received the backing of several national newspapers, which promoted it to the public.

The marchers chanted 'Stop the knives, save lives' as they walked through London. Onlookers clapped and some motorists beeped their horns in a show of support.

The minister responsible for the police spoke to the crowd, saying 'If your local community isn't doing enough, speak to your local councillor and if they don't do enough sack them at the next election or get hold of your MP, and if they don't do anything sack them.'

1   Why do you think Sharon and Gemma decided to organise a protest march?

2   What effect do you think the backing of national newspapers had?

3   What reception did the marchers get from passersby?

4   Why do you think the minister responsible for the police spoke to the crowd?

5   What advice did he give them? Why do you think he said this?

Why protest?

Protests and marches are very powerful because they attract the attention of the public and offer them the opportunity to join in or show their support in other ways. They are often used:

*   when controversial decisions are being made
*   to draw attention to an issue
*   to commemorate an anniversary.

Organisation of a march or protest should not be taken lightly. If badly planned, a protest can be a flop, upset the general public and even break the law. Making life difficult for ordinary people should be avoided. Truck drivers blocked motorways and city centres because the price of diesel was too high. Even though many people supported their cause, the resulting traffic jams upset just as many.

Whether to protest

It is only worth organising a march or a protest if:

*   public opinion is so strong that a fairly good turnout can be guaranteed
*   it can be planned sufficiently far in advance to meet the legal requirements
*   it can be well publicised and promoted
*   it can be well managed on the day.

If a full-scale march or protest is too large a project, consider a smaller event. A demonstration before a council meeting or at a supermarket that is not doing enough for the environment is much simpler to organise and can have a direct effect.

Questions to ask

Any event needs to be carefully targeted and set up to have maximum effect. Consider these questions before you begin:

- Who are you trying to reach?
- What are you trying to achieve?
- What needs to be done and who will do it?
- Are there any costs? How will they be paid?
- Have you informed the police and your school? Whatever the event, the police should be informed – and you must check with school that they are happy for you to go ahead.
- Have you checked the health and safety regulations?
- Is there likely to be opposition? If so, work out how you will deal with it.
- Can we get the media interested? The whole point of a protest is to be noticed!

Take action

Plan the action carefully. Ask yourself:
- What are you trying to achieve?
- Who is going to do what?
- Who do you need to contact?
- Who is on your side? Will they help?
- Have you checked the health and safety rules?
- How will you work out whether it has been a success?

Check point

Before you think about planning an event outside school, check with your teacher.

Publicising the event

The grand finale

The event mustn't just fizzle out at the end. The knife crime march ended in Hyde Park. The crowd was addressed by the Metropolitan Police Commissioner, a government minister and a video message from the Prime Minister. Not many events can attract such high-status people but finding a high-profile person who believes in your issue will help to get the message across.

A protest can have a big impact – particularly when it has media coverage

Planning your Campaign

The People & Planet Group

'We've spoken to the school about switching to renewable light bulbs and they've agreed as long as we find a price which will mean that within five years it's benefitting the school economically, so we're researching that. They've also said they're happy that we look into renewable energy sources for the school's electricity, and might be happy to switch if we find them a good price. We're sending a petition to various governments to encourage them to sign up to Kyoto, and we're planning a green-themed mufti day to raise money for People & Planet.'

On top of that, the group gave an assembly to the younger students at their school on how they can help to stop climate change and are currently trying to get more of them involved in their group.

1 What was the People & Planet Group's objective?
2 Draw a spider diagram to show the range of their activities.
3 What planning do you think was needed to organise these activities?

Planning the activity

Stage 1 What is our objective?

Stage 2 Who are we targeting?

Stage 3 Who is getting involved in organising?

Stage 4 What are our roles?

Stage 5 What do we need to do?

Stage 6 What resources do we need?

Stage 7 When must things happen?

Stage 8 Have we got a back up plan if things go wrong?

Stage 9 What are the deadlines?

Stage 10 Draw up the timeline.

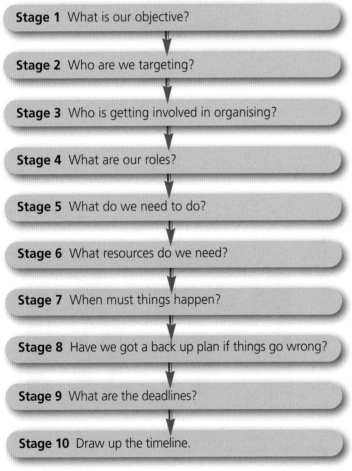

Planning means setting out what must be done and making sure that everyone knows their responsibilities. By following these ten stages, you will be on the right track. You will need to gather evidence and show how it was useful to your Campaign. The following pages will help you with the stages of organising your Campaign and gathering the evidence you need.

What will you need to collect?

- A statement of the objectives of your Campaign
- Your plan – showing how you managed time and resources
- The methods of campaigning you used – and an explanation of how they helped
- Evidence of what you did
- Evidence of how you aimed to meet your objectives
- Evidence that you have tried to persuade people in positions of power or influence and have found out what they thought
- Evidence of the views of others
- An explanation of the outcomes – and whether you met your objectives
- Your thoughts on whether you made a positive impact on your issue – using your evidence

Take action

When you have decided on your Campaign, get together with the rest of the team and work out how you are going to go about planning and putting your idea into action.

Check point

Gather evidence to show:

- the objectives of your Campaign
- the links to Citizenship
- the ways your campaign strategies will work
- your plan.

Making a plan

Brainstorm all the things that need to be done. Can you divide these things easily into groups? Who has the skills needed for each activity? Should people work in pairs or on their own? Then, when you have made these decisions, draw up a list to explain exactly what everyone has to do.

You will need your list throughout the Campaign to check whether everything has been done and to put in your records.

You will need to add the plan to your report form – so make it very clear and keep it safe.

Planning a timeline

Look carefully at your plan and draw up your timeline, putting the name of the person responsible beside every point.

This will give you markers to check whether everything is on track. It will also give everyone target dates for getting things done.

Remember that dealing with people outside school can take time so make this a priority.

Example: Planning a Campaign

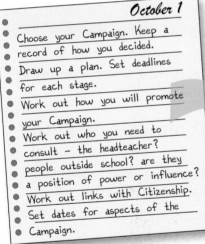

October 1

Choose your Campaign. Keep a record of how you decided.
Draw up a plan. Set deadlines for each stage.
Work out how you will promote your Campaign.
Work out who you need to consult – the headteacher? people outside school? are they a position of power or influence?
Work out links with Citizenship.
Set dates for aspects of the Campaign.

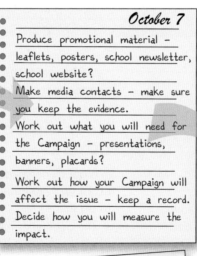

October 7

Produce promotional material – leaflets, posters, school newsletter, school website?
Make media contacts – make sure you keep the evidence.
Work out what you will need for the Campaign – presentations, banners, placards?
Work out how your Campaign will affect the issue – keep a record.
Decide how you will measure the impact.

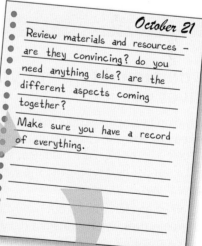

October 21

Review materials and resources – are they convincing? do you need anything else? are the different aspects coming together?
Make sure you have a record of everything.

November 21

Review what happened.
Have you got enough evidence?
Do you need to find out more about whether you influenced people?
Use the evidence to decide whether the Campaign has been a success.

November 14

The event – or the conclusion of the Campaign.
Keep a record of what happened – photographs of your involvement, of the posters, the presentations, people's comments – has the event changed their minds? record/video them?

October 28

Is everything in place?
Work out the impact of your action – a questionnaire?

Participation in action

Save my school!

Aimee said: 'I was racing to save my school. It's such a good school – it is really unfair to close it down.

'I tried to use the success of the triathlon to highlight what I see as a failure of the council in their decision to shut the school.'

1 How is Aimee showing her Citizenship skills?
2 Why does she want to make a difference?
3 Why did she pick this strategy?
4 What do you think she had to do to plan this activity?
5 What sort of evidence do you think she collected?
6 How does her activity relate to the content of the course?

How you aimed to meet your objectives

Aimee really didn't want her school to close. She and her group worked out how she could communicate the issue to as many people as possible. As a triathlete, she knew that the press would cover her next race – and she was right, as the picture above shows.

In your Campaign plan you set out how you planned to meet your objectives. What strategies did you use? Did you:

- produce leaflets, posters, banners or placards?
- set up a website?
- run an assembly?
- put on a play?
- send letters or emails?
- talk to local radio or newspapers?
- hold a meeting?
- hold a protest?
- lobby your councillors, MP or MEP?
- use any other strategy?

Whichever strategies you used, you need know why you selected them and how you participated.

How did you communicate with others?

In order to persuade people in positions of power, you might want to influence other groups. Did you try to persuade:

- the general public?
- other school students?
- parents?

Which strategies did you use for each group?

When you set about persuading people, you need to be able to present a good argument. There are moments when making a lot of noise can be useful. If you want to raise the issue with a lot of people, a demonstration might work well. If you want to persuade people in power, you need to have very good arguments on your side. You also need to know their point of view, as it is much easier to fight if you know how the opposition thinks.

Think about how your participation meets these needs.

Gather evidence of your action and how you made a contribution

There are all sorts of ways in which you can submit your supporting evidence. It doesn't just have to be in the form of written documents.

- Photos are great because they can show you were involved. Placards and banners are too big but you can take pictures of them being used as evidence of participation and communication.
- A video can show the work involved in your Campaign.
- An audio recording of a meeting or a presentation about carrying out your activity gives a clear picture of how you worked.
- A PowerPoint presentation that explains or persuades people of your point of view makes a good piece of evidence.
- A website that lets people know your plans or persuades them to support you is helpful as it shows just what you were trying to do and how you went about it.
- If you investigate what people think, you may use a questionnaire. This, together with the results, makes a good piece of evidence as it shows the way you worked and what you found out.
- You might write letters or emails to explain, persuade or justify your point of view. These are useful pieces of supporting evidence, as they give people a good picture of the Campaign

Gathering all the information as you go along will help you to put it all together. It's very easy to forget exactly what happened and when!

What views did others hold?

You need to keep a record of other people's views, but rather than writing about them, you can use other forms of evidence:

- The local media can be a useful source of other people's points of view. If you are campaigning about something local, you can be sure that they will be involved. Look out for press cuttings.
- Has the opposition got a website? These provide an easy source of evidence – but make sure that you only include what is relevant.
- You could interview people and record the conversations.

Take action

Work out how you are going to campaign and how you are hoping to change people's thinking.

Work out how you are going to gather the evidence. Make sure you keep it safe!

If any problems cropped up during your Campaign, explain how you helped your team to overcome them.

If you changed your plans, describe how you helped your team to do this and explain why these changes had to be made.

Check point

Get organised! The evidence is important so build it into every part of your action.

You should describe how each piece of evidence helped you to campaign and why you used it. For example, a letter or email to a person in a position of power would show your arguments. A questionnaire would help you to find out what people think – and how best to persuade them. It is also important that you show how the evidence you have gathered can be used to support arguments and make judgements.

When Oxford University built a new centre for medical research, animal rights protestors tried to prevent it happening. Supporters of the development took to the streets as well.

What was the impact?

When St Brendan's had such great success with their Fairtrade gig (see page 40), they decided more needed to be done.

The students realised that they needed more to make Fairtrade an integral part of their college. They wrote a policy, which went to the governors for approval – and it was passed.

1 Why do you think the students thought Fairtrade should be integral to the college?

2 How did they decide to go about it?

3 Are the governors people in a position of power?

4 What was the impact of the St Brendan's students' Campaign?

5 Have they changed people's minds?

6 Were governors important in your Campaign? If so, explain how.

What were the outcomes?

Whatever the topic of your Campaign, things will have happened. Your evidence will help you to explain the effects of your Campaign. Go through your evidence and explain the outcomes.

What were the reasons?

If it all went according to plan, just explain what happened. You might include a mention of who helped and why it was straightforward.

If things went wrong or you had to change your plans, explain why and how you sorted things out.

Were there things you did particularly well, or would do better next time?

Did you achieve your objectives?

The object of a campaign is to change things – but you can't expect to get your way all the time. Negotiation is part of most political activity.

If you changed your objectives during the Campaign, explain how and why. Did it make your objectives more achievable?

Don't worry if you weren't successful. There are always two sides to an argument and not every campaign makes change happen immediately – but it might have an effect at a later date. If you didn't win, did you change people's ideas? Very often, the outcome is a compromise.

- A new supermarket might want to cut down trees to build an access road. Perhaps they changed the line of the road and saved some of the trees.
- The council want to close the skate park. Perhaps it might just be open at the weekend instead.
- The school wants students to wear a more formal uniform. Perhaps it might be redesigned to keep everyone happy.

Explain what happened and what elements of your Campaign were achieved.

Evidence that you made an impact

Your evidence might be letters or emails that show how people have accepted your point of view. The students from St Brendan's would have had the minutes of the governors' meeting and their Fairtrade policy to show what they had achieved.

Perhaps you have pictures to show what you achieved. A pedestrian crossing outside the school? Some lights in the underpass – or at least agreement that the council will install them? Look back at the case studies on previous pages and think about the sort of evidence that other students might have had to show their achievements.

Your evaluation

You will have one hour to write up your evaluation. Here are the things that you will have to think about:

- describe the impact of your Campaign with evidence to back up your points
- describe what you learnt about the issue
- evaluate your plan. To what extent did it help you to achieve your aims?
- describe what went well and explain how you might do things differently if you took part in another Campaign
- describe the next steps that could be taken by you or others in seeking to influence decision-makers.

Once this is clear, the writing up should be straightforward. Remember that the controlled assessment is worth 60 per cent of the whole GCSE, so you can get lots of marks for doing things rather than just taking an exam.

Campaign success

Derbyshire County Council announced that they will be reducing the speed limit to 40mph on the road outside part of the Derby College campus. This follows a five-month campaign by Derby College students. The students and staff of the college and local residents are ecstatic with the results and look forward to using a safer road.

Unit 2: Identity,

democracy and justice

understanding our role as citizens

A national culture

Getting you thinking

1 Many people who visit Britain have a very traditional vision of the country. How would you describe it?

2 If you had to describe British culture to people, what would you include?

3 Do you think other people might have a different picture? How might their vision differ from yours?

What does it mean to be British?

This is a difficult question and it has many possible answers. Do you think it means that:

- you share a geographical boundary with other British people?
- you share a history that links the separate parts of England, Wales, Scotland and Northern Ireland?
- you share a common language?
- you identify with many common habits, values and pastimes?
- you have the right to have a British passport so you can move freely in and out of the United Kingdom?

A national identity is often easier to describe when you are in a different country. How might you feel if you went abroad on holiday? In Spain, for example, you would come across a different language, a different kind of diet, different kinds of schooling and different games played by children and adults.

A sense of belonging

A sense of belonging comes from growing up and living in a particular place. Parents, schools and the media pass on common ideas of British culture. Different generations are also influenced by their own personal experiences. People who have fought in wars for their country are likely to feel a different sense of belonging from those who only feel British when they are away on holiday.

Which community?

People may also identify with different kinds of national community. People from ethnic minorities may feel more comfortable with members of their own ethnic community than with other **British nationals**. Similarly, people from particular regions such as the Midlands or the South West might identify more with people from their own region than with people from other regions.

It is possible to belong to many different communities at the same time. Sports fans may feel quite comfortable supporting a British team in one competition, an English or Welsh team in another, and their local team in a third.

You will explore the meaning of national identity and culture, and discover that Britain's community is very diverse.

A multicultural community

Population of Great Britain by ethnic group (millions)

White	43.8
Black Caribbean	0.6
Black African	0.6
Indian	1.2
Pakistani	0.8
Bangladeshi	0.3
Chinese	0.3
Mixed	0.8
Other groups	0.3

Source: Social Trends 2008, Office of National Statistics

The ethnic mix of the national community has changed steadily over the years to include a significant number of people of Afro-Caribbean, African and Asian descent. In some areas, the majority of the local population is now of one of these groups. Many of these people have developed a sense of belonging and feel British, as the chart on the right shows.

In a **multicultural community**:

- a local school may serve a community with several different home languages and different festivals to celebrate
- welfare services often provide information printed in several languages
- hospitals and clinics work with a variety of traditions and expectations surrounding births and deaths
- local councils have to take account of different community needs for shops and religious buildings
- businesses may have staff and customers from a range of cultural backgrounds.

Who feels British?

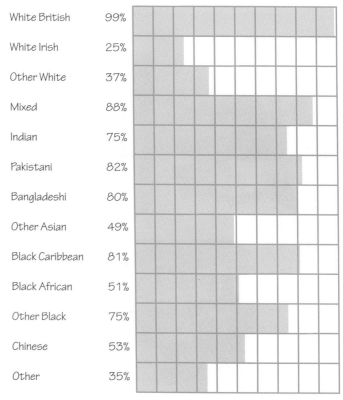

White British	99%
White Irish	25%
Other White	37%
Mixed	88%
Indian	75%
Pakistani	82%
Bangladeshi	80%
Other Asian	49%
Black Caribbean	81%
Black African	51%
Other Black	75%
Chinese	53%
Other	35%

Source: Office of National Statistics

Action

What do your friends and family mean by 'being British'? Share your findings with the class.

Check your understanding

1 What does it mean to say that Britain is a multicultural community?
2 List as many different aspects of British culture as you can that you think help define British national identity.

... another point of view?

'The region I live in is more important to me than my national culture.'

Do you agree with this statement? Give reasons for your opinion, showing you have considered another point of view.

Key Terms

British nationals: citizens of the United Kingdom

multicultural community: a community made up of people from many different cultural or ethnic groups

What makes us free?

Getting you thinking

1 Which of these pictures show things that are unlikely to happen in the UK?

2 Which one shows a situation in which a business would be held responsible?

3 Which ones show people taking responsibility for others or the environment?

4 Explain why you have made your choices.

5 Why do you think things might be different in other countries?

Putting our values into practice

My rights – my responsibilities

We all have a vote

No one is above the law

Equal in law

Tolerance is the key

1 Explain each of these headlines and give an example of each one.
2 What effect does each one have on your view of how we live?
3 Why do you think tolerance is the key?

What do we mean by values?

Values are the principles we generally live by. In the UK these are generally thought to be personal freedom, tolerance, respect for diversity, decency and fair play. Together, they mean we have respect for each other and should be able to resolve any conflict peacefully.

What makes values work?

We have personal freedom because of:

- **The rule of law**

  Everyone must obey the law. No one, not even the Queen or the Prime Minister, can break the law and avoid prosecution. In a community where the law only applies to some people and others can get away with committing crimes there is likely to be little respect for individuals or the law.

You will explore the value systems that help people to live together.

- **Representative democracy**

  In the UK, laws are made by Parliament. Everyone who has a vote (see pages 84–5) can play their part in choosing and electing their representatives. This is known as representative democracy. At 18 you will be able to vote in elections to choose your representative in your local area, the whole country and the European Union. These people then have the task of deciding how we are governed.

From the age of 18, all UK citizens have the right to vote

- **Equality of opportunity**

  People who discriminate against others are breaking the law. The following laws protect people from discrimination. You can find out more about them on page 23.
  - The Equal Pay Act
  - The Sex Discrimination Act
  - The Race Relations Act
  - The Employment Equality Regulations
  - The Disability Discrimination Act

Why do these people have equality of opportunity?

Not just the law

As UK citizens, we have rights, many of which are covered by our laws, but we also have responsibilities. Many of these responsibilities (but not all of them) are also covered by our laws. Some responsibilities are just part of living in the UK and make the country a better place in which to live.

There is no law that says you should offer your seat on the bus or train to someone who has a greater need for it. There is no law that says you should help someone who needs assistance crossing the road or getting downstairs with a buggy. You just have to decide whether you are going to do the decent thing. Respecting others, however, generally means that everyone feels more secure and helping others generally means that everyone feels better.

Action

Make a list of all the things you have done in the last 24 hours and work out when values have played a part. Were your actions the result of legal rights and responsibilities or just part of the way you live?

... another point of view?

'The law by itself can always ensure that values are upheld.'

Do you agree with this statement? Give reasons for your opinion, showing you have considered another point of view.

Check your understanding

1 What are values?
2 What is the rule of law?
3 What is a representative democracy?
4 Explain why we have equality of opportunity.
5 How do rights and responsibilities affect our values?

Key Terms

representative democracy: a type of democracy in which citizens have the right to choose someone to represent them on a council or in Parliament as an MP

rule of law: the law applies to everyone in the country – no one is above the law

Religious understanding

Getting you thinking

1 Which symbol represents the religion represented by each building?
2 Think of some other religions that are not shown.
3 What do all these religions have in common? List as many factors as you can.

Diverse views

Although most UK citizens would probably claim to be Christians, there are many other diverse religious groups in the UK. The majority of these are found in large cities, such as London, Birmingham, Manchester and Leeds, where most of the UK's ethnic **minority** communities live. This religious diversity is the result of people settling here over many years, mostly from former British colonies.

The main ethnic minority groups and their religions are:

- **Bangladeshis**: mostly Muslim, some Hindu
- **Indians (Punjabis)**: mostly Sikh, some Hindu
- **Indians (Gujeratis)**: mostly Hindu, some Muslim
- **Pakistanis**: Muslim
- **Chinese**: Christian, Confucian and Buddhist
- **Afro-Caribbeans**: Christian and Rastafarian.

Within many religions there are different 'branches'. Anglicans, Methodists, Quakers and Catholics are all part of the wider Christian tradition but practise their religion in different ways. Similarly, Orthodox and Reform Jews share many beliefs but worship in separate synagogues.

Sometimes an individual's clothes, the food they eat or the language they speak gives a clue to their religion. But this is not always the case. Think about all the UK citizens with Indian roots. Some of them are Sikhs, but what about the others?

UK citizens with Indian roots: different religions

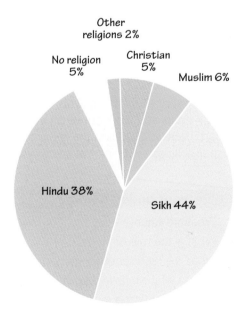

Other religions 2%
No religion 5%
Christian 5%
Muslim 6%
Hindu 38%
Sikh 44%

Source: www.statistics.gov.uk

You will find out about the religious diversity of the UK and why religious tolerance is important.

Religion in conflict

Threatened for converting

A Bradford man who faced threats and harassment for converting to Christianity from Islam was told by police to 'stop being a crusader and move to another place'.

Nissar Hussein and his wife, Qubra, converted from Islam to Christianity in 1996. They were subsequently alienated from family and friends.

As news of the couple's conversion spread, their Bradford home was vandalised and their car was set on fire. In 2001, one man told Mr Hussein that if he did not return to Islam, he would burn down his house.

I go to an Asian church

I go to church with my family every Sunday. We can wear our Indian clothes and meet other Asian and English friends that we may not see during the week. Going to an Asian church means we worship God in both the English and the Indian traditions.

During the service, one person usually stands up at the front and leads the service. We sing in different languages, including English, as many of the church members are Asian, although people from other nationalities sometimes come along.

We also have Indian instruments to help with the singing and worship. People pray in different languages too. Both men and women pray. In most Asian churches the men and women usually sit on separate sides. The young people sit on both sides, depending on their age, and whether both of their parents come to church.

1   Why do you think Nisssar and Qubra's friends and family disliked them converting?
2   The Asian church is a Christian church. How is it trying to bring people together?

Everyone's rights

The United Nations (UN), an international organisation to which most countries belong, put together the Universal Declaration of Human Rights (see page 9). This declaration includes a section on religion, which states that everyone is free to follow any religion or to choose to follow none. The declaration also states that everyone has the right to join an established religion, or to start a sect or cult of their own.

... another point of view?

'It is always important to be **tolerant** of other people's religious beliefs.'

Do you agree with this statement? Give reasons for your opinion, showing you have considered another point of view.

Check your understanding

1   Why does the UK have such a diversity of religions? Can you name any other countries where you find a similar religious diversity?
2   What does the Universal Declaration of Human Rights say about your religious freedom? Is this always observed?

Key Terms

minority: a small part of a larger group of people

tolerant: open-minded, accepting

Where are your roots?

Getting you thinking

Whose genes?

1 Many of us know where our grandparents lived, and perhaps our great grandparents. Where did yours come from?

2 Do you think it is important for you to know your roots? Explain your answer.

I live in Cheddar in Somerset. My DNA tells me I'm related to a man who lived here 40,000 years ago.

I thought I was British but my DNA tells me I'm descended from Native Americans. They must have been brought here as slaves.

I live in London and I know my family came from Yorkshire. My DNA tells me I have relations who were Mongolian, Brazilian, a Russian and a woman who lived near the Mediterranean 117,000 years ago.

'To forget your ancestors is to be a tree without roots.' Chinese proverb

3 If we know we have lots of different roots, does it help us to understand others?

A pick-and-mix people

Throughout its history, people have settled in Britain from many different countries. They bring their language, ideas and customs, all of which have mixed together to make up the country's culture.

Warlike invasions of Romans, Saxons, Vikings and Normans were followed by peaceful migrations from Europe and many former British colonies. Just look in the dictionary, phone book or map to find words and names from many languages.

➤ In the past 250 years, about six million people have come from Ireland in search of a better life. Many came to the UK during the potato famine of the 1840s.

➤ In 1860, one-quarter of the population of Liverpool were Irish migrants.

➤ Poles have lived here ever since the reign of Queen Elizabeth I, but the majority of UK Poles settled here after the Second World War when Poland was occupied first by the Nazis, and then by the Soviet army.

➤ There has been a Jewish population in the UK for hundreds of years, but most arrived in the 1930s and 40s. They came to the UK to escape from religious and racial persecution in Russia and Europe.

➤ In the 1950s, many people from British colonies in Africa, Asia and the Caribbean settled in the UK looking for work, as there was a shortage of manual and semi-skilled employees in Britain during this period.

➤ In the 1970s, thousands of Ugandan Asians arrived here after being expelled from Uganda.

➤ As more countries have joined the European Union, people from Eastern Europe, including Poland, have moved here to work because there are more opportunities.

Immigration today is more restricted for people from many parts of the world.

In the same way that people from other countries come to Britain, people emigrate from Britain to go and live in other countries. The table below shows some reasons for **immigration** and **emigration** in Britain.

Why do people come and go? (thousands)			
	Immigration	Emigration	Balance
For work	103.4	92.8	10.6
With a partner	77.2	51.1	26.1
For study	91.2	13.7	77.5
Other	164.6	99.3	65.3
No reason	27.7	49.2	−21.5
All reasons	464.0	306.0	158.0

Source: Office of National Statistics

You will find out about the diverse communities that make up the UK.

Ethnic minorities in each region

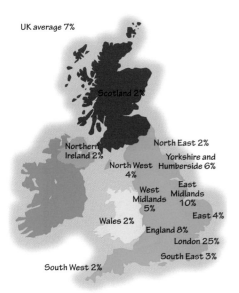

UK average 7%

Scotland 2%

Northern Ireland 2%

North East 2%

North West 4%

Yorkshire and Humberside 6%

West Midlands 5%

East Midlands 10%

East 4%

Wales 2%

England 8%

London 25%

South East 3%

South West 2%

Source: 2001 Census, Office of National Statistics

Leicester: a lesson in racial understanding

When rioting has taken place in other cities, Leicester has remained calm. Many people living in Leicester have non-white roots, and the city is proud of its **cultural diversity**. However, in the 1970s, it was labelled one of the most racist cities in Britain. There were adverts in the local papers telling immigrants not to come to Leicester and racial tension was high.

The city council took the lead by outlawing racism. It promoted Leicester as a city that welcomes everybody. The council created Britain's first-ever race relations committee. A public education programme made people aware of others' hopes and fears. Since then, various groups have worked hard to promote good race relations in the city.

There are now over 1,500 Asian businesses in the city, and many Asian councillors on the city council. Festivals such as Diwali now attract over 25,000 people to the city.

Action

Research the background and culture of any immigrant groups that have settled in your local area. Find out why they left their homelands, and to what extent they have been able to retain their language and culture. Present your findings to the class

Check your understanding

1 Suggest two reasons why the UK is a culturally diverse society.
2 Why did many immigrants come to Britain in the 1950s?
3 Why do people immigrate and emigrate?
4 In which regions, outside London, would you find the most culturally diverse communities?
5 Describe two things the council did to improve race relations in Leicester.
6 Why do you think there have been no riots in Leicester when there has been trouble in other cities?
7 Do you think other regions of the UK will become more culturally diverse in future? Give reasons.
8 What do you think can be done to bring different ethnic groups together?

... another point of view?

'Immigration benefits a country.'

Do you agree with this statement? Give reasons for your opinion, showing you have considered another point of view.

Key Terms

cultural diversity: the range of different groups that make up a wider population

emigration: leaving your homeland to live in another country

immigration: coming to live in another country

Identities

Getting you thinking

I've got Asian roots. I love sport, have loads of mates and I'm always having fun.

I come from Brighton. My parents are divorced. I've got one brother and two half-sisters. I like watching TV and listening to music. I spend loads of time at the beach with my friends.

I'm from Newcastle. I'm 15, an only child and a huge fan of EastEnders and reality TV shows.

1 What has contributed to the identity of each of these people?

2 How do you think these factors have affected them?

3 How much does your identity depend on where you live, on your family's roots or on your religion?

4 If you had been asked the question, 'Who are you?' when you were five years old, what would you have said? How would you answer this question now?

5 Make a list of factors that will shape your identity as you get older.

Who am I?

In some countries, such as France, all citizens must carry an **identity card**. There are plans to introduce one in the UK. This card gives details such as name, address and date of birth. But the word '**identity**' has another, broader meaning. The identity of a person is a combination of where they come from and the influences on their life.

Your identity develops and changes as you develop and change. Can you remember how you felt when you first went to school? You've learnt a lot about yourself in the ten or more years since

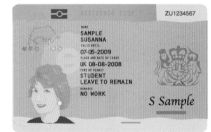

then. You now have a better understanding of your good and bad points; you are more self-aware and better aware of how other people see you. Looking back, that five-year-old 'you' will seem like a very different person. Your identity will continue to develop further as you grow older and as you become an employee, a parent, a partner, wife or husband and so on.

Identity cards obviously can't show all this information about you. However, some governments like them because it means that people can be easily identified. There are plans to introduce them in the UK.

You will discover the meaning of identity and how complex it can be.

Conflicting loyalties

Britain has one of the highest rates of mixed-race relationships in the world. By 2010, it is estimated that London will be made up of more **dual heritage** and black people than white people. While most people would agree that cultural diversity is a good thing, the mixing of races and nationalities can occasionally produce conflict.

If your mother is Chinese, your father is Irish, you were born in Paris but you live in London, how would you answer the question 'Where are you from?'

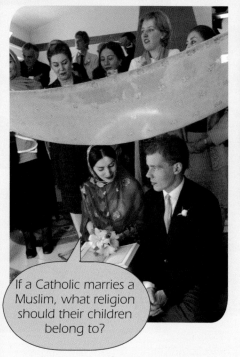

If a Catholic marries a Muslim, what religion should their children belong to?

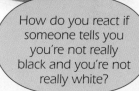

How do you react if someone tells you you're not really black and you're not really white?

If your mother is German and your father is English, who should you support in the World Cup?

1 In your own words, describe the conflicting loyalties felt by each of these people.

2 Which person has the most difficult situation to resolve, and why?

3 Suggest other situations that involve conflicting loyalties.

Check your understanding

What does 'dual heritage' mean? Describe how dual heritage can sometimes lead to a conflict of identity.

... another point of view?

'People are more alike than different.'

Do you agree with this statement? Give reasons for your opinion, showing you have considered another point of view.

Key Terms

dual heritage: people with parents or ancestors of different origins

identity: who or what someone or something is

identity card: a card that establishes someone's identity

What is a community?

Getting you thinking

1 How many of these communities do you belong to?
2 What other communities do you belong to?
3 How many of these communities do you share with people of different ages and/or interests?
4 If you don't belong to some of these communities, do you know people who do? How do you know these people?
5 What do these communities give you and what do you give them?

Belonging to a community

A **community** is a group of people who are connected in some way. Most people belong to several communities. Someone your age living in the UK could be a member of all these communities: a school, the local neighbourhood, the country, the European Union, a religious group, and others.

Neighbourhoods

There is a lot of overlap between different communities.

A **neighbourhood** community refers to those people who share local interests because of where they live. A neighbourhood might be the whole of a village or small town, but in a city a neighbourhood can be more difficult to identify. For example, someone living in Whitechapel in London might think of the neighbourhood as 'London', 'Whitechapel', 'the East End' or even just their own particular street.

You will discover the meaning of community and understand how communities work together.

'I belong to…'

As well as belonging to a neighbourhood, people are also connected by their lifestyle, religion, ethnicity or nationality.

The Chinese community

The Chinese community in the UK dates back to the mid-1800s. They live in all parts of the UK and there are well-established 'Chinatowns' in Birmingham, Liverpool, London, Manchester and Newcastle. There are over 400 Chinese organisations that serve the needs of the Chinese community in the UK, including language schools, women's groups, and art and business associations. Chinese New Year, food, martial arts, medicine and Feng Shui have all become part of British life.

Irish travellers

There are about 1,300 Irish travellers in Northern Ireland. They are a centuries-old ethnic community that travels around in mobile homes. They have their own culture, customs, traditions and language.

The Christian community

There are almost 49,000 Christian churches in the United Kingdom across more than ten different denominations, ranging from Church of England and Roman Catholic to Methodist and Greek Orthodox. As well as involving people in the wider Christian community, many churches are a focus for local people, offering facilities and events open to Christians and non-Christians alike.

The Muslim community

Almost all of the Muslim population in Britain are descendants of the families of people who came to Britain in the 1950s, 60s and 70s. However, Islam has been followed in Britain for centuries. At least 300 years ago, Indian-Muslim sailors, recruited by the East India Company, settled in port towns. The first mosque in Britain probably opened in Cardiff in 1860. Today, there are Muslim communities all over Britain.

Getting along together

Many towns and cities have a great mix of religious and ethnic groups. Leicester has successfully dealt with the issues of **community cohesion** and other cities are developing strategies to encourage people to live together in harmony. The government also works hard to promote ways in which people's voices can be heard in their communities.

People work together in all sorts of ways. Just think about where you meet people from different communities. A trip to hospital often leads to meeting people whose roots are all over the world. On television there are entertainers from many different backgrounds. Sports teams are often a great ethnic mix.

Check your understanding

1 Explain why people can belong to more than one community and why there is an overlap between communities.
2 Describe what each of the communities described above has in common. What makes each one a community?

… another point of view?

'It is easier to feel part of a community if you live in a village or small town rather than a city.'

Do you agree with this statement? Give reasons for your opinion, showing you have considered another point of view.

Key Terms

community: a group of people who are in close contact and who share common interests and values

community cohesion: the glue that holds communities together

neighbourhood: a local area within which people live as neighbours, sharing living space and interests

What's the point of law?

Getting you thinking

At the beginning of Year 11, Annie, Sanjay, Mikael, Deb, Steve and Al know that they have a hard year ahead if they are to get the GCSEs they want. They are dreaming of the summer when they know it will all be over. The plan is to go on holiday together – somewhere in the sun. It will not be cheap but they are cleaning cars together while saving up on their own.

1 Why might the friends fall out before July?

2 What rules might they need to set to stop them falling out?

3 Who sets your school rules?

4 Are people more likely to keep the rules if they have been involved in setting them?

5 What problems would there be if there were no laws?

Why do people obey the law?

Law-abiding citizens obey the law for a variety of reasons. They may:

- have strong religious or moral views about breaking the law
- be afraid of being caught and arrested
- fear the shame that going to prison would bring on them and their family
- be worried about damaging their 'good name' (their reputation).

In some situations it is obvious why a law is needed. If drivers drove through traffic lights on 'stop', they could be seriously injured or killed, or cause injury or death to someone else.

Breaking the law can damage your good name

You will understand why we need laws.

Why do we need laws?

The short answer is: try imagining life without them! Your life would be chaotic, and the most vulnerable members of society, such as the very young, the elderly, the ill and some minorities, would suffer most. What would happen to children, for example, if there were no laws on divorce?

For laws to work properly they need the support of the majority of the population. Most people agree that child abuse is a shocking crime and abusers must be punished. But public opinion is more divided on euthanasia. Some think it is wrong to treat doctors as criminals if they help terminally ill patients who are in pain to die. Others would argue that it is morally wrong as well as unlawful.

The law is a common code for us all to abide by and gives us a way of resolving disputes between people.

Who's the loser?

A shoplifter who has stolen a couple of T-shirts might argue that their actions won't put a big company like Marks and Spencer out of business, but:

- if everybody stole from them it would push up prices for everyone else who shops there, because Marks and Spencer had to pay for the T-shirts
- if you steal from Marks and Spencer, you steal from the people who own the business, so it's just like stealing a mobile phone or a car.

In the same way, if people don't pay income tax when they should, the government will have less money to pay for schools and hospitals; so many people are affected indirectly by tax evasion.

Why do laws change?

There are laws to cover a vast range of activities, including adoption, marriage and divorce, terrorism, discrimination, motoring, banking, sex, drugs, theft and assault. New developments, such as cloning or the internet, often require new laws.

Action

1 In groups, think about your usual daily routine and list how many times during the day you come across a rule or law. Why do you choose to obey, or not to obey, these rules and laws?
2 You sometimes hear people say 'But it's a bad law.' Make a list of your reasons for laws being good or bad. Be ready to explain your ideas.
3 Find out what new laws have been passed recently. Why do you think they are necessary?

Check your understanding

1 In your own words, give four reasons why people obey the law. Suggest one more reason not mentioned on these pages.
2 Make a list of crimes that have immediate consequences for the general public. List others that may have long-term and less immediate consequences.
3 Why do you think it is important that the majority of citizens support a particular law? Suggest one law that probably has majority support. Suggest one that probably doesn't, and give a reason.

... another point of view?

'You should never break the law.'

Do you agree with this statement? Give reasons for your opinion, showing you have considered another point of view.

How are laws made?

Getting you thinking

Climate change law: reduce greenhouse gas emissions by 80 per cent by 2050

The Community Rehabilitation Order aims to:

- ensure young people take responsibility for their crimes
- help young people to resolve any personal difficulties which may have contributed to their offending
- help young people become law-abiding and responsible members of the community

Smoking ban: no one can smoke in enclosed public places

School leaving age: from 2013 everyone will have to stay in education or training until they are 17

1 Why do you think the government wanted to make laws like these?

2 What, in your opinion, would happen if the government passed laws that the population did not like?

3 Why do people, in general, keep the laws that are passed by Parliament?

Power

Parliament passes laws that determine how we live our lives. By electing a government, we give it the power to do this. If people break the laws, they can be punished. The government is given authority (a mandate) because the population accepts that an election is a fair way of deciding who will hold power for a five-year period.

The government is **accountable** because it has to answer to the voters. If voters do not like what is happening, the government will not be re-elected.

How are laws made?

Laws go through several stages before coming into force. The government often puts out a **Green Paper**, which puts forward ideas for future laws. Once the ideas have been made final, a **White Paper** is published. This lays out the government's policy. To turn policy into law, the proposals are introduced to Parliament in the form of a **bill**. To change the school leaving age, for example, the government would have to introduce an Education Bill. Having gone through the process shown in the diagram opposite, the bill becomes an **Act** of Parliament and, therefore, part of the law of the country. The government is accountable to the population so it needs to be sure that everyone has had an opportunity to comment.

It is important that laws are carefully put together, or 'drafted', because there are always some people who want to find a way of avoiding them. If a law can be interpreted in a different way, it will be very hard to enforce. The law to ban hunting, for example, is proving difficult to enforce.

You will understand the process that a bill goes through before it becomes law.

The debate

Most bills are introduced by the government. Sometimes the two parties are in agreement and all goes smoothly but often the opposition seriously disagrees either on the policy as a whole or on aspects of it. This leads to lengthy debate as the opposition tries to persuade the government to accept changes – or amendments – to the bill.

Passing through Parliament

First reading
The bill is introduced formally in the House of Commons. Before it reaches this stage, it has been worked on by a Drafting Committee to make sure that it is correctly put together. A bill can be many pages long. At this stage there is no debate.

Second reading
A few weeks after the first reading stage, the bill is debated fully in the House of Commons. A vote is taken and if the majority of MPs approve of the bill, it is passed.

Standing committee
A group of 16 to 20 MPs look at the bill carefully and make any alterations that came up at the second reading, or which they now think are appropriate.

House of Lords
The bill goes through the same process as in the Commons. If the Lords want to change anything, the bill is returned to the Commons.

Report stage
The committee sends a report to the House of Commons with all its amendments. These amendments are either approved or changed. Changes are made when there is a lot of opposition to the bill or if there is strong public pressure to do so.

Third reading
The amended bill is presented to the House of Commons. A debate is held and a vote is taken on whether to approve it.

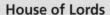

Royal assent
Once the bill has passed all its stages in the Commons and the Lords, it is sent to the Queen for her signature. This is really a formality, as the Queen would never refuse to sign a bill that had been through the democratic process. The bill then becomes an Act of Parliament and part of the law of the country.

Action

Decide on a new law that you would like to see passed. Put your proposals into a 'bill'. Work out what the opposition is likely to say and prepare your arguments.

Check your understanding

1 What is the difference between a bill and an Act?
2 What sort of things do committees have to pay attention to when making amendments to bills?
3 Why do you think there are so many stages before a law is made?

Key Terms

accountable: if you are accountable for something, you are responsible for it and have to explain your actions

Act: a law passed by Parliament

bill: a proposal to change something into law

Green Paper: this puts forward ideas that the government wants discussed before a policy is developed

White Paper: this puts government policy up for discussion before it becomes law

Civil and criminal law: what's the difference?

Getting you thinking

Grant Raphael, a cameraman, made fake entries on his old school friend Mathew Firsht's Facebook profile. The entries were not very polite! Mathew **sued** his old friend for libel and misuse of private information. He was awarded £22,000 damages against his friend, who had to pay the cost of the case as well.

Mathew Firsht won his case at the High Court

Biker's murderers jailed for life

1 Which case is a private issue?
2 Which case involved the police?
3 Which case is more worrying for the general public? Why?
4 Can you think of some other examples of private issues and some which involve the police?

Two kinds of law

Over many centuries of law making, two separate but related branches of the law have evolved to meet changing circumstances: **civil law** and **criminal law**.

Most civil cases are about disputes between individuals or groups, and very often these arguments are about rights. Examples include company law, adoption, accidents at work and consumer rights.

Criminal law deals with offences such as murder, theft and drug dealing. In a criminal case, the conflict is between the government (acting for all citizens) and the lawbreakers.

Who's right?

The person who brings a case to a civil court is called the claimant. The person accused of doing wrong is called the defendant. In some civil cases, the claimant sets out to sue the defendant. If the claimant wins, the defendant will have to give them money, which are known as damages.

Katie Price and Peter Andre won large libel damages after they took action over claims they were uncaring parents. They sued the owners of the newspaper after a story appeared in the *News of the World*. The story was based on an interview with former nanny Rebecca Gauld. In a new development, the newspaper's solicitor apologised and accepted the allegations were untrue, adding that the couple were decent and responsible parents who cared deeply for their children.

1 Who is the claimant in this case? Who is the defendant?
2 Why was this case heard in a civil court?

You will find out about the difference between civil and criminal law.

Civil courts

A civil court

Most civil cases are heard in a **county court**. Because a court case can be very expensive, most people try to settle the dispute before it gets to court. A **judge** sitting without a **jury** decides almost all civil cases.

A small number of civil cases are heard in a **High Court**. These courts deal with complex family disputes and other complicated financial and legal matters, such as bankruptcy and large claims for damages. Any case involving £50,000 or more is heard in the High Court.

If a civil case involves a claim of less than £5,000, it will be heard in a **small claims court**. About 90,000 cases a year are heard in these courts.

Action

Make a list of the different kinds of cases that appear in civil courts. Which human rights are involved in each type?

Check your understanding

1 What are the main differences between civil and criminal cases?
2 What is a) a claimant, b) a defendant and c) a small claims court?
3 What type of crime is dealt with in either the magistrates' or Crown Courts?
4 Why are most civil cases settled before they reach court?

... another point of view?

'Neighbours should sort things out instead of going to court.'
Do you agree with this statement? Give reasons for your opinion, showing you have considered another point of view.

Criminal courts

There is a separate system of courts to deal with criminal cases. Less serious offences are dealt with in **magistrates' courts**. Serious offences are dealt with in **Crown Courts** before a judge and a jury.

A criminal court

Key Terms

civil law: this covers disputes between individuals or groups. Civil law cases are often about rights between people

county court: a local court that has limited powers in civil cases

criminal law: this deals with offences such as murder and drug dealing. These cases are between the Crown Prosecution Service (acting for all citizens) and the offender

Crown Court: courts held in towns in England and Wales where judges hear cases

High Court: the court where judges hear cases on serious crimes

judge: a person who decides questions of law in a court

jury: a group of people who decide if someone is guilty in a court of law

magistrates' court: a court held before two or more public officers dealing with minor crimes

small claims court: a local court, which hears civil cases involving small amounts of money

sue: to make a claim against someone or something

Criminal courts

Getting you thinking

1 Which of the two courtrooms above is the most 'child-friendly' and why?
2 Should courts be made more 'adult-friendly'? Give reasons.
3 Is it good idea that courts are open to the public? Give reasons.
4 The results of court cases are published in the paper. What effect might this have on people who think about committing a crime?

Two types of court

Courts are formal places. Everyone involved must take the process very seriously. In some countries, youth courts are more informal because people think young people are more likely to tell the truth in a more relaxed environment.

There are two types of court for criminal cases: magistrates' courts and Crown Courts.

A magistrates' court

Over 95 per cent of all criminal trials take place in magistrates' courts. Specially trained magistrates also run youth courts for offenders aged between 10 and 17. Magistrates, who sit in court with at least one other magistrate, also deal with a small number of civil cases.

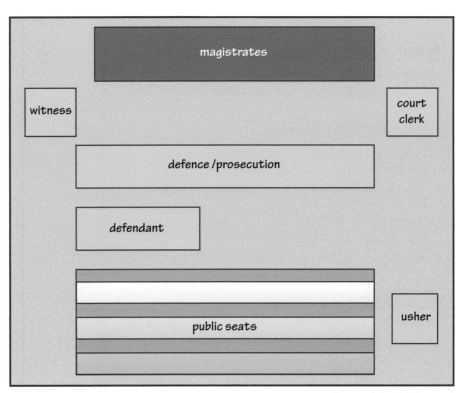

A magistrates' court

Mitigating factors

There is no jury in a magistrates' court, so magistrates must be absolutely sure 'beyond reasonable doubt' that the accused is guilty. They must also take into account any **mitigating** factors. If, for example, a woman stole from a supermarket because she had no money to buy food for herself and her children, magistrates would take this into account and might give her a lesser sentence.

A Crown Court

The most serious criminal cases are heard in a Crown Court. The atmosphere is more solemn and the proceedings are more formal than in a magistrates' court. The judges and barristers wear wigs and gowns. A jury decides if the defendant is guilty or not (unless the defendant pleads guilty, in which case no jury is involved).

Crown Court judges can have different powers. Only High Court judges, who sit in the larger courts, can try very serious cases, such as murder and rape. Others, known as circuit judges and **recorders**, try less serious cases such as theft, for example.

Crown Court judges and juries must also take into account any mitigating factors, in the same way that magistrates do. The maximum sentence in a Crown Court is life imprisonment.

What sentences can magistrates give?

Magistrates have the power to give the following penalties:

- prison: up to a maximum of six months
- community sentences
- Antisocial Behaviour Orders (ASBOs)
- fines: up to a maximum of £5,000.

Magistrates can also give a conditional or absolute discharge.

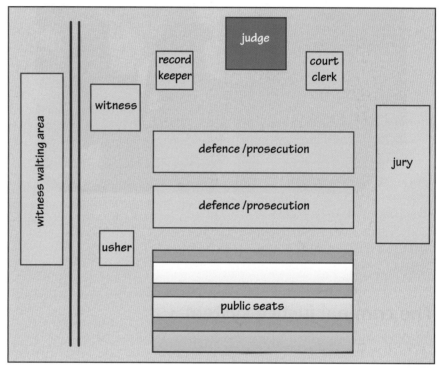

A Crown Court

2.2 Fairness and justice in decision making and the law

Check your understanding

1 What are 'mitigating factors'? Support your answer with an example.
2 What kinds of mitigating factors might influence magistrates' decisions when sentencing young offenders?
3 List the differences between a magistrates' court and Crown Court.
4 What is the maximum sentence each type of court can impose?
5 When is a jury used in a Crown Court case?

... another point of view?

'Courts should be friendlier places.'
Do you agree with this statement? Give reasons for your opinion, showing you have considered another point of view.

Action

Visit your local court. What sort of cases were being tried? What were the outcomes?

Key Terms

mitigating: making something less intense or severe

recorder: a barrister or solicitor with at least ten years' experience, who acts as a part-time judge in a Crown Court

Who puts the law into practice?

Getting you thinking

1 You've broken the law and have to appear in court. Which of the following would you prefer as your 'judge and jury', and why:

- your teachers
- your classmates
- your parents
- the police
- other young people who've been in trouble themselves
- the victims of your crime
- a group of people chosen at random, who do not know you?

2 Which group do you think the victim would prefer? Give reasons.

3 Which group do you think would give the fairest outcome? Give reasons.

The criminal justice system

The criminal justice system is large and complex. These are the roles within it:

Judges

The judges who work in both criminal and civil courts are known collectively as the **judiciary**. Most judges have worked for at least ten years as a barrister, but a few solicitors also become judges. In a jury trial, it is the jury who decide if the accused is guilty or not, but the judge who determines the sentence.

Senior judges (who sit in the higher courts) are very powerful. They don't make laws; Parliament does that. You found out how laws are made on pages 70–1. But if there is an argument about how a law should be interpreted, it is the senior judges who decide.

Magistrates

Full-time magistrates are called district judges and are paid for their work. They are usually barristers or solicitors with at least seven years' experience. They sit alone.

Part-time magistrates come from all walks of life. They are not legally qualified and are not paid. They work with other magistrates.

Jury

A jury is made up of 12 adults, who sit in a Crown Court and decide whether the accused person is innocent or guilty. A jury is made up of members of the public chosen at random.

You will find out about the various roles of people who work within the criminal justice system.

Police

The police do not make laws, they enforce them. Their job is to protect the public, arrest lawbreakers and bring them before the courts.

The Crown Prosecution Service

The Crown Prosecution Service is the government department responsible for prosecuting criminal cases that have been investigated by the police in England and Wales. It is responsible for:

- advising the police on cases for possible prosecution
- reviewing cases submitted by the police
- determining any charges in all but minor cases
- preparing cases for court
- presenting cases at court.

Solicitors

All **solicitors** must pass law exams because, among other things, they give legal advice to people who have to go to court. Some solicitors also speak in court on behalf of their clients.

Barristers

Barristers undergo a long legal training too, but they spend most of their time in court representing their clients. They are the only lawyers qualified to speak in all types of court.

A new uniform has been designed for judges in civil cases. It aims to make them less remote from the public. Do you think it works? If so, explain why

Action

1. Research the entry requirements (age, qualifications, etc.) of either a police officer or a solicitor.
2. Interview a probation officer to find out about the work they do with offenders in the community. You may wish to research a specific aspect of their work. For example, probation officers often work with young offenders who have problems with alcohol and other drugs.
3. Research who can be called for jury service and what serving on a jury involves.

Check your understanding

1. What do judges do in trials where there is a jury?
2. What powers do senior judges have?
3. What is the most important difference between the role of the police and the role of judges?
4. What is the difference between a barrister and a solicitor?
5. What skills and personal qualities do you think you need to be a good magistrate?
6. Can you think of any reasons why people don't apply to be magistrates?

Probation officers

Offenders who are given community sentences work with local **probation officers**. Probation officers are professionally qualified. They write court reports on offenders and supervise them in the community once they've been sentenced.

Key Terms

barrister: a lawyer who represents and speaks for their clients in court

judiciary: all the judges in a country

probation officer: someone who writes court reports on offenders and supervises them in the community

solicitor: a lawyer who gives legal advice and may speak for their clients in court

One person's freedom...

Getting you thinking

The Communications Data Bill

This bill allows the authorities to collect and retain details of every phone number we have called or texted, as well as every address to which we have sent emails and the address of every website we have accessed. The information could be used by government departments, local government and all government agencies.

The Transport minister said:

If they're going to use the internet to communicate with each other and we don't have the power to deal with that, then you're giving a licence to terrorists to kill people. The biggest civil liberty of all is not to be killed by a terrorist.

Liberty, the human rights pressure group, said:

The balance between the privacy of the individual and interests such as national security, crime prevention, and freedom of expression, is far from settled.

The extent of a right to privacy in the UK and its weight in relation to competing values is unclear. Liberty is concerned with how the state, the press and others strike the balance between privacy and other interests.

Radio Frequency Identification

A tag on everyday products

Right now, you can buy a hammer, a pair of jeans, or a razor blade with anonymity. With radio frequency identification (RFID) tags, that may be a thing of the past. Once you buy your RFID-tagged jeans at a store with RFID-tagged money, walk out of the store wearing RFID-tagged shoes, and get into your car with its RFID-tagged tyres, you could be tracked anywhere you travel.

There is no law requiring a label to indicate that an RFID chip is in a product.

1 What is a radio frequency identification tag?

2 Why are people concerned about their use?

3 Think of some situations in which they could be useful.

4 What does the government want to be able to look at? Why?

5 Why does Liberty question the government's plan?

You will find out how human rights can conflict with each other.

Contradictions?

European Convention on Human Rights

The right to live, as far as one wishes, protected from publicity.

United Nations Declaration of Human Rights, Article 12

No one shall be subjected to arbitrary interference with his privacy, family, home or correspondence, nor to attacks upon his honour and reputation. Everyone has the right to the protection of the law against such interference or attacks.

United Nations Declaration of Human Rights, Article 3

Everyone has the right to life, liberty and security of person.

Check your understanding

1 What does the UNDHR have to say about privacy and security?
2 Why are there always trade-offs when we decide where to draw the line on privacy and security?
3 What rules would you set up regarding the government's freedom to look at our emails?
4 What rules would you set up for the use of RFID tags?
5 Explain your reasons for the rules you have devised in questions 3 and 4.

... another point of view?

'The government should have the freedom to do whatever it wants to protect us from terrorism.'

Do you agree with this statement? Give reasons for your opinion, showing you have considered another point of view.

The United Nations Declaration of Human Rights (UNDHR) expects that we should have both privacy and security. The two objectives, however, can be contradictory. The government argues that we need to give up some of our rights if we are going to be safe. Liberty, the human rights **pressure group**, wants these issues to be looked at very carefully before we decide where to draw the line. The boundaries on what is acceptable are very difficult to define

Trade-offs

Every decision we make about the level of intrusion into our lives involves trade-offs. The RFID tag referred to in 'Getting you thinking' could be regarded as snooping on our every move but there are situations in which it can be useful. If a person who has Alzheimer's disease wanders off and gets lost, it would be good to be able to track their whereabouts.

Whatever the area of intrusion, it needs to be investigated carefully before new laws are passed. It is important to look at the ways laws might be used in future. The government might want the right to monitor emails in order to prevent terrorism now, but it may use this right for other reasons in the future. It is also important to consider the effect on society in general. Sections of the population, for example, who feel they are being targeted by such laws may be alienated.

We all have different points of view on these issues but it is important to weigh up the advantages and disadvantages before we come to a conclusion.

Key Terms

pressure group: a group of people that tries to change public opinion or government policy to its own views or beliefs

Who will help?

Getting you thinking

I've been subjected to harassment on the grounds of race and religion. I was provoked into fighting with a colleague and, as a result, was threatened with dismissal.

I've got three young children and have just lost my husband. I can't make ends meet anymore. I really need some help.

I went out with my mates on Saturday night and I reckon someone spiked my drink. I ended up hitting the girl who was after my boyfriend. Someone called the police and I'm sitting in the cells.

1 What sort of help does each of these people need?
2 Should they go to:
  a a solicitor
  b the **Citizens Advice Bureau**
  c a trade union?

Dealing with the law

The law can be complicated and it is important to get the right support. Otherwise, situations can become more difficult. Some services are free and others have to be paid for. The organisation you choose will depend on the nature of the problem.

Trade unions

Trade unions support their members when things go wrong at work. Different unions offer different levels of support, but many will help at the earliest signs of difficulty with an employer, arranging counselling or other support services.

If there is a dispute, the trade union will provide a trained representative to advise the member, attend meetings and help the member to make the right decision at each stage.

In the case of an unfair dismissal where the sacked worker decides to take the case against an employer to an employment tribunal, the trade union will provide legal advice and a solicitor to represent the worker, as long as, having investigated the case, they believe him or her to be in the right.

The Citizens Advice Bureau

You can find a Citizens Advice Bureau in most towns and cities. Trained volunteers provide free advice to people about their rights and responsibilities. The advice is available face to face, on the telephone, via email or online. The diagram on page 81 shows the range of support on offer.

You will discover who to turn to if you need help in dealing with the law.

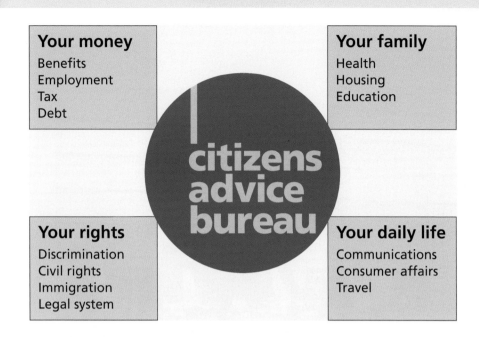

Your money
Benefits
Employment
Tax
Debt

Your family
Health
Housing
Education

citizens advice bureau

Your rights
Discrimination
Civil rights
Immigration
Legal system

Your daily life
Communications
Consumer affairs
Travel

Solicitors

Most people need expert legal help at some time in their lives. Some of the most common issues are to do with buying a house, getting a divorce or making a will. Sometimes, people need help if they are setting up home with a partner, starting a business or organising an elderly person's finances.

If you are accused of committing a crime, a solicitor will be called if requested. You can defend yourself but it is often sensible to speak to a solicitor. Everything you say will be part of the evidence the police use if the case comes to court – so it is useful to get some advice.

Legal aid

The government provides funding for **legal aid** to help people with both civil and criminal cases. It is only available for people on low incomes who could not afford to pay for legal help themselves.

The legal aid scheme aims to:

- protect basic rights and get a fair hearing
- sort out disputes in court
- solve problems that contribute to social exclusion.

In a criminal case, legal aid will provide:

- advice and assistance from a solicitor
- free legal advice from a solicitor at the police station during questioning
- the cost of a solicitor preparing a case and initial representation for certain proceedings at a magistrates' or Crown Court
- full legal representation for defence in criminal cases at all court levels
- a duty solicitor to provide free legal advice and representation at a magistrates' court.

Other sources of help

A variety of other organisations will provide legal advice on housing, money or motoring. Many people belong to a professional organisation related to their work, which will often offer help with problems in that area.

Action

Find out where your nearest Citizens Advice Bureau is. How do you become a volunteer?

Check your understanding

1. How can a trade union help if you have a problem?
2. What can the CAB do?
3. When do you need a solicitor?
4. Who can receive legal aid?
5. What other organisations might you turn to if you need help?

... another point of view?

'You can find out all you need to know from the internet so I won't need legal advice.'

Do you agree with this statement? Give reasons for your opinion, showing you have considered another point of view.

Key Terms

Citizens Advice Bureau: an organisation of trained volunteers who offer free advice to the public

legal aid: a government service that provides free legal support to people who have low earnings

International justice

Getting you thinking

Humanitarian horror

Hundreds of fighters, including children under the age of 15, attacked Bogoro – a village in the Democratic Republic of Congo. They were armed with semi-automatic weapons, rocket-propelled grenades and knives. The soldiers circled the village and converged towards the centre, killing at least 200 civilians and imprisoning survivors in a room filled with corpses. Some residents of the village were killed when their houses were set on fire, and others were hacked to death with machetes.

Two suspects, Germain Katanga and Mathieu Ngudjolo Chui, have been surrendered to the International Criminal Court (ICC – see above) by the Congolese authorities. Both men are charged with six counts of war crimes and three counts of crimes against humanity, relating to the attack on the village of Bogoro.

1 Which human rights did the fighters deprive people of?

2 Why do you think the Congolese authorities handed the men over to the ICC?

International Criminal Court

The International Criminal Court was set up in 2002. It is entirely independent but was born out of the United Nations, which can refer issues to the court.

Over 100 countries have signed up and more are committed to joining. However, some important countries have refused to join because they are critical of the court. These include the USA, China, Russia and India.

The court only deals with the most serious crimes, including **genocide**, crimes against humanity and war crimes.

The court is a 'last resort' as it will not deal with cases that countries are dealing with themselves. It will, however, take on cases if a country is holding a trial but is really protecting the offenders.

If the court is going to be understood by the people in the countries affected by its activities, it must communicate with the local people. In the Congo, for example, it has used TV docudramas and interactive radio programmes in local languages, as well as holding discussions with ethnic communities.

You will find out how people who commit humanitarian crimes are dealt with.

What law?

For a court to make a ruling, it needs laws on which to base its decisions. The **Geneva Convention** sets out the rules for how people should be treated in war. Most countries have signed up to the Geneva Convention. There have been some additional rules since the Convention was set up in 1949. These include rules related to the use of biological and chemical weapons, and anti-personnel mines.

The Geneva Convention

1 People who are not involved in hostilities must be protected and treated humanely.
2 It is forbidden to kill or injure an enemy who surrenders.
3 The wounded and sick shall be collected and cared for by the people which has them in its power.
4 Captured combatants and civilians are entitled to respect for their lives, dignity, personal rights and convictions. They shall have the right to correspond with their families and to receive relief.
5 No one shall be held responsible for an act he has not committed. No one shall be subjected to physical or mental torture, corporal punishment, or cruel or degrading treatment.
6 It is prohibited to employ weapons or methods of warfare of a nature to cause unnecessary losses or excessive suffering.
7 The civilian population must not be attacked. Attacks shall be directed solely against military objectives.

The International Court of Justice

The International Court of Justice is a UN organisation. Its objective is to settle disputes between member countries. It was asked to rule on the West Bank Barrier, which Israel claimed it had built to protect the country from terrorism. The opposition claimed that Israel was taking land that wasn't theirs and preventing Palestinians moving freely – including going to work – in the area. The International Court of Justice ruled that the wall was illegal. Israel rejected the ruling and the wall is still there.

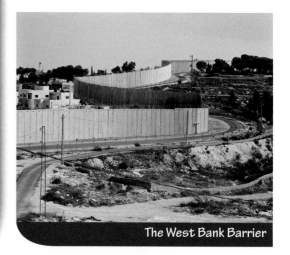

The West Bank Barrier

Action

1 What conflicts are going on in the world today?
2 Find out how people's human rights are affected.
3 Find out whether the UN's Security Council expressed a view.
4 Has anyone been referred to the International Criminal Court?
5 Find out about the trials that are going on.

Check your understanding

1 How was the International Criminal Court set up?
2 What issues does it deal with?
3 Which countries have refused to join?
4 How does it try to explain its activities to local people?
5 What rules does the Geneva Convention set out?
6 What does the International Court of Justice do?

... another point of view?

'Countries should be left to sort out their own humanitarian criminals.'

Do you agree with this statement? Give reasons for your opinion, showing you have considered another point of view.

Key Terms

Geneva Convention: an internationally accepted set of rules on the treatment of people in war

genocide: mass murder of a racial, national or religious group

We want to vote!

Getting you thinking

1 How many years ago did a greater number of men start to get the vote?
2 What had happened before these changes took place?
3 In what year did some women get the vote?
4 What had happened before any women got the vote?
5 In what year did all adults get the vote?
6 Do you think people should be able to vote at 16?

In 1819 in Manchester, the army massacred people protesting for the vote

In 1905 women were arrested for campaigning for the vote

VOTES AT 16

There is a campaign for the voting age to be lowered to 16

Who can vote?

Before 1832
1 in 10 men

1832
1 in 5 men over 21

1867
1 in 3 men over 21

1884
2 in 3 men

1918
all men aged 21 and over, and women aged 30 and over

1928
all men and women aged 21 and over

1970
all men and women aged 18 and over

20??
all men and women aged 16 and over?

The struggle

Being able to **vote** is very important. If you can't, you have no say in what goes on in the country where you live. If only the rich have the vote, they may not choose to look after people who need support. Both healthcare and education for all were introduced in the UK after everyone could vote.

It hasn't been very long since landowners were the only people who could vote. It has been a long struggle to gain the freedoms that we have today. In 1819 many protesters were killed and injured when troops were sent in to break up the 50,000 people demonstrating in Manchester. This became known as the Peterloo Massacre. This was just one example of the campaign to give ordinary people representation in Parliament.

You will discover just how hard people have fought for the right to vote.

Votes for women

Once most men were able to vote, the focus shifted to women. The **suffragettes**, as they were known, took to the streets. Many were arrested and locked up.

Election Day!

Some went on hunger strike and were force fed so that they would not die and become martyrs for the cause of women's votes. They chained themselves to the railings of Downing Street, where the Prime Minister lives. One died when she threw herself under the King's horse at the races. Many men didn't really want women to vote as the cartoon above shows.

Eventually women aged 30 and over were given the vote. It took another ten years for women to catch up with men and be able to vote at 21. The UK at last had universal **suffrage**.

Britain was the first country in the world to lower the voting age to 18 and there is now a fierce debate on whether to reduce it to 16.

Other sorts of freedom

All sorts of freedom have taken a long time to achieve in the UK. Things we just accept today have been fought for over a long period as the diagram below shows.

Speech
1215 King John is forced to sign the Magna Carta by the barons. It is later regarded as the cornerstone of liberty in England.

1689 Bill of Rights grants 'freedom of speech in Parliament'.

Association
1834 If trade unions were to be set up, people needed the right to meet together. As the government wanted to prevent working people from becoming organised, it banned 'association'. Not until 1834 is this law repealed. Even then, the government still tried to prevent trade unions being set up.

Religion
1829 The Catholic Relief Act allows Catholics to have a seat in Parliament.

1948 The Universal Declaration of Human Rights is adopted virtually unanimously by the UN General Assembly. It urges member nations to promote human, civil, economic and social rights, including freedom of expression and religion.

1998 Human Rights Act becomes part of UK law.

In 1834, the government attempted to prevent unions forming by arresting six agricultural labourers from the village of Tolpuddle in Dorsetshire, who became known as the Tolpuddle Martyrs. In a show trial, these six men were accused and found guilty of 'administering illegal oaths'. They were transported to Australia but public outcry led to them being pardoned.

... another point of view?

'People have fought so hard to get the vote, it is irresponsible not to use it.'

Do you agree with this statement? Give reasons for your opinion, showing you have considered another point of view.

Check your understanding

1 What does suffrage mean?
2 Why is it important to have the vote?
3 When did men and women get the vote in the UK?
4 What did they have to do to achieve it?
5 What other rights did people have to fight for?

Key Terms

suffrage: the right to vote
suffragette: a person who campaigned for the right of women to vote
vote: to choose a candidate in an election

2.3 Democracy and voting

Struggles – lost and won

Getting you thinking

People applaud their president

Azerbaijan, a country on the Caspian Sea – next door to Russia – has been run by Heydar Aliyev and then his son Ilham since 1993. Heydar Aliyev ruled Azerbaijan with an iron fist. His record on human rights and media freedom was often criticised in the West.

From a very early age, children in Azerbaijan learn about how Heydar Aliyev brought stability to the country and got the West to invest in the country's oil resources. This made him very popular. Children in school even recite poems about him.

He died of a heart attack – on television.

Before Heydar died he announced that his son Ilham was his successor. Ilham won the 2003 presidential elections by a huge majority. He was already Prime Minister and vice chairman of the national oil company. Observers were very critical of the election campaign in which they said there had been voter intimidation, violence and media bias. Demonstrations by the opposition were met with police violence and there were many arrests.

Ilham runs a country that has great oil wealth, but there is also widespread poverty, much corruption and mass unemployment.

1 What do you think it means to run a country with an 'iron fist'?

2 Why had Heydar Aliyev become very popular?

3 How democratic is Azerbaijan? Explain your answer.

4 What difficulties do people face when countries do not have democratic processes?

What a way to run a country!

Democracy is quite a new idea for most countries. In the UK, it is less than 100 years since every adult gained the right to vote. Countries all over the world have different ways of organising their government. Some are more democratic than others. Although Azerbaijan (see 'Getting you thinking') has **elections**, there is clearly little choice for the population.

There are many countries that have elections but where the ruling party takes control and ensures that it wins. Zimbabwe hit the headlines because Mr Mugabe, the president (see page 106), wanted to stay in power despite everyone being aware that the population wanted the opposition to take over.

You will discover that countries are ruled in different ways.

The political spectrum

In a democracy, power is held by the people under a free electoral system. They have equal access to power and enjoy freedoms and liberties that are recognised by everyone. In general, the UK is accepted as a democratic country.

Dictatorship is at the other end of the scale. A dictator has total power and can make decisions about what happens in the country without consulting anyone else. There is often a group of people who support a dictator because they benefit from being part of the ruling elite.

Questions are often asked about human rights in countries ruled by a dictator. People's political freedoms are limited and opponents are often badly treated to keep them and others quiet.

There are many stages in between democracy and dictatorship. Countries that are moving towards democracy often have a mix of the two systems.

Struggles around the world

Gender

In the UK, gender was the main issue when it came to gaining a vote. This has been the case in many countries. In Switzerland, women didn't get the vote until 1971. In some countries, it depends on who is in power. Afghan women were able to vote from 1965 until 1996 but then lost the right until 2001. They still have to vote in separate areas from men.

Afghan women voting

Race

Some countries have not allowed people from ethnic minorities to have the vote. In the USA, the constitution says everyone should be free to vote, but all sorts of rules were used to stop African Americans voting until the 1960s, when the government passed a law putting an end to such practices.

In South Africa, black people were not allowed to vote until 1994. In the first election, when Nelson Mandela became President, people queued for hours to cast their vote.

In South Africa, voting was so important people waited in line for hours

Action

Choose three countries outside the EU and western Europe and find out how democratic they are. What effect do their systems have on people living there? Are there any human rights issues in the countries you have chosen?

Check your understanding

1 What is a democracy?
2 What is a dictatorship?
3 Why do some people question the degree of democracy in the UK?
4 What drawbacks are there to a dictatorship?
5 Why do some people work hard to keep a dictator in place?
6 How does a lack of democracy affect people's human rights?
7 Which countries have been successful in achieving votes for women and other excluded groups?

... another point of view?

'Countries should be allowed to run whatever political system they want.'

Do you agree with this statement? Give reasons for your opinion, showing you have considered another point of view.

Key Terms

democracy: government by the people, either directly or through elected representatives

dictatorship: a country's leader makes all the decisions with no reference to the population

election: selection of one or more people for an official position by voting

2.3 Democracy and voting

Political rights

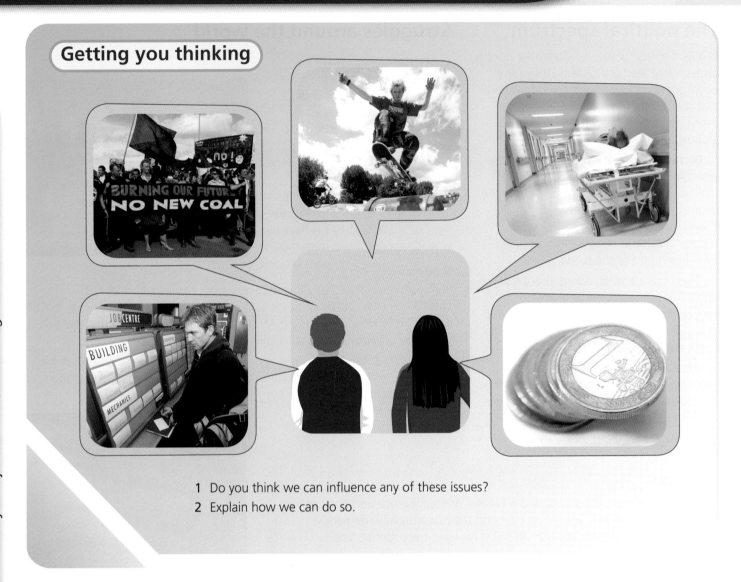

Getting you thinking

1. Do you think we can influence any of these issues?
2. Explain how we can do so.

You can make a difference!

In the UK we have **political rights**. This means that people can have their say and make a real difference. Just as the United Nations has set down everyone's human rights, it has done the same for political rights. According to the International Covenant of Political Rights, we are all entitled 'to vote and to be elected at genuine elections which shall be held by secret ballot'.

This means that we live in a democracy in which almost everyone over the age of 18 can vote and also stand as a candidate in an election.

Who can we vote for?

- **Locally**

  Whether you live in a town or a rural community, you can vote for people to represent your area. These people are known as **councillors** and are your first source of help if you are concerned about a local issue.

- **Nationally**

  Every part of the country is represented by a **Member of Parliament**. Most people decide to vote for a candidate who has views they agree with.

- **Internationally**

  The European Union has a parliament which represents all members of the European Union. We elect **Members of the European Parliament** to have a say in the plans that are developed for Europe.

You will find out about your right to influence the way the country is run.

A group of young people in Aldbourne got together to campaign for a BMX track in their village. After raising funds and representing their views at the Parish Council, they achieved their objective – and won the Philip Lawrence award for Good Citizenship. This was just the beginning of their activities. The group has become an official Youth Council, which is elected by the young people in the area.

Political parties – why should you join?

If you are interested in politics, you might decide to join the **political party** that holds views closest to your own. The major political parties all have youth sections. They encourage young people to take part because they want them to remain committed to the party throughout their lives. If you want to find out about any of the political parties, have a look at their websites, where you will find their manifestos and information about their youth sections.

A referendum?

Big decisions can be made by a **referendum**. They do not happen often in the UK, although a referendum was held in 1975 to test public opinion on EU membership. There was pressure for another one to decide whether the UK should accept new rules on the running of the EU but the government decided against it.

The power of your voice

A government has more power when it has a large majority in the House of Commons. A large majority means that the government always has enough MPs to vote for the actions it wants to be passed.

When the parties are more evenly balanced, the government has to work harder to convince the opposition and may have to compromise. The combination of a strong opposition and public opinion can make a difference to government policy.

When you vote, you help to decide the balance of power, so your vote really does count.

Check your understanding

1 What is meant by political rights?
2 How can we use our political rights?
3 How would the UK be different without these rights?
4 What cause have people protested for, or against, recently?
5 Why are freedom of speech and the freedom to campaign important if people are to put their rights into practice?
6 When does Parliament have more influence over government policy? When does it have less?

… another point of view?

'We don't need political rights. The government can decide what happens to us.'

Do you agree with this statement? Give reasons for your opinion, showing that you have considered another point of view.

Key Terms

councillor: a member of a local council, elected by people in the area

Member of Parliament: a person who has been elected to represent a part of the country in Parliament

Member of the European Parliament: a person who has been elected to represent a part of the country in the European Parliament

political party: an organised group of people with common aims who put up candidates for elections

political rights: the right to take part in elections and other democratic activities

referendum: a vote on a particular issue by all those registered to vote

Putting on the pressure

Getting you thinking

I will never forget the day when Jay, a boy from the village, was killed. He wasn't the first person to be hit by a car that was speeding through the village. The council seemed to think that 40mph was quite slow enough, but drivers always thought they could get away with more. What we really needed was a 30mph limit and some rumble strips so everyone noticed.

When Jay died, I realised it was time to act. I started a petition. There were copies in all the local shops and the pub, and with all the local organisations. Soon we had over 5,000 signatures and we were ready to make our mark.

I took the advice of our local councillor, who suggested that I should go to the council meeting to make my point. I sent a letter and the petition in advance so they would be prepared. At the meeting I stood up and explained what we were asking for. The council members listened carefully.

The council members understood what we wanted and why we wanted it. Within a few months, we, like other villages, had the 30mph limit that has made our lives safer.

Why was it a good idea to:

1 organise a petition
2 talk to the local councillor
3 send a letter and the petition before the meeting
4 go to the meeting in person?

Pressure groups

People who have a message that they want to get across often form a pressure group. A group of people who want something to change can often have more effect than a single person. Pressure groups want to influence people in government – local, national and even international.

Pressure groups come in all shapes and sizes, but they are usually concerned with one issue or area of policy. For example, the petition for a 30mph limit was started by one person, but in order to put pressure on the local council,

other people got involved. They formed a small pressure group, which had one objective. Once the work was done and the group had succeeded in getting the 30mph limit, they could then stop campaigning.

Many pressure groups work on a much larger scale. Major pressure groups such as Greenpeace and Shelter have objectives that often lead them to put pressure on national government and big businesses, as well as organising activities at a local level.

You will find out how pressure groups can influence local decisions.

Is there a group of people who care about the issue?
Organise the group and give people responsibilities.

Getting your voice heard
The key to getting your voice heard is to put together a campaign that reaches as many people as possible.

Is the message clear?
Make sure that everyone understands what you are trying to achieve.

Who do you need to talk to?
Find out who is responsible for the things you want to change.

Have you got good evidence?
Do you need a petition to show that lots of people care about the issue? Have you got the facts and figures right?

How do you get the message across?
You might give out leaflets in the high street, put out a press release so the local media know what is happening, campaign in public about the issue, or prepare a presentation for the council. You will need to fit the method to the audience that you are trying to influence.

Can you make your argument more persuasive?
Look at all the material you have. Test it out on people. Make sure that the key points are very clear. Are there any key issues that will make people take notice? Use them!

Is there a local radio station or newspaper?
Local radio stations and papers are always looking for news. How do you get in touch with them?

Action
Is there a local issue that you really care about? Work out what you would do in order to change things.

Check your understanding
1 What is the aim of pressure groups?
2 How can members of a pressure group get their voices heard?
3 Why might a pressure group only exist for a short length of time?

... another point of view?
'Some pressure groups have too much power.'

Do you agree with this statement? Give reasons for your opinion, showing you have considered another point of view.

A louder voice

Getting you thinking

What's happening to identity cards?

The government says it wants to give people a sure-fire way of proving they are who they say they are. It argues ID cards will boost national security, tackle identity fraud, prevent illegal working and improve border controls.

Liberty, the human rights pressure group, expressed concern about the government's ability to safeguard individuals' intimate details on the National Identity Register after government departments last year lost 30 million pieces of personal data, including those of 25 million child benefit claimants.

It's been delayed. Under the original plans, the first British citizens would have been issued with ID cards in 2008, with the widespread roll-out taking place in 2010. This has now been put back to 2012. Even then, people applying for passports will no longer be forced to have an ID card, although their details will still be entered into a central identity database.

NO2ID is a campaigning organisation. They say: 'We are a single-issue group focused on the threat to liberty and privacy posed by the rapid growth of the database state, of which ID cards are the most visible part. We are entirely independent. We do not endorse any party, nor do we campaign on any other topic.'

Stop ID cards and the database state

NO2ID

www.no2id.net • 07005 800 651

Published by NO2ID, Box 412, 19-21 Crawford Street, London W1H 1PJ

1 Why does the government think identity cards should be introduced?

2 Why does NO2ID disagree?

3 What does it mean to be a 'single issue' group?

4 Do you think there is a connection between the actions of the pressure groups and the delay in the introduction of identity cards?

5 How strong do you think the connection is between public opinion and government policy?

What do pressure groups do?

Pressure groups often work to promote a cause such as looking after the environment (World Wide Fund for Nature and Friends of the Earth) or helping relieve housing problems (Shelter). Trade unions and other organisations are pressure groups that work to protect the interest of their members.

How do pressure groups work?

Pressure groups look for the best ways to get their message across and find support. They might:

- use adverts, press releases, special days or media stunts to bring an issue into the public eye
- **lobby** MPs by writing to them, meeting them, organising petitions and trying to involve them in the work of the organisation
- try to influence changes in the law
- sponsor MPs and finance political parties.

People often say 'they' when referring to government, big business and other organisations which they don't think they can affect: '*They* must do something about …'.

An increasing number of people want to make their voice heard. Have a look at the Number 10 e-petition website http://petitions.number10.gov.uk/. Anyone can start a petition on a topic of their choice. If there's something you feel strongly about, why wait for someone else to do something about it?

You will investigate how people and pressure groups can influence government decisions.

The pros and cons of pressure groups

Pros

Pressure groups provide information for the public

They give a voice to a wide range of views

They represent issues that cross party lines, like capital punishment and abortion

They let governments know what people think

They help people to persuade governments

They provide public services like legal aid or housing

They keep a check on government, especially when the opposition is weak

They represent people without a voice, like the old or the homeless

Pressure groups might influence government at the expense of the majority interest

They might be undemocratic because a small group of people can decide what is to be done

They might bribe or corrupt MPs to get their way

They might influence government leaders and therefore reduce the influence of backbench MPs

They might break the law through their campaigns

They might have more power than individual voters

Action

1 Find out about the work of a national or international pressure group. What are their current campaigns? What successes have they had in the past? How do they encourage individuals to join in with their work?
2 What issue would you want to support? Explain why.

Check your understanding

1 What can individuals do if they want to help shape the way things are done?
2 Why could it be argued that pressure groups help democracy? Why could it be said that they harm democracy?

... another point of view?

'An individual can have an effect, but you can make a bigger difference if you work with others.'

Do you agree with this statement? Give reasons for your opinion, showing you have considered another point of view.

Key Terms

lobby: to try to persuade MPs to support a particular point of view. This used to happen in the 'lobby', or hallway, on the way into Parliament

2.3 Democracy and voting

Influencing change

Getting you thinking

Breaking the law to change the law

Members of a gang involved in campaigning for animal rights were warned today they would be jailed for up to 12 years. They had admitted blackmail against the owners of a farm breeding guinea pigs for medical research. The owners had faced a six-year campaign of terror ending in the theft of an elderly relative's dead body.

1 Who is influencing change in each of these stories?
2 How are they attempting to do so?
3 Is it always right to campaign for things you believe in?
4 Does your strategy matter?
5 What effect do such activities have on people's human rights?

Campaigning for change

The UK Youth Parliament launched a petition calling for the government to ensure that every young person receives Sex and Relationship Education within Personal, Social, Health and Economic Education (PSHEe), by making it a compulsory part of the National Curriculum.

The government has accepted the arguments that PSHEe should be compulsory and agreed to undertake a review to consider how to turn the decision into a practicable way forward.

Ways to change things

People, by themselves or in groups, can bring about change. It's going on all the time. Just Google 'pressure groups' and you will find all sorts of organisations that are working to change things.

It is often more effective to work together because a larger group of people makes a louder noise than an individual, and the people who are being targeted have to recognise that a larger number of people are looking for change.

Change for the better?

The strategies that are chosen to influence change need to fit the objective. Deciding whether the results of actions make things better or worse often depends on your point of view.

The UK Youth Parliament's actions are controversial. While many support the government's decision, there are people who think sex education should happen at home and certainly not in primary schools.

Animal rights campaigners firmly believe that we should not use animals in experiments, whatever the benefit to people with health problems. Many people agree with this point of view, but there are others who think that the laws the government has in place are sufficient to ensure that the use of animals is strictly controlled and is worth the benefits to medical research.

It's all a question of perspectives.

International pressure

Amnesty International uses the power of the individual to put on pressure. The organisation publicises human rights abuses and asks its members to write to the relevant governments or authorities in protest. One letter would have little effect but hundreds or thousands might make people listen. These are the sorts of strategies used by many large pressure groups.

You will explore how people can influence change.

Young man missing in the Russian Federation

Ibragim Gazdiev was 29 years old when he 'disappeared'. On 8 August 2007 he was reportedly seized by armed men in camouflage. He has not been seen since, and his family believe that he is – or was – held incommunicado.

The authorities deny that they are holding him. Amnesty International fears that Ibragim Gazdiev is in real danger of being tortured or killed in secret or incommunicado detention.

Send your appeal to the Prosecutor General of the Russian Federation, by post or fax, requesting a thorough investigation into Ibragim Gazdiev's disappearance.

TORTURE is wrong, unjust and it should never happen to anyone.

EVERYONE has the right not to be tortured. Everyone also has the right to be free of the threat of torture. But in the world in which we live, many people are tortured. In fact, in more than 150 countries, torture is used to hurt, frighten and punish people.

Stop Torture

This booklet is about torture and what you can do to stop torture. It has been written by an organisation called Amnesty International. Please help us to make the world free of torture.

1 Why are people tortured?

2 How many countries use torture?

3 Why is it wrong?

4 How do you think you can help Amnesty International to end torture?

Check your understanding

1 How can people influence change?
2 Why is change not always welcomed by everyone?
3 Draw spider diagrams for the stories to show how different groups of people are affected by the change that that has taken place. Use a black pen for the positive influences and a red pen for the negative ones.
4 Choose a campaigning organisation that has been trying to change things. Select one change they want to make and draw a spider diagram like the ones you did for Question 3.

… another point of view?

'Change is always for the better.'
Do you agree with this statement? Give reasons for your opinion, showing you have considered another point of view.

Action

Choose a pressure group that you support. Find out what you could do to help.

Political change

Getting you thinking

Local and national

Council shuts down speed cameras

Swindon council took action after councillors became frustrated that local residents were having to pay for the upkeep of cameras through their council tax, while central government retained the money from fines. In a single year, nearly 30,000 people in Wiltshire received speeding tickets, generating £1.76 million – £252,300 in Swindon alone.

Council responds to local needs

The ruling Lib Dem group in Sheffield says that every attempt will be made to replace a centralised council bureaucracy with a system that responds to individual requirements.

'This is a huge sea change in the way the city is run, moving from a one-size-fits-all approach to meeting the needs of the individual, from the Town Hall taking decisions to giving choice to local people and putting business and environment at the heart of what we do.

'What's right for Burngreave might not be right for Broomhill. What's right for Stocksbridge might not be right for Southey.'

Local, national or international?

The decisions in 'Getting you thinking' are being made by both local and national government. Local government is making decisions that affect their own area. In London, the boroughs all have their own councils. In other big cities, there is one council that represents the city as a whole. Other parts of the country have county councils or district councils.

Making changes

Political change comes about in a variety of ways.

Before a general election, every party writes a manifesto setting out the plans it will put into action if it wins. Voters can look at the manifestos of the parties to decide which one is closest to their views. They then make a democratic choice, and the party that most people agree with is elected.

Sometimes the winning party can be taken to task because it hasn't kept all its promises. This may affect how people decide to vote in the next election. Sometimes circumstances change, so it would be unreasonable to expect all the promises to be kept. If the economy changes and unemployment goes up, the government will get less income from taxes and it will have to spend more on unemployment benefits. There will be less to spend on other things – so it may be impossible to do everything that was promised.

Once in power, a government can make decisions about all aspects of running the country, but ministers must always remember that they are accountable to the **electorate** who can decide whether to re-elect them at the end of the term of office. This can be no more than five years.

You will explore how political parties in the UK can influence policy and the public.

What would happen to...

Taxes?

Conservatives will cut some taxes, and look for more efficient ways of running some government services.

Liberal Democrats will cut 4p off income tax, raise taxes on the rich and cut services.

Labour will raise taxes for some people and some businesses in order to spend more.

Trains?

Conservatives want a new high-speed train network

Liberal democrats want a new high-speed train network

Labour wants 100,000 more train seats.

Hunting?

Conservatives want to repeal the hunting ban

Liberal Democrats will keep the hunting ban

Labour will keep the hunting ban.

1 Are the decisions being made at the local or national level?

2 Who wins and loses from each of these examples of political parties causing change?

3 How can the parties justify making changes?

4 What reasons might each party give for each of the changes? You might want to do a little research.

5 Choose a change that is happening at the moment. Work out who gains and who loses.

Check your understanding

1 How do political parties tell the public about their plans before an election?
2 How does democracy influence change?
3 Why do governments have to think about the electorate when they decide to make changes?
4 What effect does the media have on people's points of view?
5 How do you think the electorate will measure the success of changes made by the government? Use an example to help you explain.

... another point of view?

'It is important that governments are accountable to the electorate.'

Do you agree with this statement? Give reasons for your opinion, showing you have considered another point of view.

Action

Find out about issues in your local community. What are the points of view of the political parties? Which do you support and why?

Key Terms

electorate: all those registered to vote

The impact of public opinion

Getting you thinking

Western extension stopped after consultation

The **public consultation** on the congestion charging zone ran for six weeks and attracted nearly 28,000 responses. The results showed that 69 per cent of individuals and businesses supported the removal of the western extension; 19 per cent wanted the extension kept as it is and 12 per cent supported changing the scheme to improve the way that it operates.

What do we mean by campaigns?

'You might call it influencing, **advocacy** or campaigning but it is all about change. Whether you are trying to save a local community centre from closing or lobbying government, you are trying to produce a change.

NCVO is a highly effective lobbying organisation and represents the views of its members, and the wider voluntary sector, to government, the European Union and other bodies.'

National Council for Voluntary Organisations

Making a difference

'Our mission is to drive the change to make our society the first in which disabled people achieve equality. Human rights are a powerful tool in trying to achieve this change through our campaigning.'

Scope

1 Why did the Greater London council decide to scrap the western extension of the congestion charging zone?

2 Why do organisations campaign?

3 Whose opinion does the National Council for Voluntary Organisations want to change? Explain why.

4 How could they go about campaigning?

5 What is Scope's mission?

6 Why do they think human rights are a powerful tool?

What is public opinion?

Public opinion sums up the views of the population. It can give the government strong messages about people's views on current issues. This can affect how laws are changed. Governments aim to be re-elected and therefore generally take public opinion into account when they make decisions.

Opinion polls are often held in order to find out what people think. They may be organised by people who want their views to be heard and think some hard evidence of people's views will help to persuade the government to listen.

Newspapers often run opinion polls to find out which political party has most public support.

You will find out how interest groups and government consultations affect decisions made by the government.

Should we change the clocks in March and October?

There is often discussion about whether we should have British summer time all the year round.

Here is what people thought:

Don't know: 2.71%

No – change clocks twice a year as now: 36.89%

Yes – keep a standard time all year: 60.40%

1. Did people want to change the clocks?
2. How might this help to persuade the government to change the time?
3. Can you think of reasons why people might want to stop changing the clocks?

What is an interest group?

Interest groups are usually run by people with a mission to change something. Scope, in 'Getting you thinking', want to make life better for people with disabilities. There is a close link between interest groups and pressure groups – they both want to change aspects of life.

Because interest groups have a mission, they work hard to persuade the government to make changes to accept their proposals. They also want to influence public opinion in order to encourage the government to listen.

Why consult?

The government and local councils consult people on a range of issues. Local government is required to do so. There are a variety of benefits of doing so.

- It allows people to have their say and can lead to a more democratic society.
- People may come up with innovative ideas.
- If the services that are provided are what people want, more people will use them.

If consultation comes up with answers that oppose the government's view, it can be difficult to handle. The same is true of a school council. If students are asked their opinion, the headteacher must be prepared to accept their views or have a very good reason to explain why their wishes cannot be carried out!

Scope looks after people with disabilities and acts as a pressure group

Check your understanding

1. What is public opinion?
2. What are interest groups? Give some examples.
3. What is advocacy?
4. How can governments test public opinion?
5. Why does the government carry out public consultations?
6. What influence can interest groups have on public opinion?

... another point of view?

'The government always knows best and looks after people, so we don't need interest groups.'

Do you agree with this statement? Give reasons for your opinion, showing you have considered another point of view.

Key Terms

advocacy: arguing on behalf of a particular issue

interest groups: bodies whose activities are carried out for reasons other than profit, but do not include any public or local authority

public consultation: involves asking the public about their opinions on changes in the law, policies or large-scale developments

public opinion: the popular view

What is the media?

Getting you thinking

Let's all chill out together this evening.

Let's have a quiet night at home.

Let's plan a holiday.

Let's find out the latest news.

Let's find out if my team won.

Let's choose which new car we want.

Let's find out about fair trade.

1 Choose two different types of **media** that you might use for each activity. Explain your choices.

2 Put the types of media into groups that show their main use, for example, 'entertainment' and 'information'.

3 Do you believe or trust more of what you learn from one kind of media than what you learn from another?

4 How do you decide what to trust?

5 What effect does reading, seeing or hearing material that you don't trust have on your views?

Mass media

The media has become a massive industry during the last 50 years. One hundred years ago, newspapers were the only form of information about what was happening in people's locality, in the UK and beyond. In the days when many people couldn't read, they only knew what they were told by other people.

Today, there is information everywhere. Newspapers and magazines are widely available. You can watch television 24 hours a day. Cable television and the digital revolution have changed things too. They provide news, entertainment and education whenever you want it, even on your mobile phone.

Viewers, listeners and readers

Habits change. A hundred years ago, politicians could expect to speak to a packed hall at election time. There was no television, so it was the only way people could ever see who they were voting for. Today, the numbers watching party political broadcasts are in decline. Perhaps there is so much exposure that people are no longer curious about who governs them.

As new methods of communication become available, people move on. When radio was introduced, families would sit together listening carefully. When television broadcasts started, radio listening declined. Now we have over 50 television channels, so each company has to work extra hard to attract our attention. With more families having the internet at home or on the road, television watching may take different forms. What will come next?

You will develop an understanding of the scope and influence of the media.

Who does what?

Despite all the changes, people still buy newspapers, books and magazines, listen to the radio, and watch television. The choice of media means that we select the ways of finding out information that suit us best. Although the patterns change, most people use most media most of the time. They simply adjust the amount of time they spend on each one.

The internet

Political parties use the internet to provide information and organise online surveys of public opinion. More people might want to vote if they could join in debates and had easier access to information.

Products for people

All forms of media aim to provide what the customer wants. There are television channels that are aimed at young people and others aimed at an older population. There is also a growing number aimed at people with specific interests, ranging from music to gardening, cooking to history.

Adult participation in selected leisure activities (%): by age							
Age	16–19	20–24	25–29	30–44	45–59	60–69	70 +
Watching TV	100	99	99	99	99	99	99
Listening to radio	92	93	93	92	89	82	76
Listening to CDs	98	97	95	91	83	71	57
Reading books	63	67	66	65	67	64	64

Source: Social Trends

Action

1. Look at a range of papers from the same day. Do they tell stories in different ways? How are they different?
2. Watch the news on various television channels on the same day. Does each channel give the same picture? Do different channels take a different approach?
3. Do you prefer one newspaper's or television channel's way of telling the story? Do you believe one more than the other? Explain why.

Check your understanding

1. What is meant by 'the media'?
2. How has the media changed over the last 100 years?
3. What does the media provide?
4. Why is the media powerful?

... another point of view?

'Newspapers are more powerful now than they were a hundred years ago.' Do you agree with the statement? Give reasons for your opinion, showing you have considered another point of view.

Key Terms

media: ways of communicating with large numbers of people

Legal, decent, honest and truthful?

Getting you thinking

1 Identify the different sorts of people in these pictures.
2 What sorts of thing does the press do to give people cause for complaint?
3 Do you think that these complaints are always justified?
4 Make a list of things you feel the press should not do.
5 Make suggestions about how to stop the press doing this sort of thing.

What are the rules?

Anyone in the public eye can be pestered by the press. People find themselves being looked at through the long lens of a camera and on the front page the next day. Ordinary people who have had some good luck or experienced misfortune are just as vulnerable as the famous.

The Press Complaints Commission attempts to prevent this invasion of privacy but it is not always successful. It has drawn up the **Press Code** as guidance for journalists working in the media. Although it can look at complaints and decide if the code has been broken, it can do little to prevent it happening again.

The wrong side of the law?

Sometimes the media is guilty of invading people's privacy, and on other occasions the media gets its facts wrong. A paper or television channel can then find itself in court facing a **libel** or **slander** case.

There are laws that prevent anyone from making public statements about people that are not true. Footballers have challenged people who said they fixed a game, politicians have challenged newspapers that said they received money for asking particular questions in Parliament. *Private Eye*, the magazine that takes a satirical look at the world, often finds itself in court because it has pushed the limits too far.

The Press Code

Newspapers:

- must not publish inaccurate, misleading or distorted information or pictures
- must give a right to reply to any inaccurate reporting
- must respect people's private and family life
- must not harass people for information
- must not intrude on grief or shock
- must not intrude on children during their schooling
- must not use hidden bugs to find things out
- must avoid prejudice
- must not make payments to people involved in criminal cases
- must not profit from financial information
- must not identify victims of sexual assault
- must protect confidential sources.

You will explore the media's attitude towards accuracy and respect for people's privacy and dignity.

Popular or quality?

People buy four times more popular papers than quality papers. The quality press tends to take a more serious view of the world and its headlines reflect this. In contrast, on days when dramatic world events are taking place, popular papers have put stories about footballers, sex and money in their headlines.

Average sales of daily newspapers in the UK

	Daily sales	Percentage change
The Sun	3,045,899	-0.72
Daily Express	752,181	-6.39
Daily Mail	2,193,715	-4.98
Daily Mirror	1,400,206	-7.56
Daily Star	714,192	-8.32
Financial Times	448,532	-0.68
The Times	636,946	-3.04
The Guardian	358,379	-4.24
The Independent	201,113	-8.29
Daily Telegraph	835,497	-3.95

1 Which is the bestselling quality paper?
2 Which is the bestselling popular paper?
3 Why do you think newspaper owners might be worried?
4 What do you think has happened to the way people find out about the news?

Action

1 What decisions has the Press Complaints Commission made recently? Do you agree with their findings? Why?
2 Look at the headlines in a range of newspapers on the same day. How do the popular and quality papers compare? You will find newspapers on the internet as well as in newsagents.

Check your understanding

1 How should people's privacy be protected?
2 How effective do you think the Press Complaints Commission is?
3 Can you think of any examples when their rules have been broken?
4 Why is it important for journalists to protect confidential sources of information?
5 How do quality papers differ from the popular papers?
6 How does the law limit what newspapers can say?

... another point of view?

'Celebrities work hard to attract media attention but they should be protected when the press invades their privacy.'

Do you agree with this statement? Give reasons for your opinion, showing you have considered another point of view.

Legal limits

Just like anyone else, the media has to obey laws about decency. Discrimination is against the law, and some parts of the media have to be very careful not to overstep the limits. The popular papers find themselves in front of the Press Complaints Commission or in court more often than the quality press. But who is responsible? After all, the more sensational the story, the more we want to buy the paper.

Key Terms

libel: writing incorrect things about people

Press Code: guidelines for the media and journalists about the information they gather, and how they obtain and use it

slander: saying incorrect things about people

What news?

Getting you thinking

More than just the papers

1 Which media company owns the most papers?

2 Which companies also have a share in television companies?

3 If the people who run the companies have strong views, what effect might this have on the news in the papers and on television?

4 Do you think a media company could affect decisions made by the government?

5 Why do you think the government limits the number of papers and television stations that can be owned by one company?

News Corp
The Sun, News of the World, The Times, The Sunday Times, Sky TV

Trinity Mirror
The Mirror, Sunday Mirror, The People

Guardian News Group
The Guardian, The Observer, 37 radio stations, interest in Auto Trader and many trade magazines

Daily Mail & General Trust
Daily Mail, Mail on Sunday, London Lite, Metro, 20 per cent interest in Independent Television News

Barclay Brothers
The Daily Telegraph, The Telegraph on Sunday

Where does the power lie?

A newspaper or television news programme can choose the stories it wants to run. It can also decide how to tell the story. The owners of a paper appoint an **editor** to run it for them. The editor has the power to make these decisions. Often, an editor is chosen because they have the same points of view as the owners. This means that the way the news is presented reflects the owners' point of view. Television news has editors too. They put the programme together in just the same way.

Most newspapers belong to companies that are owned by shareholders. The objective is to make a profit, so sales are a top priority. Lots of sales means lots of advertising and selling advertising helps to increase profits. Businesses that want to sell their products will buy space in papers with many readers.

All these factors combine to make newspapers and television very powerful. They can influence public opinion and affect decisions made by both local and central government.

Who buys what?

Most people read a paper that agrees with their own views. Conservative voters often buy *The Daily Telegraph* or *Daily Express*, while Labour voters might buy *The Guardian* or *Daily Mirror*. The way the news is presented depends on the views of the papers. The cartoons are often the giveaway. They are always ruder about the party they don't support!

You will explore how the media can influence our opinions.

The influence of advertising

Advertising pays for commercial television and the papers. If you were the editor, what would you do if you were faced with a story that showed one of your main advertisers in a bad light? Would you:

- run the story?
- hold it for a day when there were no adverts from that business?
- rewrite the story so it was less critical?
- just ignore it?

It's a tough decision to make.

In a spin?

Politicians often want to be at the top of the news and shown in a good light. Political parties employ **spin doctors** who write the stories and work hard to get them in the news. A common story is about new government spending on health, education or other areas that people care about. When journalists look carefully, however, they often find that the spending has been announced several times before! This is the work of spin doctors.

Whose views?

Everyone has a point of view, and often it is hard to hide it. If, as a reader or viewer, you are aware of the **bias** of a television programme or newspaper, you can take it into account. If not, you may just believe it all. In a country where only one point of view is permitted, people are unlikely to know what is really going on.

Under control

Every time one media company wants to take over another, their plans are reviewed. If the takeover puts too much power in too few hands, it won't be allowed to go ahead. News Corp, a company listed in both Australia and America and run by an Australian, owns media businesses in 100 countries. It covers newspapers, books, films and digital media. If it wanted to buy another UK newspaper, it would be investigated by the Office of Fair Trading.

A few of News Corp's titles and companies

Twentieth Century Fox · Sky TV · National Geographic Channel · HarperCollins · MySpace · News Corp · The Sun · The Times · thelondonpaper · News of the World · The Sunday Times

Action

Compare articles about the same story or event in two different newspapers. Is there a difference in the way the stories are told? Is there any bias?

Check your understanding

1 What does an editor do?
2 Why are media owners powerful?
3 What factors influence the contents of a newspaper?
4 How is media ownership controlled?

... another point of view?

'Media owners have too much influence on the way we think.'

Do you agree with this statement? Give reasons for your opinion, showing you have considered another point of view.

Key Terms

bias: to favour one thing over another unfairly

editor: the person who is responsible for the content of a newspaper, or television or radio programme

spin doctor: someone who tries to get certain stories into the public eye and to make bad news sound better

Why should the press be free?

Getting you thinking

Journalists protest in Namibia about the clampdown on press freedom in Zimbabwe, the country next door. They would have been arrested if they had protested in Zimbabwe

ZIMBABWE
Laws passed that:

- only allow foreign journalists into the country to cover specific events
- only allow registered journalists to work
- require media organisations to be registered
- stop people criticising the President
- limit the publication of important information
- stop stories that discriminate against a political party
- only allow demonstrations that have government approval.

International journalist arrested

The Independent newspaper's Zimbabwe reporter has been arrested under new laws. His house had been ransacked and he was told that the order for his arrest had come from the highest level in the government.

'The worst-ever attack on the liberties of the people.'

A member of the Zimbabwean parliament

Zimbabwe was about to have an election when these laws were passed.

1 What did these laws prevent?

2 Why do you think the government brought them into force?

3 What effect do you think this had on the results of the election?

4 Explain why the laws were seen as 'the worst-ever attack on the liberties of the people'.

5 Why is it important for the media to be free to report on events?

6 Do you think there should be any limit on what the media can say?

What is freedom?

'Everyone has the right to freedom of opinion and expression; this right includes freedom to hold opinions without interference and to seek, receive and impart information and ideas through any media, regardless of frontiers.'

Universal Declaration of Human Rights

One of every human being's rights is to have their say. If they don't like the government, they should be free to say so. If people think the government should spend more or less on health, education or defence, laws should not prevent them from saying so. If people want to know what is going on, they should be free to find out. Information and data should not be kept secret unless there is a good reason. In a democracy, people need to be able to hear others' points of view and know what is going on if they are to use their vote effectively.

You will understand the importance of a free press.

Why control the press?

If information is kept from people, they will find it hard to decide whether the government is keeping its promises or breaking the law in order to stay in power. If a government is determined to stay in power, preventing people from knowing the truth can be very effective. **Censorship** means that people will only know what you want them to know.

Press freedom is often the first thing to go when the government of a country wants to prevent democracy working. A country that controls the press cannot really be democratic. There are examples throughout history. In the last century, the Soviet Union controlled all forms of media. Even today, there are no television channels that are free from government control in Russia (as part of the former Soviet Union is now known). China also has strong controls on what the people are told. There are examples of press control throughout the world.

A voter in Zimbabwe reading a government-owned paper, which accuses the opposition party of terrorism. All media output is controlled by the government

In Russia the government controls all television output

Is it ever right to control the media?

When the UK was fighting Argentina over the Falkland Islands in 1981, there was a complete news blackout. Every night a government spokesman appeared on the television and gave a report. He read a message in a slow, serious manner, telling us what the government thought we should know.

When people are caught spying, very often much of the information that is provided in court is not published.

These are both examples of occasions when national security is thought more important than press freedom. Sometimes, by telling people everything, you may be giving the game away. There is, however, always a debate about how much information should be given out.

Check your understanding

1 What does the Universal Declaration of Human Rights have to say about press freedom?
2 Why might a government that wants to be re-elected decide to control the press?
3 Why can democracy not work effectively if the press is controlled?
4 Are there reasons why press freedom should sometimes be limited? Explain your answer.
5 Draw up a list of issues that you think the press should be free to discuss and any that you think it should not be allowed to print stories about. Use your list to draw up a law on press freedom.

... another point of view?

'The media must always be free to express a point of view.'
Do you agree with this statement? Give reasons for your opinion, showing you have considered another point of view.

Key Terms

censorship: limiting the information given to the general public

press freedom: the ability of the press to give information and express an opinion

What is the European Union?

Getting you thinking

Fish catches in Europe are limited to preserve fish stocks

The European Union (EU) is a trading area. When countries sell things to each other, taxes often have to be paid on products before they are allowed into the other country. The EU removed these taxes between countries within the EU so that they could trade freely with each other.

In order to allow this trade to be as free as possible, rules have been drawn up about a range of things that affect how businesses work. The rules aim to make competition fairer between countries so they are all working on a level playing field.

The rules are about:

- **Protecting employees**

  Without EU regulations, one country could allow children to work in factories. That country could make things more cheaply because wages would be lower.

- **Protecting the environment**

  If one country allowed businesses to pollute the environment, production would be cheaper there because they wouldn't have to clean up the mess that was made.

- **Guaranteeing product standards**

  Poor-quality products can be dangerous.

- **Promoting fair competition**

  Businesses are not allowed to have too much power. For example, if a business controlled prices unfairly, this would hurt the customer.

1 Why do you think the European Union has rules like this?

2 If one country broke the rules, how might this affect other countries in the EU?

3 Why is it necessary to have rules for all European countries about things like fishing?

4 What other things do you think Europe should have rules about?

5 If one country breaks the rules, how would it affect the others?

How the EU was formed

At the end of the Second World War in 1945, the countries of Europe were anxious that war should not break out again. By joining together more closely, it was felt that war would be less likely. Ever since 1958, more countries have become involved and have worked together more closely in all sorts of areas, including economics, politics, the environment and social issues.

What the EU does

The European Union:

- promotes economic and social progress
- gives the EU a voice on the international scene
- introduced EU citizenship
- develops an area of freedom, security and justice
- maintains and establishes EU regulations.

You will explore the structure of the European Union, what it does and how its power is distributed among its institutions.

How the EU works

All member countries, or **member states**, of the EU elect Members of the European Parliament (MEPs). MEPs have much bigger constituencies than MPs in each country because the European Parliament has to represent all the member countries: 380 million people in total. The European Parliament has 732 members altogether. The UK has 646 MPs compared with 78 MEPs.

The European Parliament is one of the five organisations that run the EU. It is, however, not quite like the UK Parliament, which has power to make laws. Look at the diagram below to decide where the power lies.

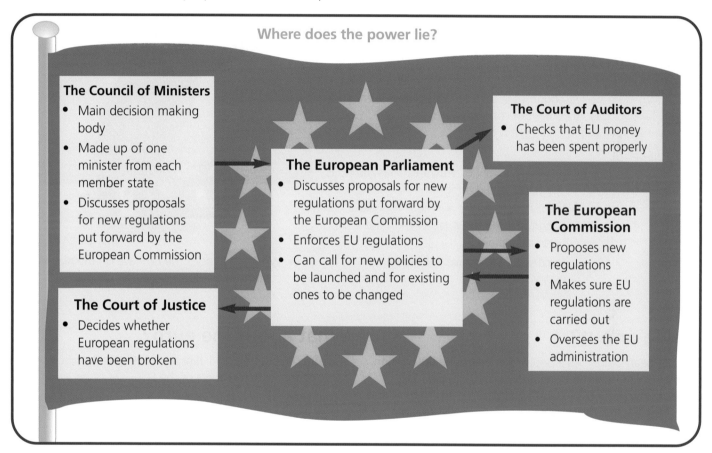

Where does the power lie?

The Council of Ministers
- Main decision making body
- Made up of one minister from each member state
- Discusses proposals for new regulations put forward by the European Commission

The Court of Justice
- Decides whether European regulations have been broken

The European Parliament
- Discusses proposals for new regulations put forward by the European Commission
- Enforces EU regulations
- Can call for new policies to be launched and for existing ones to be changed

The Court of Auditors
- Checks that EU money has been spent properly

The European Commission
- Proposes new regulations
- Makes sure EU regulations are carried out
- Oversees the EU administration

Action

1 Who is your MEP?
2 Which political party does your MEP belong to?

Check your understanding

1 What are the organisations that run the EU?
2 Which organisation in the EU holds most power?
3 How is the EU different from the UK in this respect?
4 How democratic is decision making in the EU compared with the UK?

... another point of view?

'Countries that trade together should all have the same rules for running businesses.'

Do you agree with this statement? Give reasons for your opinion, showing you have considered another point of view.

Key Terms

member state: a country that is a member of the EU

Citizens of Europe

Getting you thinking

A bigger market

Roy Stewart turned his hobby into a business when he developed remote-controlled golf bags. At first he thought he would just sell to the UK market through his internet site. Once he had set up his website, however, he found that he started to trade internationally. He now has a growing business in both the UK and Europe. There is lots of competition in the golf market so Roy must keep his costs down and his prices competitive.

When he sells to countries in the European Union there are no taxes to pay. An American company selling to the EU would have to pay taxes on their products.

1 Do you think Roy Stewart thinks the EU is a good or bad thing?

2 What advantages are there in making products in the UK rather than the USA, for example?

3 Why does Roy have to keep his costs down?

4 What effect does the EU have on the prices customers pay?

Inside or out?

The European Union has a population of around 500 million people – more than the US and Japan put together. This makes for one very big market for businesses to sell to. It also means there is lots of competition, which should reduce prices.

A tax, or **customs duty**, has to be paid on goods from parts of the world outside the EU, however, so these goods would probably cost more for an EU consumer.

These factors have meant that the UK buys and sells more products to EU countries than any other part of the world.

What about the euro?

The **euro** was set up on 1 January 1999. It is the single currency for some members of the EU.

When the euro was launched, the UK decided not to join because, among other things, the UK economy was not in line with other European countries.

The euro makes things:

- more straightforward. People and businesses don't have to change money from one currency to another when they travel to different countries within the European Union.
- cheaper. Banks charge for changing money from one currency to another.
- more certain. The value of currencies change against each other. If you go on holiday to the USA, the number of dollars you can buy with your pounds will change from day to day. If everyone in Europe uses the euro, a business knows that there will be no change in the price it receives for products sold in other European Union countries.

Not everyone is in favour of the euro, however. The main concern is that it reduces a country's control over its own economy. If a lot of people are unemployed, the government might want to use policies that help to create jobs. This might be difficult if these policies did not fit with EU policy.

You will investigate how the economy and citizenship in the UK are affected by European Union regulations.

Citizens of the European Union

Any citizen of a country within the EU is automatically an EU citizen. This does not interfere with your national rights but adds four special rights to them.

- **Freedom to move and take up residence anywhere in the Union**

  You can get a job anywhere in the EU. It is much harder to get work in other parts of the world.

- **The right to vote and stand in local government and European Parliament elections in the country of residence**

  A British citizen living in another member state could stand for election there.

- **The right for EU citizens to be protected by representatives of any member state in countries where an individual's country is not represented**

  Wherever you are in the world, an EU representative can help you out if you are in difficulties.

- **The right of appeal to the European ombudsman**

  If you feel that EU rulings have not been carried out properly, you can appeal to the **European Ombudsman** to investigate.

Ken Tatham, an Englishman, became mayor of his village in France

Action

1 Collect as much information about the euro as possible. Make a display, using the evidence you have collected, about how the euro is affecting the UK.
2 What does European citizenship mean to people who you know?
3 Would they describe themselves as Europeans? Are there any situations in which they would be more or less likely to call themselves Europeans?

... another point of view?

'I am a European.'
Do you agree with this statement? Give reasons for your opinion, showing you have considered another point of view.

Check your understanding

1 Give two reasons why it can be cheaper to buy goods from within the European Union than from outside it.
2 Why could belonging to the euro be a problem for individual EU countries?
3 As a British citizen, would you be allowed to work in Spain? Give reasons.
4 If you were travelling outside the European Union and you needed help from officials, who could you go to if you found there was no British embassy or representative in that area?

Key Terms

customs duty: taxes on products bought from other countries

euro: the name of the single currency used by a group of countries within the European Union

European Ombudsman: a person who investigates complaints against the EU

The Commonwealth

Human rights training

Human rights are at the heart of the Commonwealth's values. To support the work of member countries' police forces, the Commonwealth has developed a programme of training in human rights. It covers all aspects from arresting people to dealing with vulnerable people.

'Most Commonwealth police officers would no doubt see themselves as servants of the public: as protectors, not violators, of human rights.'

1 Why do police need to be trained in human rights?

2 What difference does this training make to the way a country is run?

3 How has the Commonwealth helped Abigail?

4 How has the Commonwealth helped Zambia by helping Abigail?

Commonwealth grant supports pupils

When Abigail was just a child, both her parents died. Her elderly grandmother took her in, but Abigail could not afford to buy the clothes, the books or the stationery she needed to go to school.

A £20,000 grant from the Commonwealth Secretariat is supporting 60 young women like Abigail to continue their education at rural schools in Zambia. Poverty makes it difficult for girls in rural Africa to stay in school and gain qualifications, which in turn makes it harder for them to find employment to break out of the cycle of poverty.

Abigail says: 'When I start working, I want to help other orphaned children and put them through school. Teaching a girl is a very beautiful thing.'

The Commonwealth today

The **Commonwealth of Nations**, usually just called the Commonwealth, is an association of countries, most of which were, in the past, ruled by Britain. All the countries in the Commonwealth have English as a common working language, and similar systems of law, public administration and education. The Queen, like her predecessors, is head of the Commonwealth.

Today's Commonwealth has built on its shared history to become a vibrant and growing association of states, and is a world away from the handful of countries that were the first members. From Africa and Asia to the Pacific and the Caribbean, the Commonwealth's 1.7 billion people make up 30 per cent of the world's population.

The modern Commonwealth helps to advance democracy, human rights and sustainable economic and social development within its member countries and beyond. Zimbabwe was thrown out of the Commonwealth in 2003 because it infringed human rights and its elections were not very democratic.

You will find out how the countries of the Commonwealth share a mission and work together.

How does the Commonwealth do its work?

The Commonwealth has all sorts of ways of helping people and encouraging them to work together. Here are two examples:

The Commonwealth Fund for Technical Cooperation (CFTC)

The CFTC promotes economic and social development, and helps to overcome poverty in member countries. The skills of member countries are used to help others. Advisors go to other countries to provide help with agriculture, enterprise, trade, legal issues, etc.

The Commonwealth Youth Credit Initiative (CYCI)

The CYCI is a small enterprise scheme providing 'micro-credit' (small-scale lending), training and enterprise development to bring economic self-sufficiency to the poorest young people. The CYCI offers:

- low interest rates
- support to encourage saving and the paying back of loans
- ongoing training at a low cost
- ongoing monitoring.

The members of the Commonwealth

The members of the Commonwealth: Canada, United Kingdom, Antigua and Barbuda, The Bahamas, Barbados, Dominica, Grenada, Jamaica, St Kitts and Nevis, St Lucia, St Vincent and the Grenadines, Trinidad and Tobago, Belize, Guyana, Malta, Cyprus, Pakistan, India, Bangladesh, Sri Lanka, Maldives, Malaysia, Brunei, Singapore, Fiji, Kiribati, Nauru, Samoa, Solomon Islands, Tonga, Tuvalu, Vanuatu, Papua New Guinea, Australia, New Zealand, The Gambia, Sierra Leone, Ghana, Nigeria, Cameroon, Uganda, Kenya, Seychelles, Tanzania, Malawi, Zambia, Botswana, Namibia, Mauritius, Mozambique, Swaziland, Lesotho, South Africa

The Commonwealth

The Commonwealth's mission

A source of practical help for sustainable development
The Commonwealth helps people to work so they can look after themselves, and has programmes that aim to look after the environment.

A platform for building global agreement
The Commonwealth holds conferences which bring all the countries together to discuss major issues. This helps everyone to work together better.

A force for making democracy work
The Commonwealth helps its members to develop a working democracy. It sends observers to check that elections are carried out properly.

Action

1 Have any countries joined the Commonwealth recently?
2 What are the conditions for joining the Commonwealth?
3 Why do countries want to be members of the Commonwealth?
4 Find an example of a recent Commonwealth sustainable development.

Check your understanding

1 What are the origins of the Commonwealth?
2 How has it changed over the years?
3 What is its mission today?
4 Describe some ways in which it achieves its mission.

... another point of view?

'The Commonwealth is the same as it has always been.'
Do you agree with this statement? Give reasons for your opinion, showing you have considered another point of view.

Key Terms

Commonwealth of Nations: a voluntary group of independent countries

The United Nations

Getting you thinking

UNICEF

In Sri Lanka, thousands of families have fled from the civil war. Vithuskya and her friends at least have school to go to. The United Nations Children's Fund (UNICEF) has provided a school-in-a-box with basic materials such as notebooks, pens and pencils.

'I had no luggage with me, just the clothes I was wearing. I was happy to get these supplies, especially the notebooks. I put them in a plastic bag when I am at home, so that they don't get wet when it rains heavily and rain leaks into the shelter.'

For the displaced children, going to school every day is more important than ever. It gives them a sense of normality. They can play with their friends, learn and be out of their shelters for part of the day.

1 How has UNICEF helped individual students like Vithuskya?
2 How has this project helped the community?
3 Why does the United Nations spend money on projects like this?

The aims of the United Nations

Nearly every nation in the world belongs to the **United Nations** (UN). Its membership totals 192 countries. When states join, they agree to accept the UN charter. The aims of the charter are:

- to maintain international peace and security
- to develop friendly relations among nations
- to cooperate in solving international problems and in promoting respect for human rights
- to be a centre for harmonising the actions of nations.

The UN is not a world government and it does not make laws. It does, however, help to resolve international conflict and makes policies on matters affecting us all. At the UN, all the member states have a voice and can vote in this process.

The organisation of the UN

The UN's General Assembly is made up of representatives of all the member countries. Each country has one vote. The General Assembly makes recommendations which are approved by the Security Council and put into action by the Secretary General.

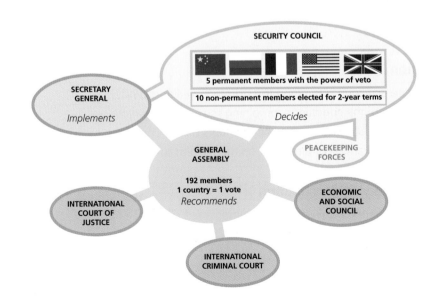

You will explore the work of the United Nations and consider its role in the world.

The agencies

The UN has agencies that deal with the whole range of human and economic development. They carry out the activities agreed by the General Assembly and the Security Council. Some of the agencies are listed below.

UNDP	United Nations Development Programme
UNIFEM	United Nations Development Fund for Women
UNEP	United Nations Environment Programme
UNFPA	United Nations Fund for Population Activities
UNHCR	Office of the United Nations High Commissioner for Refugees
UNICEF	United Nations Children's Fund
WFP	World Food Programme
FAO	Food and Agriculture Organization
UNESCO	United Nations Educational, Scientific and Cultural Organization
WB	World Bank
WHO	World Health Organization
UNWTO	World Tourism Organization
IMF	International Monetary Fund

Action

1 Check how countries are progressing towards achieving the Millennium Goals.
2 Which agencies are likely to be useful in achieving the goals? Explain how.
3 Make a presentation to others explaining the Goals and how the UN is helping to achieve them.

Check your understanding

1 What is the UN?
2 Who are the members?
3 Explain the structure and responsibilities of the main organisations of the UN.
4 Why did the UN set up the Millennium Goals?
5 Which agencies will help countries to achieve them?

... another point of view?

'There are too many challenges for the UN to be any use.'
Do you agree with this statement? Give reasons for your opinion, showing you have considered another point of view.

UN's Millennium Goals

In the year 2000, world leaders agreed that development in the poorer parts of the world was moving too slowly. They all agreed to promote eight Millennium Goals, which aim to encourage and support further development. The target year for change is 2015. Some regions are being more successful than others. China, for example, is doing well but much of sub-Saharan Africa is not making a great deal of progress,

Prevent extreme poverty and hunger
Reduce hunger and poverty by a half

Achieve universal primary education
Primary education for all girls and boys

Promote gender equality and empower women
Access to secondary education for all women

Reduce child mortality
Reduce by two-thirds the number of children who die before they are five

Improve maternal health
Reduce by three-quarters the number of mothers who die during childbirth

Combat HIV/AIDS, malaria and other diseases
Halt the growth and reverse the incidence of diseases

Ensure environmental sustainability
Integrate sustainability into government policies

Develop a global partnership for development
Address the needs of countries in order to achieve economic growth through trade and development

Key Terms

United Nations: an international organisation that tries to encourage peace, cooperation and friendship between countries

The UN at work

Getting you thinking

When civil war broke out in Liberia, 340,000 people fled in fear. Once peace was established, the Office of the United Nations High Commissioner for Refugees (UNHCR) began to bring them home.

The UNHCR also worked with communities to rehabilitate and construct schools, water and sanitation systems, shelter, bridges and roads, which were all severely damaged during the 14-year conflict.

A Dutch soldier helps the returning refugees

1   Why do you think people left Liberia?

2   Why do you think **refugees** needed help to return home?

3   How did the UN help Liberian communities?

4   Why do you think people respect the soldiers from the UN?

Peacekeeping: the work of the UN Security Council

The Security Council:

- can investigate any international dispute
- can recommend ways of reaching a settlement
- is responsible for peacekeeping forces.

When war breaks out and people are suffering, the UN's Security Council discusses what to do. There is a long list of issues and resolutions (as they call the decisions) every year.

The civil war in Liberia (see 'Getting you thinking') led to a resolution to help:

'The Security Council decides to establish the United Nations Mission in Liberia for a period of 12 months. It will consist of up to 15,000 United Nations military personnel, including up to 250 military observers and 160 staff officers, and up to 1,115 civilian police officers, including units to assist in the maintenance of law and order.'

Their role was peacekeeping and providing humanitarian aid:

'They will contribute towards international efforts to protect and promote human rights in Liberia, with particular attention to vulnerable groups, including refugees, returning refugees and internally displaced persons, women, children, and demobilised child soldiers.'

The Members of the Security Council

All representatives must be in New York, where the Security Council is based, all the time to deal with emergencies.

The five permanent members

France	USA	Russia
UK	China	

The ten elected members (each serves for two years)

Africa	3 members
Asia	2 members
Western Europe and 'Others'	2 members
Eastern Europe	1 member
Latin America and the Caribbean	2 members

Humanitarian action and human rights

People throughout the world are deprived of their human rights when war breaks out. As in Liberia, UN troops, who come from member countries, are sent in to help solve the problems.

You will investigate the ways in which the United Nations carries out its peacekeeping and humanitarian work.

Refugees

For more than five decades, the Office of the United Nations High Commissioner for Refugees has been helping the world's uprooted peoples.

The agency's first task was to help an estimated one million people after the Second World War. During the 1950s, the refugee crisis spread to Africa, Asia and then back to Europe. It had become a global problem.

During its lifetime the agency has assisted an estimated 50 million refugees to restart their lives.

The UN helps refugees all over the world

Child soldiers

Child soldiers in Africa are often looked after by the UN and educated in order to help them to fit into society again. Often their families can't be found. This is just one of many projects to help people in difficulties.

A former child soldier at a rehabilitation centre

'The soldiers gave me training. They gave me a gun. I took drugs. I killed civilians. Lots. It was just war, what I did then. I only took orders. I knew it was bad. It was not my wish.'

Action

1 Research a current UN peacekeeping operation. Why are people fighting? How is the UN helping? Is it 'maintaining international peace and security'?

2 Find a recent example of work done by the Office of the United Nations High Commissioner for Refugees. Why had the refugees left home? How has the UNHCR helped?

Check your understanding

1 What kind of work does the UN do?

2 Is the UN a government? Explain your answer.

3 Describe the Security Council's responsibilities.

4 Why is the UK important in the Security Council?

5 Why do you think the UN needs to intervene in the conflicts mentioned?

6 Why might the UN be able to help refugees more effectively than individual countries?

7 Which human rights are the child soldiers being denied?

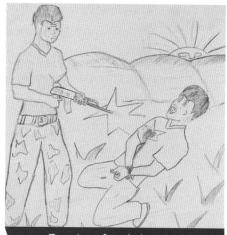

Drawing often helps children to recover from the trauma

... another point of view?

'Countries should not be allowed to be members of the UN if their populations' human rights are not respected.'

Do you agree with this statement? Give reasons for your opinion, showing you have considered another point of view.

Key Terms

refugees: people who have been forced to leave their country and must live somewhere else

Exam questions

After you have studied all of the theory for this unit you will have to take an exam. The exam lasts for 1 hour. You need to revise all of the work you have covered. The questions below give you an idea of what to expect when you take this exam.

Section A

Leave margin blank

Answer all questions.

Spend about 30 minutes on this section.

For Questions 1–5, put a ring around the number of the definition (i, ii, iii or iv) that matches the term.

1 What is meant by the term European Union?

    i A European political party aiming to create a single European nation.

    ii Another name for the European Court of Human Rights.

    iii An alliance of European credit unions.

    (iv) A partnership of member countries in Europe. *(1 mark)*

2 What is the best description of a magistrates' court?

    i A court for disputes about ownership and contracts.

    (ii) A court through which all criminal cases pass.

> Make sure you clearly circle just one answer.

    iii A court with a judge and jury.

    iv A court which hears about only minor criminal offences. *(1 mark)*

3 Which term best fits the following description, 'People with similar views who form an organisation to get representatives elected to Parliament'?

    i Charity.

    ii Pressure group.

> If you are not sure which is correct, decide which ones are not correct first to narrow down your choice.

    iii Trade Union.

    (iv) Political party. *(1 mark)*

4 What is meant by the term free press?

    i Media that is free of charge, allowing everyone to keep up with the news.

    ii Media where journalists have no contracts and so can work for anyone.

    (iii) Media where politicians do not control what can be spoken or written.

    iv Media that is totally free to say anything about anybody even if it is untrue. *(1 mark)*

5 Which of the following best describes the work of the United Kingdom Parliament?

    i It makes all the important decisions in the United Kingdom.

    ii It is a meeting of the Scottish Parliament and the Assemblies of Wales and Northern Ireland.

    iii It advises the Queen.

    (iv) It discusses and votes on ideas put forward by the government. *(1 mark)*

6 State one reason why people should vote in an election.   *(1 mark)*

To have a say

> You could have written: it's your responsibility as a citizen or you have no right to complain if you do not vote.

7 Apart from detecting crime and arresting criminals, state one responsibility of the police.   *(1 mark)*

Giving evidence in court

> You could have written: keeping the peace or advising on crime prevention.

8 State one legal way in which a pressure group may try to influence the government.   *(1 mark)*

Campaigning

> You could have written: carrying out research or influencing MPs.

9 State one example of an international issue where the United Nations has tried to help.   *(1 mark)*

War

> You could have written: global warming or famine.

10 State one source of legal advice and support.   *(1 mark)*

Citizens Advice Bureau

> You could have written: police or solicitor.

> These questions have many correct answers. You only need to write one down.

> All of these questions ask you to state – that means you do not have to explain.

11 Explain why people's human rights are more likely to
    be protected in a democracy than in a dictatorship.
    In your answer you should:

    Make sure you complete all of the bullet points. You can tick them off as you do them so you do not miss anything out.

    • describe the differences between
      democracy and dictatorship
    • explain which human rights are more likely to be protected in a democracy. *(4 marks)*

> In a democracy, the government is voted for
> by the people and they are consulted
> about the way the country is run. In a
> dictatorship, there is no voting or consultation and the dictator has total power.
> According to the United Nations Declaration of Human Rights, everyone has
> the right to take part in the government of their
> country and everyone's vote is equal. These
> rights are more likely to be protected in a
> democracy because when we are old enough anyone can stand for election and
> vote for who they want to run the country.

The candidate has described the differences between democracy and dictatorship.

Specific rights have been mentioned to back up the explanation.

Study Document 1 and answer questions 12 and 13 that follow.

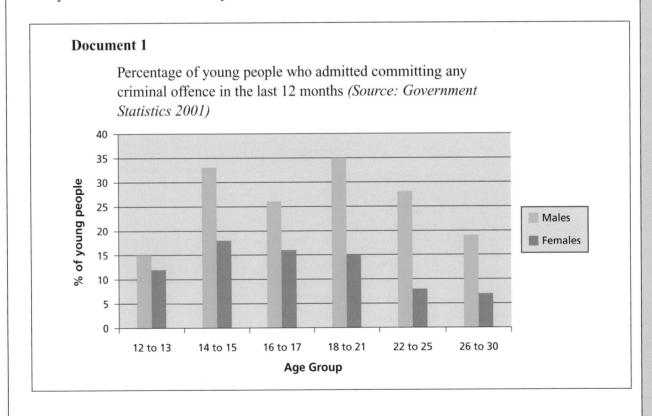

Document 1

Percentage of young people who admitted committing any
criminal offence in the last 12 months *(Source: Government
Statistics 2001)*

12 Study each of the sentences below.
    Put a ring around the number of the statement (i, ii, iii or iv) that gives the best description of
    the differences in youth offending according to Document 1.

    i Young people are more likely to offend as they get older. Males are more likely to offend at
       any age than females.

    ii Males are more likely to offend, especially those who are 18 years of age or older. Older
        females are also more likely to offend.

    (iii) Male crime is highest for 18 to 21 year olds. 14 to 15 is the peak for females.

    iv The youngest groups are more likely to offend. This is the case for males and females.

    (1 mark)

13 Study each of sentences below.
    Put a ring around the number of the statement (i, ii, iii or iv) that gives the most suitable
    warning about our use of the statistics in Document 1 to know about youth crime.

    i There are fewer females than males in the study so Document 1 gives a false impression
       about the extent of female crime.

    ii The number of arrests by the police underestimates the true amount of crime.

    iii All age groups should have been included, not just the young.

    (iv) It may not be wise to rely on the honesty of young people in admitting to their own crimes.

    (1 mark)

14 Explain why crime threatens human rights.
    In your answer you should:
    • give suitable examples of crime to support   ⟨ Have you covered all of the bullet points? ⟩
      your answer
    • mention specific human rights that may be threatened by crime.   *(4 marks)*

    In the United Nations Declaration of Human Rights, everyone has the right to
    privacy and no one may enter your house without good reason. If you were a
    victim of a burglary at home then
    these human rights would be   ⟨ The candidate has given specific examples of
    threatened. We also have the right to   crimes and human rights in this answer. ⟩
    security. If someone threatens you then you don't feel secure so this also
    threatens your human rights.

    (Total marks: 20)

Section B

Answer all the questions in this section.

Spend about 10 minutes on this section.

Study Document 2 and answer the questions that follow.

The two questions in this section will always come from 2.2 Fairness and justice in decision making and the law.

Document 2

Your friend phones you. She has been arrested by the police for shoplifting and needs your advice. She received a police caution two months ago for a similar offence.

She asks you what is likely to happen to her.

15 Study each of the alternatives below.

  i Shoplifting is not a criminal offence so it will only go further if the shop manager decides to take it to court.

  (ii) People with a recent caution for a similar offence are likely to have their case referred to the Crown Prosecution Service. Her best option is to be honest and apologise.

  iii She cannot be charged by the police as she has received a caution for a similar offence within the last three months. Further punishment would be against her human rights.

Evaluate the case and explain what is likely to happen in this case.

In your answer you should:

  • state clearly what your advice would be by putting a ring around i, ii, or iii above

  • describe your friend's rights or responsibilities in this case

  • evaluate the case and explain the reasons for your choice of alternative.

You do not have to write about both rights and responsibilities. Think about which one you know most about in this case before you start to answer the question.

(4 marks)

Shoplifting is a criminal offence and as your friend has a recent conviction for a similar offence she will have this new offence regarded more seriously. This is why I have chosen option ii. After she is arrested she needs to be honest and apologise as she might be treated more leniently. She has the right to remain silent and the right to a solicitor.

The candidate clearly understands the law in this case and has given good advice.

Do not worry if you select the wrong piece of advice above. You can still gain some marks for knowing about the rights or responsibilities.

16 Analyse Document 3 and answer the questions that follow.

Document 3

Jasmine (aged 18) is on holiday and early one morning finds a quiet beach from which to go swimming. She does not like to let other people see her swim but nobody seems to be around and she makes the most of it.

The next day she sees a large photo of herself on the beach in the local newspaper with the headline 'Keeping cool when the heat is on'.

Jasmine is offended, and upset. She thought she was alone on the beach and nobody asked permission to take the photo. Her family will be angry if they see it.

Study each of the three pieces of advice below.

   i Forget it. This could happen to anybody in a public place.

  ii Seek legal advice and consider making a complaint.

 iii Insist that the newspaper prints an apology.

Evaluate the case and explain what advice you would give to Jasmine.

In your answer you should:

- state clearly what your advice would be by putting a ring around i, ii, or iii above

  > You do not have to write about both rights and responsibilities. Think about which one you know most about in this case before you start to answer the question.

- describe Jasmine's rights or the newspaper's responsibilities in this case

- evaluate the case and explain the reasons for your choice of alternative. *(4 marks)*

This case is not clear cut because Jasmine has not been identified by name in the photograph. This is why I have chosen option ii because she needs legal advice to clarify this matter. Jasmine has the right to privacy and this case could be an invasion of her privacy. Newspapers must respect people's private life and it could be argued that they were not doing this when they printed the picture.

> Not all of these questions are going to have a clear cut answer. The candidate has shown their understanding of rights and responsibilities by putting together this answer.

(Total marks: 8)

> Do not worry if you select the wrong piece of advice above. You can still gain some marks for knowing about the rights or responsibilities.

Section C

Answer all the questions in this section.

Spend about 20 minutes on this section.

If you see a star (*) by a question this means the examiner is looking at the quality of your written communication, as well as whether or not you can answer the question.

17* Evaluate the following viewpoint:
'There is little point in voting. There are better ways of making your voice heard in a democracy.'

In your answer, you should:

- explain how far you agree that 'there is little point in voting'
- evaluate the other ways of making your voice heard in a democracy
- use evidence or examples to support the points you make
- sum up your response to the viewpoint.

(12 marks)

You may use this space to plan your evaluation.

This is the last question on the exam but it is worth a lot of marks so spend a few minutes planning your answer. Jot down some of your ideas in this box so you don't miss out any important points in your answer.

People fought to get everyone the right to vote so we should all use our vote so I disagree that there is little point in voting. We can't vote every year for who we want to run the country, it can be up to five years between elections in the UK. This means that sometimes we have to do other things to get our voice heard.

The candidate has expressed their opinion at the beginning so it is clear to the examiner they disagree with the viewpoint.

124

We can join pressure groups and campaign about issues. When the ban on fox hunting was made law there were many pressure groups campaigning against this, such as the Countryside Alliance. The Conservatives have said that if they win the next general election they will repeal the law. I could vote for the Conservatives in the hope that they win and then repeal the law but I could also sign up at supportfoxhunting.co.uk to say I want the law repealed. This way would get my voice heard straightaway and not rely on a particular party winning an election. In this situation I think the best thing to do is to vote and also be involved with pressure groups.

> The candidate has used examples to support the points made.

The media can be an effective method of getting your voice heard in a democracy. Recently a celebrity, Joanna Lumley, has gone to Gordon Brown to ask him to allow Gurkhas who fought for Britain to settle in the UK. The Daily Telegraph supported her campaign and this meant that the story was in the newspaper a lot more. Her campaign has been successful. The fact that she was a celebrity and had media backing helped her to get her voice heard.

> Again, the candidate has used examples to support the points made.

In a democracy, the government does listen to pressure groups and the media on particular issues, but if you want the country to be run in a certain way then you must vote so you get the government you want.

> The candidate has referred to other ways of making your voice heard and has summed up their response.

Unit 3:

Rights and

3.1 Our rights and responsibilities at school/college and within the wider community

3.2 Our rights and responsibilities as citizens within the economy and welfare systems

responsibilities
extending our knowledge and understanding

Rights and responsibilities at school

Getting you thinking

1 How are these young people affecting others?

2 What human rights are they affecting?

3 What responsibilities do you think you have as a student?

4 Are there any legal rights that affect your life in school?

Rights for all

The students in a school are not the only ones to have rights. Everyone who works there has rights too. The students have rights. The parents have rights. They all have responsibilities to each other.

- Parents have a responsibility to ensure their children receive an education.
- Teachers have a duty of care to their students and are expected to use their professional judgement when making decisions.
- The students are responsible for ensuring that they do not prevent others from learning.
- The school has a responsibility to ensure that the treatment of everyone in the school is within the law.

The students in the picture above are certainly not respecting the rights of others. There will be students in the class who want to learn and those who are behaving badly are preventing this from happening.

When rights become legal

In many cases in school, rights and responsibilities are the result of school rules and a culture of respect that everyone develops for everyone else. Sometimes things go wrong in different ways.

Teachers have a range of rights in their contract of employment. These include:

- the right not to be treated less favourably on grounds of race, sex, disability, sexual orientation, religion or belief
- the right not to be unfairly dismissed
- the right to be treated with appropriate trust and confidence
- the right to be provided with a reasonably safe working environment.

These rights are based in the laws concerning discrimination and health and safety. There are also criminal matters that must be taken into account. The two case studies below provide examples of this.

Science teacher's career in ruins

A Science teacher was found guilty of assaulting a pupil. He had snapped when the teenagers insulted and swore at him in a torrent of abuse. The judge sympathised with the 51-year-old's plight, because of the extreme abuse from the schoolboys, but he had no alternative but to find him guilty. The teacher is now likely to be struck off the register and will be unable to teach again.

I'll never work again

When a Year 10 boy swore at me, I asked him to leave the classroom but he came up to me in a very threatening way and pinned me against the wall. I tried to push him away but couldn't because he was much bigger than me. Some members of the class cheered him on and things got worse. He manhandled me across the room and pushed me against the desk with such force that I fell and damaged my back. I'm in pain every day and there's nothing to be done about it.

You will explore the balance of rights and responsibilities within the school community.

When rights conflict

- Should the playground be a quiet place or can we play football there?
- Does the school uniform allow me to demonstrate my religious beliefs?
- I want to do Business Studies and PE GCSEs but the timetable won't let me.
- My mum never gets me here on time and I keep getting put in detention.

These are all examples of situations in which people's rights conflict. Sometimes it is hard to weigh up who is in the right and who is in the wrong. When there are different points of view it can be hard to decide. The following questions are helpful when trying to come to a conclusion.

- Which action results in the most good and least harm?
- Which action respects the rights of everyone involved?
- Which action treats people fairly?
- Which action contributes most to the quality of life of the people affected?

Abare Girls' School in Wales has a no jewellery rule and only allows students to wear watches and ear studs. Sakira Watkins-Singh refused to take off her bangle because she said it was a religious symbol of Sikhism and she therefore had to wear it. She was suspended.

Should Sakira have been suspended?

Whose results?

Hurstpierpoint College in West Sussex has paid what is believed to be a five-figure sum after Katherine Norfolk took the school to the High Court, claiming that poor teaching had left her with a low grade in her A-levels.

If it all goes wrong?

Schools usually have a range of penalties for students who break the rules. At worst, students can be excluded from school for a fixed number of days or permanently. The school must give the reasons for exclusion in writing.

Parents usually have a right of appeal when things go wrong and the governors may be the people who make the final decision. If the issue cannot be resolved, it may end up in court.

Action

1. Write a charter of rights for school students.
2. From the charter of rights, devise a code that spells out people's responsibilities.

Check your understanding

1. Who has rights and responsibilities in schools?
2. Give some examples of these rights and explain how they affect people.
3. What is the role of the law?
4. Give some examples of how the law might be used in school?

... another point of view?

'A school that has to resort to the law has failed.'

Do you agree with this statement? Give reasons for your opinion, showing you have considered another point of view.

Evaluating advice

Getting you thinking

From the Department for Children, Schools and Families website

The Government has announced new standards for school food in all local authority schools in England. The new standards cover all food sold or served in schools:

- breakfast, lunch and after-school meals
- tuck, vending, mid-morning break and after-school clubs.

A newspaper article on an Ofsted Report

A £17m school is thought to have become the first of its kind to fail an Ofsted inspection.

Previously praised as a 'beacon' school by the Government, it reopened ten months ago and the Ofsted report said pupils were proud of their new buildings. But inspectors found the building work caused disruption and found too few students had made the expected level of progress between the ages of 14 and 16, with underachievement particularly marked among boys.

Citizens Advice Bureau on holiday travel

Some contract terms can be unfair to the customer. Examples of this include contract terms written in such a way that you cannot understand them, or terms which take away your legal rights. If you believe that a term in the contract with your holiday trader is unfair, you should consult an experienced adviser, for example, at a Citizens Advice Bureau.

Which?, the consumers' advice organisation, on digital cameras

No advertising, no bias, no hidden agenda

Great cameras that will help you take better photos. All our Best Buy cameras are easy to use too.

If you're looking for the best digital camera, check out the Which? digital camera reviews. The best digital cameras we've tested have good picture quality and ease of use, while other cameras take mediocre photos and have poor shutter delay. So pick a Which? Best Buy digital camera from our digital camera reviews to avoid missing your best photo shot!

1 Where does this information come from?

2 Which would you trust? Explain why.

3 What are the motives behind each one?

4 Are there any organisations that you would not trust when looking for advice?

You will consider the reasons for trusting different sources of advice.

Advice for citizens

There is a mass of advice out there. Just Google 'going green' and you will find millions of pages. They come from all sorts of organisations, from central and local government, pressure groups, community organisations, businesses that sell green products, and many more.

There are some questions to be asked before you can decide whether the advice is reliable. The most important is about motives.

Pressure groups' motives are:
- wanting to persuade us to adopt their point of view
- wanting us to join the group.

The government's motives are:
- wanting to persuade us that its policies work
- wanting to achieve its targets.

What are the motives?

Businesses' motives are:
- wanting to sell their products
- wanting to have a good image.

Community groups' motives are:
- wanting us to participate
- having a view about the local community.

Fact or fiction?

Organisations such as the Citizens Advice Bureau and Which? are less likely to be biased than many others. Their customers rely on getting good advice – and if they prove to be wrong, people will stop asking them. Which? depends on consumers buying their reports and must live up to their catch phrase 'No advertising, no bias, no hidden agenda'.

When businesses give advice, they often have a hidden agenda. They want to sell their products – so of course they say they are the best. If an insurance company offers information on its website about the prices charged by other companies, why do you think it is doing so?

Pressure groups very often take a particular view on an issue and therefore do not represent other perspectives. If you want independent advice, you might need to check a variety of sites, in search of different points of view.

Having decided that healthy eating is important in schools, the government wanted to change things. It offered good sound advice – but wasn't very persuasive. As a result, the number of children having school meals fell because they didn't like the food. The papers had pictures of mothers taking orders for junk food through the school fence. Might it have been better to suggest that school councils discuss the type of meals that students want? Many students want to stay healthy but don't like the authoritarian approach. The advice might be good – but the approach could have been better.

Action

Find as many reports as you can about the performance of your school. Do you think they are accurate? Explain your reasons.

Check your understanding

1 What sorts of organisations offer advice to the public?
2 Why is the advice likely to be of variable quality?
3 What motives do the different sorts of organisations have?
4 Why might you have to look at different sources of advice?

... another point of view?

'You can never trust the advice given by organisations.'
Do you agree with this statement? Give reasons for your opinion, showing you have considered another point of view.

Protecting human rights

Getting you thinking

'S' was arrested and charged with attempted robbery. He was only eleven at the time. He was acquitted of the charge.

Mr Marper was charged with harassment of his partner. The case was formally discontinued as he and his partner had become reconciled.

Both 'S' and Mr Marper had their fingerprints and DNA samples taken.

Despite the fact that neither person was found guilty of any offence, their fingerprints and DNA samples were kept by the British authorities. The information had been stored on the basis of a law that says it could be kept with no time limit. Both people asked for the information to be removed from the database, but their requests were turned down.

They decided to take the case to the European Court of Human Rights, where it was decided that keeping the fingerprints, cellular samples and DNA profiles of people who were suspected but not convicted of offences:

- did not strike a fair balance between the competing public and private interests
- failed to respect private life
- could not be regarded as necessary in a democratic society.

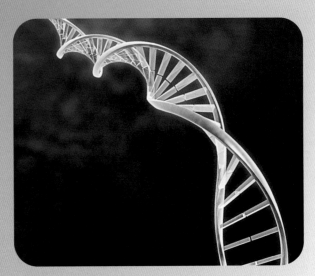

1 Why does the British government want to keep fingerprints and DNA samples?

2 Why did 'S' and Mr Marper want their information removed from the database?

3 Why did the court say that the UK government was in the wrong?

4 What effect might this have on UK law?

What rights?

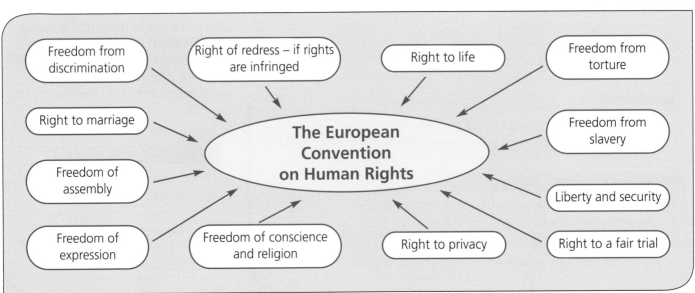

- Freedom from discrimination
- Right of redress – if rights are infringed
- Right to life
- Freedom from torture
- Right to marriage
- Freedom from slavery
- Freedom of assembly
- **The European Convention on Human Rights**
- Liberty and security
- Freedom of expression
- Freedom of conscience and religion
- Right to privacy
- Right to a fair trial

You will find out about how people can challenge those who try to restrict their human rights.

The European Court of Human Rights

The European Court of Human Rights was set up by the **Council of Europe**.

The Council of Europe aims to protect human rights, democracy and the rule of law. All 47 member countries have signed up to the European Convention on Human Rights, which forms the basis for the court's judgements. The European Convention is based on the Universal Declaration of Human Rights and embeds it in the laws of European countries.

The Court was set up to enforce the European Convention on Human Rights, which had been drawn up by the Council of Europe. The Court can award damages but does not have the power to award other punishments. Ultimately, a country could be expelled from the Council if it did not accept the rulings. The EU also watches carefully to see what the member states are up to.

Implications for UK law

Once a ruling has been given by the European Court of Human Rights, governments are expected to change the law to take it into account.

In the case of the DNA and fingerprint records (see 'Getting you thinking'), the UK government argued that it needed to keep the information in order to fight crime. Others didn't agree.

- A human rights lawyer said: 'The government should now start destroying the DNA records of those people who are currently on the DNA database and who are innocent of any crime.'
- Liberty, the human rights pressure group, said: 'This is one of the most strongly worded judgements that Liberty has ever seen from the Court of Human Rights. The court has used human rights principles and common sense to deliver the privacy protection of innocent people that the British government has shamefully failed to deliver.'
- Scotland already destroys DNA samples taken during criminal investigations from people who are not charged or who are later acquitted of alleged offences.

42 days' detention?

Under current anti-terror laws you can be locked up and repeatedly questioned by police for up to 28 days without being charged or even being told why you are there. This maximum period of 'pre-charge detention' for an individual suspected of terrorism is seven times longer than the limit for someone suspected of murder.

On 6 December 2007, the Home Secretary announced new anti-terror proposals, which included extending this maximum limit to 42 days.

After an overwhelming defeat in the House of Lords on 12 October 2008, the government dropped this dangerous and unnecessary proposal.

1 Which human rights does this infringe?

2 Discuss whether terrorism is so serious that human rights should be ignored?

Action

Find out how UK law changed in light of the ruling on DNA and fingerprint records.

Have any other European Court rulings affected UK law?

Check your understanding

1 Which organisation set up the European Court of Human Rights?
2 What is the basis for its judgements?
3 What do governments have to do if the court finds against them?
4 What is the ultimate sanction?

... another point of view?

'A country should be free to decide its own laws.'

Do you agree with this statement? Give reasons for your opinion, showing you have considered another point of view.

Key Terms

Council of Europe: a European organisation that encourages parliamentary democracy, social and economic progress, and unity among its member states

CBI or TUC?

Getting you thinking

The Confederation of British Industry called on the government to make sure that companies can borrow more easily. It has released figures showing that more than a third of British businesses have had to shed staff in the past three months because they were refused credit.

The Trades Union Congress has attacked Marks & Spencer after it sacked an employee who 'blew the whistle' on its plans to reduce the redundancy terms for staff. 'It is truly shocking that an employee can be dismissed for exposing underhand and secretive decisions about issues that will directly affect staff in his workplace.'

1 What sort of organisations do you think the Confederation of British Industry (CBI) represents?

2 What was it trying to achieve with this statement?

3 How was it representing its members?

4 What sort of organisations do you think the Trades Union Congress (TUC) represents?

5 What does 'blew the whistle' mean?

6 What was the TUC trying to achieve with this statement?

CBI
THE VOICE OF BUSINESS

Climate change: everyone's business

CBI on climate change

CBI

Lobbying in the UK and Europe and the world

Doing business in overseas markets

Driving innovation and productivity

Improving the UK's communication networks

Balancing climate change with energy needs

Delivering effective public services

Promoting flexible labour markets

Enhancing the UK's economic and tax environments

Who represents business?

- **The Confederation of British Industry** represents big businesses. The main role of the CBI is to lobby the government and the EU, as well as representing UK business across the world. It also provides information and advice to its members. It carries out surveys on many aspects of the economic and business world and provides monthly updates.

  The annual conference is a key point of the year and always attracts the party leaders and other high-profile people from the world of economics and business. This gives the CBI considerable power as it has the ear of so many prominent people.

You will find out how trade unions and employers' organisations support and represent their members.

- **The Chambers of Commerce** are local organisations run by local businesses. They campaign locally about issues that affect businesses. The Liverpool Chamber, for example, campaigned to keep parking free after 6pm. The North East Chamber campaigns for people to buy from the North East rather than further afield.

  They also provide opportunities for networking to help members develop their businesses by meeting people from other businesses in the area.

  The British Chamber of Commerce represents all the local Chambers and lobbies for them.

- **The Institute of Directors** is an organisation for the directors of companies. It performs similar functions to the two other organisations in that it lobbies, and also offers information and networking opportunities.

Action

Choose one of the above organisations and find out what they offer to their members. In what way is the organisation currently trying to influence government policy?

Check your understanding

1 Explain the role of the CBI, Chambers of Commerce, the Institute of Directors, the TUC and Unite.
2 How are doctors, lawyers and accountants represented?
3 Why is lobbying important for all these organisations?
4 Why are organisations more powerful when they have many members?

... another point of view?

'Everyone should negotiate by themselves. These big organisations give some people more power.'

Do you agree with this statement? Give reasons for your opinion, showing you have considered another point of view.

Who represents the workers?

The Trades Union Congress (TUC) represents all the trade unions. You found out about the work of the trade unions on pages 22–3 and 80. They are organised groups of workers, which aim to protect and advance the interests of their members. They often negotiate agreements with employers on pay and conditions. Usually, they also provide legal and financial advice, sickness benefits and education facilities to their members.

The TUC lobbies government and the EU on the rights of workers. It is drawn into discussions on many issues affecting the economy, particularly when there is a threat to trade union members – such as unemployment and inflation.

Trade unions are growing larger because they are merging. Part of the reason for this is that jobs are becoming less defined as more people in more industries work in offices and use computers. As more jobs are done by machines and robots, so the nature of work has changed.

Unite, for example, was formed from the Transport and General Workers Union and Amicus. It now has more than 2 million members. The bigger the organisation, the louder its voice.

Lawyers, doctors and accountants all have unions but they go by different names. The British Medical Association, the Law Society and the Institute of Chartered Accountants all offer services to protect their members and defend them if things go wrong.

Who is the law protecting?

Getting you thinking

1 Why are these regulations necessary?
2 What do organisations have to do to stay within the law?
3 What effect might these regulations have on the costs of running a business?
4 What effect might these regulations have on the cost of the products the business sells?
5 If the business is competing with other businesses in countries where there are no such laws, what effect might the regulations have on sales or profits? Explain.
6 Why is it important for the government to weigh up the interests of different groups when making such laws?

NetRegs

What are environmental damage regulations?

Environmental damage is:

• damage to surface or underground water
• contamination of land where there is a significant risk to human health
• damage to natural habitats and species, and protected sites.

Who's responsible?

Those responsible for environmental damage might be:
• private businesses
• farming
• manufacturing
• construction and demolition
• waste management
• forestry
• the public sector – schools, hospitals, and government departments or agencies
• individuals
• voluntary organisations.

What do you have to do?

If you or your activities threaten to cause, or have caused, environmental damage you must:

• take steps to prevent the damage (or further damage) occurring
• inform the Environment Agency or other authorities who will tell you what you must do to repair the damage.

If the Environment Agency has to repair the damage for you, you will have to pay the costs. If you don't comply with the regulations, you can be prosecuted, fined and/or imprisoned. This law has come about because of changes in EU law.

Source: adapted from www.netregs.gov.uk

Whose perspective?

Making laws is not a simple process. There are always different groups of **stakeholders** who have an interest in any new law. The government has to decide on its main objective and try to work out how best to achieve this objective without hurting too many people in the process. The example in 'Getting you thinking' came about because EU law changed and the UK had to come into line.

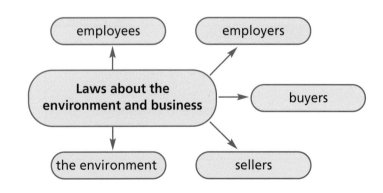

You will explore the trade-offs in the laws on employment and production.

Enforcing the rules

Sometimes new laws are the only solution. People can be more easily encouraged to look after the environment if they have to pay for damaging it. For example, you have to pay more road tax for cars that produce high levels of CO_2. Businesses are targeted by the Climate Change Levy, which is designed to persuade them to reduce their energy consumption or use energy from renewable sources by taxing their energy use. There are also taxes on the amount of waste that businesses send to landfill sites.

What about people?

There is a huge amount of legislation designed to protect people at work (see pages 22–3). The legislation covers employment, discrimination, and health and safety, among other things. Again, there are trade-offs. People clearly need protecting but it can be expensive and complicated for businesses. The rules on maternity and paternity leave, for example, may be difficult for a small business that only employs a few people because it is hard to find someone to fill the gap.

When the minimum wage was introduced, there was much debate about the effect on employment but it does not seem to have caused many problems. It may be that it has been set at a level low enough that few employers have had difficulties paying it.

The National Minimum Wage (NMW) is a minimum amount per hour, which most workers in the UK are entitled to be paid. With a few exceptions, it applies to all workers over the compulsory school-leaving age. The rate is reviewed every year. Any changes take place in October.

All employers have to pay the NMW to workers who are eligible for it – there are no exceptions for different types or size of business. Where you work in the UK makes no difference to the level of NMW you should receive.

Source: www.direct.gov.uk

Action

Find out whether any local businesses have broken environmental legislation. What happened? Were they fined? Did they rectify the damage?

Check your understanding

1 Why do we need laws to protect the environment?
2 What trade-offs do the government have to make about laws and imposing taxation?
3 Who does the government have to take into account and why?
4 Create spider diagrams to show the stakeholders for new laws about education and health.
5 What is the minimum wage and why do you think it was imposed?

... another point of view?

'The environment is more important than other stakeholders.'
Do you agree with this statement? Give reasons for your opinion, showing you have considered another point of view.

Key Terms

stakeholder: someone who has an interest in a decision that is being made

Success or failure?

Getting you thinking

1 In what ways can the business claim to be successful?

2 How might The Carphone Warehouse be contributing to the economy?

3 Why do you think The Carphone Warehouse takes its customers seriously?

4 What evidence is there to suggest that The Carphone Warehouse could be a good employer?

5 Why is it important to look after staff and customers?

6 What evidence is there that The Carphone Warehouse helps the community?

The Carphone Warehouse (CPW) started trading in 1989. It now has over 2,400 stores in nine countries, and employs over 21,000 people. Its profit is over £124 million. The Carphone Warehouse also actively supports charity work.

We want all our people to enjoy working at CPW. Parties, family days out and an annual ball are a feature of life here. We have our own Events Club with everything from paintballing and go-karting to concert and theatre trips.

The company helps Get Connected, a helpline for children and young people under 25 who are, for whatever reason, vulnerable to danger. The charity's HQ is based at the company's offices.

- If we don't look after the customer, someone else will.
- Nothing is gained by winning an argument but losing a customer.
- Always deliver what we promise. If in doubt, under promise and over deliver.
- Always treat customers as we ourselves would like to be treated.
- The reputation of the whole company is in the hands of each individual.

Going for growth

At The Carphone Warehouse, success comes from the growing market for mobile phones and providing good customer service. The mobile phone business is very competitive so The Carphone Warehouse has to invest in new buildings and equipment in order to keep ahead of competitors. The company also needs to employ, train and motivate the staff.

Supporting individuals

Employees are paid well and many receive training to develop their skills. Individuals will be able to use, or transfer, skills such as good customer service to a new job.

Supporting communities

Employees help local businesses by spending money in local shops, pubs and restaurants. Businesses pay taxes from their profits, and people pay taxes from their earnings and when they buy things. These taxes provide the government and councils with money that can be used in the community.

Supporting the wider community

A growing business helps to create or support jobs in other businesses. Some of these jobs may be in the local community, but others may be further away. A growing business:

- communicates more
- uses more energy and water
- buys extra equipment such as computers
- buys more materials from suppliers
- buys more services from other businesses.

All these contributions help the country's economy to grow. Successful businesses often create jobs and pay more taxes, so people benefit.

You will discover how the economy changes and ways in which the government can help.

Markets moving on

Businesses and industries come and go. The motor industry is a prime example. In the 1970s, almost 2 million cars per year were made in the UK. By the beginning of the 1980s, this had fallen to below 1 million. It has risen again to about 1.5 million – but the industry is very different. Instead of being full of people, the factories are now full of machinery and robots. In the Longbridge area of Birmingham, for example, most of the population used to work in the car industry. The factory is long since gone, however, and people have had to **retrain** and find other jobs.

Markets failing communities

When markets move on, people may lose their jobs. Some of the businesses that supported the declining industry also close down. Local shops and traders lose out because people have less money to spend.

Those employees made redundant may have the wrong skills for new types of business. New businesses won't start up in areas where people don't have the skills they need, or where other businesses are failing.

The market is said to have failed a community when unemployment is much higher than in other parts of the country.

Many of the jobs in the motor industry are now done by robots

Economic decline and growth

It is natural for some businesses to grow and others to decline. The market system brings about a shift of resources towards making things that are most in demand. The economy will grow if the value of the new sales of the expanding businesses is greater than the value lost from declining businesses. If it is the other way round, however, the economy will decline.

Where this happens, the government needs to step in to help. By introducing retraining schemes, and investing in roads and other communications, the government can make areas where lots of people are unemployed more attractive to new businesses.

Action

Find out about:

- a business in your area that helps the community
- businesses that have closed down: can you work out why?
- new businesses that have moved in: can you work out why?

Check your understanding

1 How can employees benefit from working for a business?
2 How might growing businesses create jobs both in the local community and beyond?
3 In what other ways can businesses help the community?
4 How do businesses and their employees provide money for local services?
5 What knock-on effects might there be when a big employer in a local community closes down?
6 How might the government reduce the impact of a big employer closing down?
7 What would happen if, across the country, more businesses were closing down than expanding?

... another point of view?

'The government must take control when the economy goes wrong.'
Do you agree with this statement? Give reasons for your opinion, showing you have considered another point of view.

Key Terms

retrain: to learn new skills that can be used in a different job

When prices rise – or fall

Getting you thinking

The changing value of money

£1,000 in 1971 would buy as much as £10,670 in 2008

£1,000 in 1981 would buy as much as £2,950 in 2008

£1,000 in 1991 would buy as much as £1,560 in 2008

1 What happens to the value of money over time?

2 If a small car cost £1,000 in 1971, what might you expect to pay for it today?

3 What do people expect to happen to their pay?

Why do prices change?

Inflation happens when things we buy get more expensive as time passes. Sometimes prices fall and this is known as **deflation**. Inflation often happens because people want to spend more.

Deflation occurs when people spend less. The diagram below shows how inflation occurs. In fact it's one big circle:

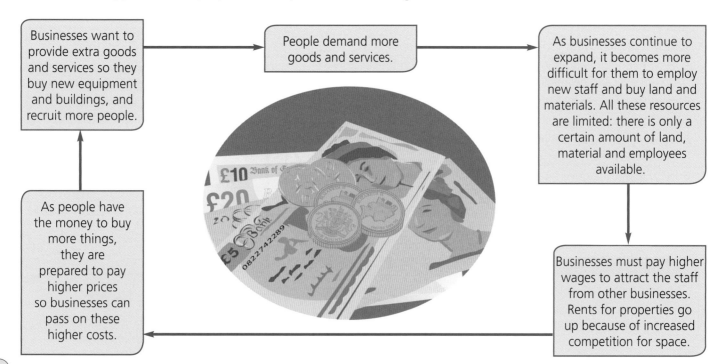

Businesses want to provide extra goods and services so they buy new equipment and buildings, and recruit more people.

People demand more goods and services.

As businesses continue to expand, it becomes more difficult for them to employ new staff and buy land and materials. All these resources are limited: there is only a certain amount of land, material and employees available.

As people have the money to buy more things, they are prepared to pay higher prices so businesses can pass on these higher costs.

Businesses must pay higher wages to attract the staff from other businesses. Rents for properties go up because of increased competition for space.

You will find out what causes inflation, the problems caused by changing prices, and ways in which prices can be controlled.

Who is affected by changing prices?

When prices rise:

- People with savings lose out because their savings will not buy so much in the future.
- People with incomes that do not grow at the **rate of inflation** also lose out. Some pensions are not linked to the inflation rate so their value falls when prices rise.
- UK businesses can also lose out if inflation in other countries is at a lower rate. The price rises make our products and services more expensive to buy.
- Borrowers gain because the value of their debt falls.

When prices fall:

- Savers gain because their money goes further.
- Borrowers lose because they have to repay money that is now worth less.

Can it go too far?

A little bit of inflation, about 2 per cent each year, doesn't do any harm. However, if prices rise too fast, businesses start losing money because people stop buying their products. To stay in business, companies cut their costs by making people redundant. This may keep the business going, but causes unemployment to rise.

When prices fall because people are buying less, the economy shrinks and businesses find it difficult to keep going because they can't sell enough. Eventually, businesses close down and unemployment rises.

The government has to work hard to keep the economy on track – often with a little bit of inflation.

If pensions don't increase at the same rate as inflation, pensioners can suffer

What can be done to control inflation?

Prices can be controlled in three ways:

- **Change interest rates**

  Every month, the Bank of England decides whether to change interest rates or keep them the same. If the Bank believes inflation will increase, it raises interest rates. This increases the cost of borrowing so people buy less.

- **Make sure there are enough staff**

  A shortage of trained people makes wages go up. One way of reducing inflation is to make sure that there are plenty of people with the right skills. The government can provide training courses and help businesses to train their staff.

- **Keep business costs down**

  In order to remain competitive, businesses try to reduce their costs. They reduce their costs by keeping their payments for materials, land and staff as low as possible. They may need to reorganise so that they are making their products as efficiently as possible. They want to keep prices down to attract consumers.

Check your understanding

1 In your own words, explain what inflation is.
2 Explain what happens when prices fall.
3 Name two things that can cause inflation. Explain why these things can lead to an increase in prices.
4 How might inflation affect someone who:
   a) is saving money?
   b) has a pension that is not linked to inflation?
   c) has trained in an area of work where there is a skills shortage, such as computer programming?
   d) is working in a business that is losing money and who doesn't have any specialist skills?
5 What can businesses do to help keep inflation rates down?

Action

What is happening to prices at the moment? Is the level of inflation seen to be good for the country? You could look at www.treasury.gov.uk.

Key Terms

deflation: the general fall in prices
inflation: the general rise in prices
rate of inflation: the rate at which prices rise

Managing the economy

Getting you thinking

1 What sort of organisation is the Tax Payers' Alliance?

2 What is it campaigning for?

3 What are taxes used for?

4 If taxes were lower, what would happen?

5 How are decisions made about how the money raised by taxes is spent?

6 Can voters have an influence?

The TaxPayers' Alliance: the mission

The TaxPayers' Alliance (TPA) is Britain's independent grassroots campaign for lower taxes. After years of being ignored by politicians of all parties, the TPA is committed to forcing politicians to listen to ordinary taxpayers.

Taxes keep on rising but there is very little improvement in the quality of schools, hospitals and transport provided by government. Most recently, British workers, employers, consumers, home-owners and pensioners have been hit by higher National Insurance contributions, huge council tax increases and higher taxes on pension funds.

Who's responsible?

If we didn't pay taxes, everyone would have to fend for themselves. They would have to pay for all the services that the government provides – from health to education and even roads, the police and the army. Some of these things are possible to provide – and some people do. Others really have to be done centrally. We have to pay to use some roads, such as the M6 relief road north of Birmingham and those in central London. It would, however, be difficult to pay for every stretch of road we use.

In the UK, there is a broad consensus about the need to pay for many things that are considered necessary but there is a debate about just how much should be provided by the state and what we should provide for ourselves. People who cannot look after themselves for a wide variety of reasons are generally looked after. If children are not properly fed and don't go to school, they are unlikely to develop the skills that mean they can look after themselves in later life.

What's changed?

Over the last 50 years the amount of support provided to various groups of people has decreased generally. Prescriptions were free, students received grants to go to university and provision for the elderly was greater. We now have to provide these things for ourselves unless we earn very little.

There are trade-offs in any decision. Look at pages 14–15 to see how the government raises and spends its money.

What should people have to pay for?

You will investigate ways in which the government plans and manages the economy.

What has caused the changes?

There are many reasons why it has become more expensive to run the country. Here are a few of them:

- The UK population is ageing so more people are paid pensions and fewer people are paying taxes.
- The cost of healthcare has risen as more treatments have been invented.
- More people go to university so more resources need to be devoted to higher education.
- The pressure to look after the environment has grown and this can be an expensive area. Council tax has to cover the costs of domestic recycling, for example.

You've got cancer. There is a drug that can help, but it's not available on the NHS. What do you do?

Do you use your life savings or remortgage your house to pay for it?

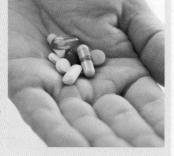

But – if you want the drug that could lengthen your life, you have to become a private patient. That means paying for all your care as you are not allowed just to top it up.

1 Why do you think the government rations healthcare?
2 What are the problems of rationing healthcare?
3 After much pressure from the media, the government changed its policy and decided that you could top up your care. Is this fair if some people cannot afford it?

Check your understanding

1 How does the government raise money? Have a look at pages 14–15.
2 How does the government spend its money? Have a look at pages 14–15.
3 Are there some things that it is difficult for people to provide as individuals?
4 Why do we need to provide some basic services for everyone?
5 Why are the spending decisions difficult?
6 Why is it difficult to balance controlling the economy and deciding on government spending?

The big picture

The government has to control inflation, keep unemployment down and encourage **economic growth** – while balancing taxes and spending. Not a small challenge!

The main difficulty is that all the decisions are linked together.

- If the government increases spending, it makes us better off so we spend more and inflation may rise.
- If the government cuts spending, we have less to spend so people may lose their jobs and unemployment rises.
- If the government reduces interest rates to encourage us to spend more, we may end up with inflation.
- If the government raises interest rates to reduce our spending, we may end up with unemployment.

All these possibilities can vary according to what is going on in the world as a whole. The world's economies are closely linked so if things go wrong in one place, they very quickly spread to others.

The decisions the government has to make are a balancing act and it is very difficult to satisfy everyone. When you next hear about a change in the government's economic policy, think about the knock-on effects.

Action

What decisions has the government made about spending recently? What effect do you think this will have on us and other parts of the economy?

Key Terms

economic growth: this happens when the country produces more goods and services from year to year

Responsible business?

Getting you thinking

The price of AIDS drugs

Glaxo announced that the prices of 14 of its HIV medicines will fall by an average of 21 per cent. In 64 of the world's poorest countries, Glaxo sells its HIV drugs at what they cost to produce. The company said improvements in manufacturing and the availability of cheaper raw ingredients have made the latest round of price cuts possible.

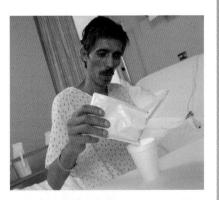

BP's sustainability review

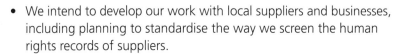

As part of its sustainability review, BP stated the following:

- We anticipate spending at least $500 million over each five-year cycle on community investment.
- We plan to continue to invest in education, from school-based projects to university research.
- We intend to develop our work with local suppliers and businesses, including planning to standardise the way we screen the human rights records of suppliers.
- We plan to continue to explore ways of using our capabilities to meet the energy needs of low-income customers.

Arriva in the community

In Liverpool, Arriva's Healthy Schools Bus, in partnership with Everton Football Club and the city council, completed more than 250 school visits in its first 18 months, giving more than 11,000 pupils a fun focus on healthy eating and exercise. The initiative includes follow-up visits and monitoring of pupils' progress in nutrition and fitness. In 2009 the project, supporting Key Stage 2 pupils, took a new step forward with the introduction of a second bus provided by Arriva.

1 In what ways are these businesses showing responsibility to the wider community?
2 How are communities being helped?
3 Why do you think the businesses are involved in this way?

Corporate responsibility

Communities work together in many different ways and businesses are no exception. On page 27 you read about Costain's staff helping to brighten up the playground of a school. The motives of businesses that work with the community are varied.

- Businesses want customers to trust them so they often work hard to develop a good name. Supporting the community contributes greatly to this agenda. When a company is caught employing children in LEDCs or polluting the environment, its good name can be damaged very quickly and may be hard to repair.

- Engaging with the community often helps staff to develop certain skills that are not easily found in the workplace. Some companies have programmes that involve members of staff going to work with students in schools – just as Arriva did with schools in Liverpool in 'Getting you thinking'.

- A business that is involved in activities that might be thought to be damaging to the environment may want to show that it has wider interests in looking after the environment. One of BP's business activities is producing and refining oil, so its sustainability review in 'Getting you thinking' shows how it sets about looking after the environment.

You will explore the need for businesses to behave responsibly towards each other and the wider community.

There is a view that corporate responsibility is just another form of marketing because having a good image helps businesses to sell their products. Others say that it is a win-win situation which does not have losers.

Legal responsibilities

Businesses have many legal responsibilities to their staff, the local community and the environment in general (see pages 20–3 and 136–7).

- There is increasingly strong legislation controlling the way businesses treat the environment.

Thames Water was fined £125,000 for polluting the River Wandle with industrial-strength bleach

- There are also laws that protect the innovative ideas of businesses. Patents protect products and copyright protects books, music and other similar material. Dyson, for example, was paid £4m damages by Hoover when Hoover produced a vacuum cleaner on the same principle as a Dyson. The model was protected by a patent and could not be copied.

Have they been about too long to receive a fee when their music is played?

Copyright is limited to 50 years, after which time royalties no longer have to be paid. Every time a Rolling Stones, Beatles or Cliff Richard track is played on the radio, the artists receives a fee – but the 50 years is nearly up for some of them and the fees will come to an end. Despite a campaign for an extension, the government has decided to stay with the present law.

Action

1 Do any businesses provide support for your school?
2 Do any businesses provide support for organisations where you live?
3 Work out how the businesses help and what the benefits are for each side.

Check your understanding

1 How do businesses help communities?
2 Why do businesses help communities?
3 How does the law influence business behaviour? Have a look at pages 18–23 to help you answer this question.
4 What is a patent? How does it protect a business?

... another point of view?

'Businesses only believe in social responsibility because it is good marketing.'
Do you agree with this statement? Give reasons for your opinion, showing you have considered another point of view

Solutions to global problems

Getting you thinking

Reduce waste

Clean up streets and parks

Create safe routes to school

Create local employment

Reduce racial harassment

Reduce pollution

Create nature reserves

1 The images show different ways of improving the local community. Which ones are relevant to where you live? Are there any others where you live?

2 Why might the list be different in different communities?

3 Do you think the list will change over time?

4 Has your school been involved in improving the environment in any of these ways – or others? If so, explain how.

Is Agenda 21 the answer?

Agenda 21 was set up to promote sustainable development. It has resulted in targets for countries and local communities. At an international level, targets have been set by the UN, the EU and individual countries. There is general acceptance of the need to reduce the output of greenhouse gases.

The Kyoto Protocol established targets for 2012 and the EU has set more ambitious ones for 2020. The UK plans to reduce carbon dioxide emissions by at least 26 per cent by 2020 and at least 60 per cent by 2050 (based on levels in 1990). The targets will be reviewed to decide whether they should be even more challenging. To achieve such targets everyone will have to make great changes to their lifestyle.

Local Agenda 21 (LA21) was developed to encourage people to make changes at local level (see page 36). Since 1992, local councils in the UK have been working with local people on a wide range of projects. LA21 has resulted in a variety of activities around the world.

Chicago, USA

Rooftop gardens in the heart of Chicago will improve the air quality in the city because the plants absorb carbon dioxide and produce oxygen. The gardens will keep the sun's heat off the buildings, making them cooler and cutting down on the energy needed for air conditioning. The gardens also encourage birds to nest in the heart of the city.

You will investigate how effectively Agenda 21 helps communities to become sustainable.

Rules for all?

The targets for cutting emissions are not popular with everyone. The USA, for example, has not signed up to the Kyoto Protocol. Reducing the output of gas can be expensive for businesses and therefore makes products more expensive. If countries don't all follow the same rules, this can make it harder to sell the products made in those countries that obey the rules.

Developing countries have argued that they should not be subjected to the same rules as the industrialised world. Preventing pollution is expensive and can push up the price of the products they make. The plan that seems to come some way to being acceptable sets pollution targets for specific industries, such as cement, steel or aluminum. If the 37 industrial countries miss their goals they are fined – but this would not be the case for the developing countries. The plan fits well with Beijing's intention to increase the efficiency of its key industries, which produce the bulk of its carbon emissions.

Enforcing the rules that are needed to hit the targets can be difficult.

- **Persuasion** is one strategy. We are encouraged to take shopping bags to the supermarket instead of using plastic bags – although many shops still offer bags to their customers. We are provided with bins to recycle all sorts of things – but many people still just throw all their rubbish away. Snooping eyes in wheelie bins have been shown not to work and have been ridiculed in the media.

- **Taxation** is another strategy. It is often not welcome but can be the only way for people to pay for the environmental damage they do. It can also stop people doing particularly damaging things.

Action

Find out if your local council is promoting LA21 projects. For example, are they trying to reduce traffic congestion, pollution and noise? Are they introducing traffic-calming schemes or trying to make streets safer for children and older residents?

Check your understanding

1 In your own words, what is the main aim of Agenda 21?
2 What targets have been set to improve sustainability?
3 Which of the LA21 aims in 'Getting you thinking' do you think is the most important for your local area? Give reasons.
4 Do the LA21 projects above offer sustainable solutions? Explain your answer.

... another point of view?

'Local solutions are likely to be more successful than global solutions.' Do you agree with this statement? Give reasons for your opinion, showing you have considered another point of view.

Want to know how much energy your electrical equipment uses?

Woking LA21 group has bought 20 energy meters for measuring the electricity consumption of household appliances. These can be borrowed from the group, who then keep a record of the results submitted to show how efficient various electrical products are. Some items are much more efficient than others and some are still using power when they seem to be turned off.

Saving energy in Sandanski, Bulgaria

- Energy-efficient street lighting – replacement of old, inefficient lamps with new energy-efficient ones
- Solar installations for hot water in four small hotels and thirty residential buildings
- Installation of six hydroelectric power plants

Key Terms

Local Agenda 21: a global plan to ask local people how they think their immediate environment could be improved

Free trade or fair trade?

Getting you thinking

Should he be at school?

The Clean Clothes Campaign code for garments workers ensures:

- freedom to join a trade union
- no discrimination
- no forced or slave labour
- health and safety checks
- 48 hours maximum working week
- a fair wage.

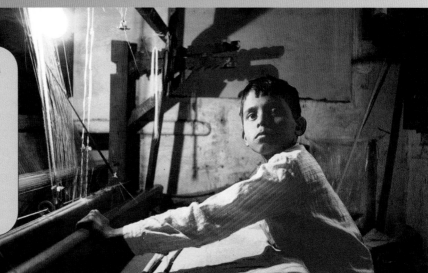

1 How do you think this boy's human rights are being violated?

2 Why is such a young child at work?

3 How can people and organisations in MEDCs help?

4 How do you think governments can help?

Making trade fairer

Trade is a very important way for any country to earn money and create jobs. People and countries have traded for thousands of years, but in today's global economy, information, goods and money can be moved around the world at an incredible speed. Companies aim to make the best products at the cheapest price.

The World Trade Organization (WTO) is responsible for negotiating international trade agreements. Most rich countries want a **free trade** system in which the prices of goods are determined by the amount that people want to buy and sell. But many people believe such a system favours richer countries like the USA and Japan, and want the WTO to be reformed. They argue that world trade must be managed so the poorest countries benefit more. In other words, they want world trade to become '**fair trade**'.

Fair trade is trade that is good for the producer. Fair trade ensures that more of the price consumers pay goes to the producer than is the case in a free trade system. Fair trade means that staff are paid a fair wage, have good working conditions and are allowed to form trade unions to defend their rights.

Who can help?

Traders' organisations

There are two types of organisations that help traders. First of all, farmers or other producers can belong to a producer group. They must make or grow products to fair trade standards and have been accepted as meeting these standards. They can then sell their products with a fair trade label.

Fair trade labelling organisations set the standards and check that producer groups meet them. In the UK, The Fairtrade Foundation is the main group. There are many others round the world.

Together, these organisations help farmers and producers to sell their output at fair prices, and therefore give them a better standard of living.

You will explore ways in which trade can be fairer.

Pressure groups

Fair trade campaigns, such as the Clean Clothes Campaign (CCC) in 'Getting you thinking', have drawn attention to the working conditions of workers all around the world. Because such activities have been brought into the public eye, people have started to ask questions.

When big companies like Gap are caught out, the news hits the headlines. Many companies now follow ethical codes for production, but it is difficult to manage production in LEDCs, especially when the work is subcontracted to small businesses that employ lots of outworkers to make clothes, and other things, in their own homes.

Governments

Governments can choose ways of supporting fair trade. The story above shows one way in which the UK government has chosen to help. In LEDCs, governments can give grants to farmers to help them achieve Fairtrade status. This can help to lift them out of poverty and help the economy to grow.

Divine was the first mainstream Fairtrade chocolate brand. The brand is even more special because the farmers who grow the cocoa beans have a share in the business that makes the bars. There is far more profit to be made from making chocolate bars than selling cocoa beans, so the farmers receive a greater reward.

Action

1 Use the internet to research UK companies that are trying to promote fair trade.
2 Find details of company 'codes' like the CCC code. Use these to create a leaflet or poster explaining the issues about fair trade and its aims for helping workers in LEDCs.
3 You could lead an assembly to explain fair trade to the rest of your school.

Check your understanding

1 Explain, in your own words, what the World Trade Organization (WTO) does.
2 Why do some people want to reform the WTO?
3 How would fair trade help workers in LEDCs?
4 What human rights do groups such as the Clean Clothes Campaign help to protect?

... another point of view?

'People in the UK should **boycott** companies that sell "dirty" clothes and trainers.'

Do you agree with this statement? Give reasons for your opinion, showing you have considered another point of view.

UK government doubles fair trade funding

The £1.2m grant will support the development of fair trade through the international Fairtrade Labelling Organisation. The funding is part of a £3m programme to increase support for the Fairtrade label internationally – and help more developing country producers export their products.

Key Terms

boycott: to refuse to use or have anything to do with something

fair trade: a way of buying and selling products that aims to pay the producer a fair price

free trade: trade between countries which is not restricted by things like high taxes on imports

Trade or aid?

Getting you thinking

Aid to the starving

Five million Afghans face serious food shortages as winter comes, but Oxfam warns that donors have put forward less than a fifth of the money needed. Oxfam believes that time is running out to avert a humanitarian crisis and it urges governments to respond to the emergency humanitarian appeal.

Aid for trade

If a country is to increase its overseas trade, it needs efficient ports and roads, trained customs officials with the right equipment, and entrepreneurs who know an opportunity when they see one. Without these, no country will be able to produce the quantity and quality of goods at the right price for world markets. Many developing countries need help to achieve this.

Why does trade help an economy to grow?

When one country sells products to another, it receives payments which help its economy to grow because people are employed and paid to make the things that are sold. These people then have more to spend so the economy grows more.

As countries grow richer:

- children get a better education and therefore grow up to take more responsible jobs
- healthcare often improves, so children can go to school more frequently and adults can go to work regularly.

Both these factors make it easier for a country to become more competitive.

How can aid help?

People usually want **aid** that helps them to help themselves (see pages 38–9). Giving food and shelter in emergencies is clearly necessary but if people are to become self-sufficient, the aid needs to be targeted more carefully. The fishermen in Chad are a good example. Working out just what will help is important, as the experiments in Kenya showed.

Working together

Both trade and aid have their places. Trade will help countries to grow and therefore lift people out of poverty. Aid can help to develop the skills and competitiveness that people need to work and make products – or provide services – that people in other countries want. They can help to ensure that development is sustainable because businesses grow on the basis of having markets to sell their products.

You will investigate whether trade or aid is a better way of supporting a country so it can develop or become more sustainable more quickly.

Aid helps you to help yourself

'If you don't have a canoe,' says Michel Adjibang, 'you'll always be poor.' Nets are essential too, along with the smoking ovens which preserve the fish for taking to market.

Walta is a community-based organisation in Chad whose name means 'to take responsibility for yourself'. With the help of aid from the UK, a new canoe-building technique has been developed using locally available planks, which are easy to use and kind to the environment. Trainers have shown local carpenters how to build the canoes, and a micro-credit scheme helps fishermen buy canoes and nets.

'With what I earn from fishing, I invest a part of it in farming,' says one fisherman. 'I even get to hire extra hands sometimes. Today my children are in school, and it is what I earn from fishing that even helps me to care for myself.'

What sort of aid?

Experiments in Kenya found that providing poor students with free uniforms or a simple porridge breakfast increased school attendance. But giving them drugs to treat the intestinal worms that infect more than a quarter of the world's population was more cost effective. It cost only $3.50 for each extra year of schooling achieved. Healthier children are more likely to go to school.

When countries trade with other countries, the population usually gets richer. To do this, they need skilled people at all levels so it's important to get them all to school.

1 In what situations is aid essential to help people survive?
2 How does aid help the fishermen of Chad? What effects does this aid have on the wider community? How does it help the economy of Chad to grow?
3 What do countries need if their trade is to grow?
4 Why do countries often need help to achieve trade growth?
5 Why is it important to target aid carefully?
6 Some people argue that aid is a waste of time. Explain why.

Why give aid?

Countries that give aid do so for a variety of reasons. They might want to:

- give aid to help in a crisis
- make political links
- help industries at home by sending their products as aid
- commit another country to buying products from them.

If both sides win, the motives may not be a problem, but if there are many strings attached to the country receiving aid, it can cost the country more than the aid is worth.

... another point of view?

'Aid is more important than trade.' Do you agree with this statement? Give reasons for your opinion, showing you have considered another point of view.

Check your understanding

1 When is aid essential?
2 Why does trade help to reduce poverty?
3 How can countries be helped to trade?
4 How can trade help development?
5 How do trade and aid help development to be sustainable?

Key Terms

aid: help given by one country to another

Politics and new media

Getting you thinking

Technologies for politics

Barack Obama's election campaign changed the way politicians organise supporters, advertise to voters, defend against attacks and communicate with constituents.

The campaign used:

- **Web2** to organise supporters into an army of volunteers and paid organisers on the ground.
- **YouTube** for free advertising. The videos were said to be much better than TV campaigning because viewers chose to watch them or received them from a friend instead of having them interrupt their television shows.

The campaign's official videos for YouTube were watched for 14.5 million hours. This level of advertising would have cost Obama's party, the Democrats, $47m.

- **the internet** for fact-checking. People used the internet to find past speeches, and if these proved a politician wrong, they then alerted their fellow citizens.

1 In what ways did the Obama campaign use technology?

2 How did it encourage people to get involved?

3 Why could this campaign reach many more people than it had been possible to reach in the past?

4 Why are people more likely to watch the YouTube clips than the TV ads?

5 What advantages did the use of the internet have for the Democratic party?

A source of power

Giving people information offers them a source of power. The decision about what to tell and what not to tell means that you can affect the way people think.

When people vote in a UK election, they make decisions that affect the country for the next five years. How do they make their voting decisions? Very often, the decisions are based on information that is provided by the media. The media therefore helps people to make decisions. If the information provided is not accurate, the effect can be very damaging. If the media presents what it wants people to know, rather than the whole truth, it is difficult for people to make informed decisions.

The power of Barack Obama's campaign was that it presented to the people what the party wanted them to hear and see. The campaign bypassed the press and used the media to the party's advantage.

You will explore ways in which the media and the internet can drive political change.

Denford Magora's Zimbabwe blog

Roy Bennet, who was to be sworn in as a government minister, has been arrested and was last seen at a fuel station on the outskirts of Marondera. The swearing in of all the other cabinet ministers continued and was finished a little while back. It was temporarily delayed as Mr Mugabe and other members of the new government met behind closed doors at State House to discuss the arrest of Bennet.

Kubatana.net speaks out from Zimbabwe 100% empowerment

Posted on 3 March 2009 by Bev Clark

'In Harare we've had several downpours since Friday. Today is overcast with intermittent drizzle. And that's where this weather report ends. So there's water all around except here at work where there's none in our taps. Usually we rely on a couple of rickety taps in the car park to fill two white plastic containers but today even they've run dry. Apparently though we can buy water from a shop nearby for US$2 per litre. Remember all those election posters and T-shirts with the slogan ... 100% empowerment ... that means a Zimbabwe with no water, no jobs and barely a meal a day.'

1 What information are these two bloggers sending to the rest of the world?
2 What effect do you think it might have on:
   a) readers   b) governments.

Action

Choose a story from the international news. Google the story and see if you can find any blogs on the subject. Can you find any local information? Is there more than one point of view? What are the bloggers trying to achieve?

Check your understanding

1 How did new technology help Barack Obama to be elected?
2 How can messages reach beyond the borders of countries where the press is not free?
3 What effect can this have on public opinion and governments in other countries?
4 Suggest some current examples of ways in which new technology is helping to promote human rights.

... another point of view?

'New media always helps to promote human rights and democracy.'
Do you agree with this statement? Give reasons for your opinion, showing you have considered another point of view.

Hearing the voice

In countries where people have few democratic rights, it can be hard to get your voice heard. A blog can let people know what's going on – and help to change opinion or make demands for change. Blogging gives everyone a voice – from ordinary people who are trying to make a living to political experts who want to let the outside world know what is happening. People in Zimbabwe have been writing blogs about what is going on in the country (see above). This has enabled the rest of the world and the UN to know far more about the problems there than it would have done 20 years ago. The UN has condemned the activities of the Zimbabwean government.

There are at least two sides to every story. A reader must be careful to look at the source of the information in blogs. People have all sorts of motives and wish to promote a range of views – so it is important not to believe everything you find in blogs.

Exam questions

After you have studied all of the theory for this unit you will have to take an exam. The exam lasts for 1 hour. You need to revise all of the work you have covered. The questions below give you an idea of what to expect when you take this exam.

Section A

Answer all questions.
Spend about 25 minutes on this section.

> These questions have many correct answers. You only need to write one down.

> All of these questions ask you to state – that means you do not have to explain.

1 (a) State one example of a direct tax.   *(1 mark)*

Income tax

> You could have written: National Insurance.

   (b) State one of the main sectors where the government spends money raised
        through taxes.   *(1 mark)*

Health

> You could have written: education or defence.

2 (a) State one source of advice for people who want information about their rights.   *(1 mark)*

Solicitor

> You could have written: Citizens Advice Bureau or police.

   (b) State an example of one government agency or official regulator that safeguards or
        promotes people's rights.   *(1 mark)*

Office of Fair Trading

> You could have written: Ofsted or Commission for Equality and Human Rights.

3 (a) State one way in which a Trade Union might support its members.   *(1 mark)*

Offer advice

> You could have written: negotiate for improved pay or attend to health and safety matters.

   (b) State one way in which the law protects the interests of employers.   *(1 mark)*

It allows them to discipline staff

> You could have written: protects copyright or may limit their liability for financial loss.

4 (a) State one way in which local authorities can encourage sustainable development. *(1 mark)*

Give everyone recycling bags

You could have written: reducing waste or fining people for environmentally unfriendly activities.

Leave margin blank

(b) State one other type of organisation, apart from a local authority, that might encourage sustainable development. *(1 mark)*

School

You could have written: pressure group or charity.

5 (a) State three different ways in which a student council or school/college council can help students to develop their rights and responsibilities. *(3 marks)*

Understanding how the school operates
Developing debating skills
Having a say

Be careful that you do not repeat yourself or you may not score all 3 marks.

(b) State one legal right of parents in connection with their child's education. *(1 mark)*

To say which school you would prefer your child to attend

You could have written: to be told about meetings involving your child.

6 Explain how more economically developed countries (MEDCs) benefit by giving aid to less economically developed countries (LEDCs).

In your answer you must:

- explain one advantage in depth or at least two advantages in outline
- use examples to support your explanation. *(6 marks)*

Make sure you complete all of the bullet points. You can tick them off as you do them so you do not miss anything out.

Read this question carefully – there are two ways to get full marks.

More economically developed countries are richer countries like the UK, whereas less economically developed countries are poorer ones like Afghanistan and Iraq. When MEDCs help LEDCs they do so to improve security. This means that the LEDC might be a country that is suffering from conflict and by giving aid there might be peace in the country. The UK helps Iraq to improve security. MEDCs also give aid to encourage the LEDC to trade. A lot of the money given to Afghanistan by the UK goes to help create jobs. Products are then produced and can be exported to the UK so we benefit from having a range of products for sale in this country. The UK government also gives aid to Pakistan. This allows both countries to ensure their own security, stability, growth and development. This benefits the UK as it helps our own national security.

> The candidate has shown they understand what MEDCs and LEDCs are.

> Two advantages have been explained in outline.

> The candidate has used examples.

(Total marks: 18)

Section B

> In this section of the exam, you will be able to find some of the answers in the documents. Read each document carefully before you look at the relevant questions.

Answer all the questions.

Spend about 35 minutes on this section.

To help you answer the questions in this section, you should use:

- the stimulus documents linked to each question
- your own knowledge, understanding and experience of Citizenship Studies.

7 Study Document 1 below and answer the questions that follow.

Document 1

BBC World Service

BBC World Service is the world's most respected voice in international broadcasting. It provides impartial news and information in 33 languages worldwide.

BBC World Service is trusted for its accuracy, editorial independence and expertise, and encourages the exchange of ideas across cultural, linguistic and national boundaries.

It promotes British values of trust, openness, fair dealing, creativity, enterprise and community.

BBC World Service is a public service funded by the UK Foreign and Commonwealth Office.

Extract adapted from the website of the British Broadcasting Corporation, www.bbc.co.uk

---

(a) State one piece of evidence from Document 1 that shows that the BBC World
    Service does not always agree with the United Kingdom (UK) Government. *(1 mark)*

It gives impartial news

> You could have written: it is trusted for its editorial independence.

(b) State one reason why the UK Government is willing to pay for the
    BBC World Service *(1 mark)*

It promotes British values

> You could have written: it promotes the exchange of ideas.

(c) State two ways in which the internet can be used to support human rights. *(2 marks)*

Allows instant worldwide communication

Easy to run campaigns

> You could have written: it makes it easy to research abuses of power.

8 Study Document 2 below and answer the questions that follow:

Document 2

HMG is a company that makes paints.

John Falder, the Managing Director, says the company is a 'family business, owned and run, with lots of families from the local community also working within the business'.

HMG respects staff as individuals, giving everyone a sense of involvement. Keen employees help give the company an advantage over its competitors. HMG has a flexible working policy, where working hours are adjusted to meet employees' needs. Around 15 per cent of the 170 staff are working flexible hours.

HMG gives employees a day off with double pay on their birthdays. It also supports company sports teams.

HMG's Social Responsibility activities include action in education, the environment and the community. Requests for paint from the local community are always met. The company provides the Rose Wood Gardens for the enjoyment of local residents.

HMG offers youth job placements for 14- to 16-year-olds. Feedback has been extremely positive, with students describing the placements as 'fantastic' to their schools.

In HMG's view, treating employees as part of a team means that people stay with the company. The average worker stays with the company for a lifetime. This saves on recruitment costs.

The company also says its excellent health and safety record – only one unsuccessful claim for industrial injury in the history of the company – is because of trust and team spirit at all levels of the business.

Adapted from www.article13.com, a website giving examples of social responsibility in business

---

(a) State one piece of evidence from Document 2 that shows HMG is a socially responsible business. *(1 mark)*

HMG maintains Rose Wood Gardens

> You could have written: HMG donates paint or HMG offers job placements to students.

(b) State two reasons why 'the average worker stays with the company a lifetime'. *(2 marks)*

HMG has an excellent health and safety record

HMG supports company teams

> You could have written: HMG offers a flexible working policy or respects staff.

> The last part of Question 8 requires you to use the theory you have studied as well as the document to get good marks.

*(c) Write a reasoned argument to oppose the viewpoint that, 'a company should do their best to make money instead of bothering with social responsibility'.

> If you see a star (*) by a question this means the examiner is looking at the quality of your written communication, as well as whether or not you can answer the question.

In your answer you must:
- explain key terms such as 'social responsibility'
- explain what it means to be a good business
- use evidence to support your argument. *(6 marks)*

> Make sure you complete all of the bullet points. You can tick them off as you do them so you do not miss anything out.

If a business is socially responsible, it obviously looks after employees but also sees the local community as important and looks after them as well.

HMG is a good example as they provide the Rose Wood Gardens for the enjoyment of local residents. This will give the company a good name in the community and make the area more attractive.

> The candidate offers a range of evidence linked to social responsibility. They show that by being socially responsible a company can potentially make more money.

As it says in the document, HMG respects staff as individuals, giving everyone a sense of involvement. This makes the employees motivated to work harder and help HMG to be successful. Because the company offers flexible work, with hours adjusted to meet employees' needs, the staff want to stay working for HMG. This means that they save money because they do not have to recruit and train new staff all the time.

I think that by being socially responsible you can save money in the long run and this is important for any business nowadays.

Their conclusion shows that they are aware of the importance of social responsibility in business today.

9 Study Documents 3 and 4 below and answer the questions that follow.

Thousands of school days were disrupted by a one-day teachers' strike in April 2008. There were different viewpoints on the strike.

Document 3

Pay cuts for teachers

Since 2004, teachers' pay has gone up by less than inflation. This means the real value of teachers' pay has gone down. At the moment, inflation is over 4 per cent. Teachers have been told their pay will go up this year by only 2.45 per cent.

How this affects education

If teachers' pay goes down, schools will find it more difficult to get the staff they need. This may mean that class sizes go up or that teachers can't be found. We know that our strike disrupted your child's education. We regret that – but we have tried everything else and the government won't listen.

Extracts adapted from a leaflet written by the National Union of Teachers (NUT) for parents, www.teachers.org.uk

---

Document 4

Jim Knight, Government Minister for Schools

I think parents are confused because the average teacher earns about £34,000. Their pay has gone up by 19 per cent in real terms since 1997 and a 2.45 per cent increase is a reasonable deal.

Martin Ward, Association of School and College Leaders

It's a bad time for the NUT to have called this strike. Head Teachers don't think it was right for teachers to strike this year, at all. But if they were going to, it would have been better to do so after the examinations. The independent review body, which governs teachers' pay, has worked very well for teachers over the last ten years or more.

Margaret Morrissey, Parent Teachers Association

Our evidence is that the strike has not really affected parents' attitudes to teachers. They are really supportive, but that is different from saying they agree with the strike. Many feel let down by not being told early enough. Some parents were only given 24 hours' notice.

Adapted from the BBC website, www.bbc.co.uk

(a) State the amount of the teachers' pay increase given in Document 3.   *(1 mark)*

2.45%

(b) State the reason that teachers think their pay increase is really a pay cut.   *(1 mark)*

Because pay has gone
up less than inflation

> You could have written: inflation is over 4% or the real value or their wages has gone down.

(c) State one person in Document 4 who disagrees with the statement in Document 3 that 'the real value of teacher's pay has gone down'.   *(1 mark)*

Jim Knight

*(d) Evaluate the viewpoint that teachers were right to strike in April 2008.

> The last part of Question 9 requires you to use the theory you have studied as well as the documents to get good marks.

In your answer you must:
- explain arguments in favour of the strike
- explain arguments against the strike
- use relevant examples to support your answer
- explain your own point of view.

> If you see a star (*) by a question this means the examiner is looking at the quality of your written communication, as well as whether or not you can answer the question.

> Make sure you complete all of the bullet points. You can tick them off as you do them so you do not miss anything out.

(6 marks)

The teachers were right to go on strike in April 2008. This is because according to the NUT, in real terms their salary had decreased as inflation was at 4% and their increase was only 2.45%. If teachers' pay decreases then schools will find it hard to recruit new staff and so there will have to be increased class sizes which is not good in the long run. The strike did not really affect parents' attitudes so going on strike did not have a negative impact.

> Evidence has been used to support the evaluation.

On the other hand, they were wrong to go on strike in April because students who had exams coming up could suffer because they would be missing lessons. This was said by Martin Ward. The teachers should have given more notice about going on strike.

> The answer is well organised and follows the bullet points.

In my opinion they were wrong to go on strike. If they wanted to get their voice heard there are other methods they could use which won't affect students' education.

Although a 2.45% increase was low, if inflation decreased then this could be seen as a better rate of pay.

> The conclusion gives the candidate's own opinion based on a balanced evaluation.

> On this exam, Questions 8c and 9d are checking you can evaluate a viewpoint. These questions could ask you to:
> - oppose
> - support
> or
> - evaluate
> Be careful when you answer these questions that you have read the question carefully and know what you are meant to do. Use the bullet points as a guide.

(Total marks: 22)

Unit 4: Identity,

democracy and justice

leading the way as an active citizen

Cultural influences

Getting you thinking

1 What cultural connections are shown here?

2 Can you think of any other ways in which different cultures have influenced life in the UK?

3 How do you think life would be if we had no influences from other countries?

Veeraswamy's Indian Restaurant opened in London's Regent Street 1927. It is still there today. There are not only millions of Indian restaurants in this country, but the flavours used in Indian cooking are now to be found in new recipes developed in the UK.

Developing a culture

In Unit 2 (page 62) you explored the mix of roots and identities of people in the UK. There is plenty of evidence on every high street, and in our language and lifestyle, of the effect of the mix of people that we really are.

If you look at the timeline of immigration to the UK, you can identify all sorts of influences that have come from different groups of people.

You will investigate the contributions of different cultures to life in the UK.

When did people arrive?

1685	Religious persecution forces 100,000 Huguenots (French Protestants) to leave France for Britain.
1840s	Famine forces thousands of people to leave Ireland.
1848	Britain becomes the destination of choice for many refugees from revolutions in Europe.
1880s	Jews seek sanctuary in Britain when they are persecuted in Europe.
1914–18	Refugees flee from First World War in Europe.
1939–45	Refugees flee from Second World War in Europe.
1946	People seek refuge from Communism in Europe.
1948	West Indians come to Britain as there are many jobs to fill after Second World War.
1972	Ugandan Asians settle in the UK after being expelled from Uganda.
1975	Many seek a new life in Britain because of political unrest and war in Southeast Asia.
1980s	Large numbers of Australians, New Zealanders and South Africans move to the UK because of opportunities for those with specialist skills and professional training.
1992–98	Ethnic disputes in the Balkans force thousands to seek refuge in Western Europe. Many seek asylum in the UK.
1998–2002	During these years, 45,000 people arrive from Africa, 22,700 from the Indian sub-continent and 25,000 from Asia.

1 Work out how each of these groups has influenced life in the UK.
2 Are there other influences that we might have brought back from our holidays or found out about in other ways?

Our World Food Day promoted tolerance, respect, cultural understanding and lovely food. We had over 20 food stalls and we raised over £1,500. Food from Indonesia to Somalia, the Middle East to Mexico represented the diversity and creativity of Drayton Manor High School. There were Dhol drums and singing. It was hot, lively and rowdy, as the students enjoyed tasting some foods for the very first time, knowing they were helping to make a difference to some of the poorest people in the world. It was truly wonderful to see young people working, eating, singing, dancing and celebrating together and realising that their actions can have such positive effects. We hope that our next FoodAid World Food Day will be even bigger and better!

Lucia Johnstone-Cowan, Drayton Manor High School, London

Action

1 Work out which aspect of life in the UK interests you most. Perhaps it is dance, or music, or food?
2 Identify as many groups as you can that have affected your choice. How has each one changed things?
3 Plan an event in school to showcase your choice. Look at pages 180–1 to find out how to go about planning your event.

Check your understanding

1 Where have people come to the UK from since 1685?
2 What aspects of our lives have they influenced?
3 How can running an event in school help people both in school and further afield?

... another point of view?

'I only like English stuff.'
Do you agree with this statement? Give reasons for your opinion, showing you have considered another point of view.

Reasons for tension

Getting you thinking

Keep calm!

Teachers' leaders yesterday appealed for calm at a school where teenagers chanted racist abuse at refugee classmates.

Ten pupils at Parkside Community Technology College, Plymouth, have been suspended after allegedly shouting 'Pakis out' in the playground. Teachers responded by herding twenty of the victims into a classroom for their own safety.

The parents of the refugee children, who were targeted by a mob of about forty pupils on Wednesday at lunchtime, are now refusing to send them back to the school.

The Minister for Borders and Immigration said:

'I think the immigration system has been too lenient and I want to make it harder, but I also want to be nice to people who do come to settle here. That's what I have wanted to do all my life since a boy from Uganda came to my school and was called Banana. I was appalled.'

Who's afraid?

The war on terror causes fear on both sides. Muslims feel targeted by the campaign in the media and by the government. It raises the level of fear in the hearts of people who had been living together peacefully for years.

Morrissey said:

'Also, with the issue of immigration, it's very difficult because, although I don't have anything against people from other countries, the higher the influx into England, the more the British identity disappears, so the price is enormous. If you travel to Germany, it's still absolutely Germany. If you travel to Sweden, it still has a Swedish identity. But travel to England and you have no idea where you are. It matters because the British identity is very attractive. I grew up into it, and I find it quaint and very amusing. But England is a memory now. Other countries have held on to their basic identity, yet it seems to me that England was thrown away.'

1 Why do you think the children at Parkside Community College behaved as they did?

2 If you were the Minister, how would you want to 'be nice to people who ... come to settle here'?

3 Morrissey complains that immigration means that the UK is losing its culture. What aspects of our culture do you think have changed because of immigration? What has stayed the same? What sorts of things have changed for other reasons?

4 How has the war on terror affected communities?

Why do people have different attitudes?

In Unit 2 you discovered that the UK has a diverse population and has had for many years (see pages 66–7). Yet people react in different ways to immigrants arriving in the country. There are a number of reasons for this:

- **Fear of change**

Many people have a fear of differences, and worry that new arrivals may change their community. If you are afraid of change you may not know how to deal with people from different backgrounds and cultures.

You will explore the reasons why groups of people react differently to people from other countries.

- **Employment**

  New people may threaten the jobs market, although there is evidence that immigrants take jobs that residents do not want. Many people from new EU countries came to pick fruit, for example. They were brought here because farmers couldn't find enough pickers. When the economy is booming, people are welcome because there are more jobs than people. If unemployment starts rising, the situation may change.

- **Inequalities**

  Inequalities work in both directions. The established community can resent people who arrive and, because they have no resources, are looked after by the state. Newcomers may resent the local population who have settled jobs and security.

  Many immigrants work very hard to make the most of their opportunities and when they become successful, this can cause tension.

Who works hardest?

Helping people to become self-sufficient so that they can participate in the local community helps to overcome difficulties. The data on GCSE A* to C grades shows how some groups are making the most of the opportunities they are offered and can therefore become successful members of the community.

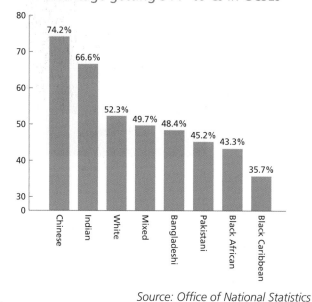

Source: Office of National Statistics

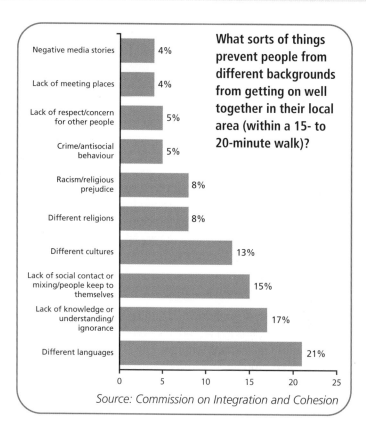

What sorts of things prevent people from different backgrounds from getting on well together in their local area (within a 15- to 20-minute walk)?

Source: Commission on Integration and Cohesion

Check your understanding

1. Why do some people not respond positively to new arrivals?
2. Why do you think others welcome them?
3. What raises tension in communities?
4. How can new arrivals help themselves?
5. How can this cause tension?

... another point of view?

'People are always afraid of change.'

Do you agree with this statement? Give reasons for your opinion, showing you have considered another point of view.

Working together

Getting you thinking

The Word is a hip hop group based at Thornhill Business and Enterprise School in Sunderland. Through powerful and highly creative performances, The Word aims to inform young people about cultural, ethnic, racial and religious diversity; to raise awareness of and tackle the problems of discrimination, racism and antisocial issues and, above all, inspire all young people to achieve their ambitions.

In **Leicester**, Sacred Heart Catholic Primary School was twinned with Bridge Junior, 80 per cent of whose pupils are Muslim children. A performance group ran workshops and organised an event for the parents from both schools to meet for the first time. The schools carried out work on identity, in which pupils explored their parents' and grandparents' experiences. Pupils and parents started communicating with each other.

Langport, a small town in Somerset, has recently attracted an increasing number of migrant workers. The local community was offered help to understand that migrant workers – mainly of Polish and Portuguese origin – were arriving to live and work in the area, and why. It offered practical support to help the newcomers to overcome problems with their day-to-day integration. An 'international' sporting event took place, at which new arrivals took part in teams with residents. There were also language classes to help new arrivals learn English.

Radio Salaam Shalom is the UK's first Muslim and Jewish online radio station. It aims to bridge the gap between Jewish and Muslim young people. Radio Salaam Shalom's key success is bringing Muslim and Jewish communities together to consider their shared local values and experiences as residents of Bristol, where it is based, and beyond.

Bradgate Bakery encourages migrant workers to improve their English language skills by giving employees substantial time off to learn English, as a wider package of learning and personal development in the workplace.

Sharing Cultural Memories brought 15 older volunteers into 10 local primary schools. Volunteers used innovative methods to help pupils with numeracy and literacy. They shared cultural memories and experiences with the children. For example, one volunteer ran a Caribbean Nature project at Rotherfield Primary School to raise children's awareness about their own and other people's heritage.

1. What is a community? Use Unit 2 pages 66–7 to help you.
2. Which groups of people did these projects aim to help?
3. In what way do you think these projects help communities?
4. Why do you think these projects are necessary?
5. Are there any activities in your area that aim to help communities work together better?

You will explore ways in which problems of community cohesion can be resolved.

What is community cohesion?

Community cohesion is the togetherness and bonding shown by members of a community. This can be described as the 'glue' that holds a community together. It might include features such as a sense of common belonging or cultural similarity. You found out about communities and identities in Unit 2 (see pages 64–7). Encouraging members of communities to work together better has been part of government policy for a number of years.

What makes communities work together?

- *Lifestyle* is top of the list. People need education, jobs, a reasonable income, healthcare and decent housing if they are to feel secure in their community. If people are in poor health or debt, have poor skills and bad living conditions, they are likely to have low self-esteem. This often leads to difficulties in getting a job and a sense of insecurity.

- *Social order* is also important. If the community is peaceful and secure, people are more likely to respect each other. Lack of social order can lead to suspicion and lack of respect.

- *Social networks* connect people and organisations, and help people to support each other by offering information, trust and friendship.

- *Sense of belonging* is important. It comes from shared experiences, values and identities.

- *Equality* – or fairness – means that people in the community have equal access to resources such as jobs, healthcare and education, which affect people's life chances.

When these factors are part of community life, there is more likely to be social inclusion. People who miss out are likely to feel excluded from society and therefore tend to drop out or become disengaged.

Achieving community cohesion

A community that really works needs:

- a common vision and a sense of belonging for all
- to value diversity
- similar life opportunities for all
- strong and positive relationships between people from different backgrounds and circumstances, in the workplace, in schools and within neighbourhoods.

Check your understanding

1 Why is it difficult for some communities to work together?
2 Explain the factors which make it easier for communities to work together. Explain why each one is important.
3 What sort of activities can help to develop community cohesion?
4 What are the characteristics of a community that works well?

... another point of view?

'Communities need help to be cohesive.'

Do you agree with this statement? Give reasons for your opinion, showing you have considered another point of view.

Key Terms

community cohesion: the glue that holds communities together

Community groups and leaders: what's the impact?

Getting you thinking

Following anti-terrorism police raids in Waltham Forest, the following letter was sent to all the residents in the borough.

Dear Resident

Last week many of us woke to the news that police had launched an anti-terrorism operation within Waltham Forest.

We were shocked by allegations that extremist groups were plotting from within our borough. Now that the eyes of the world are on the part of East London that we call home, it is important that we all renew our commitment to forge strong community links whilst wholeheartedly condemning all forms of extremism and violence.

Our borough is privileged to be home for a large number of ethnic and faith groups. The vast majority of people living here enjoy the diversity of our neighbourhoods.

We must continue to work together to ensure the events of last week do not have an adverse effect on our way of life in Waltham Forest.

Since the raids occurred, Waltham Forest Council has been continuing its close work with representatives of the local mosques, community leaders and the police.

Signed by the following community leaders:

8 councillors of the 3 main political parties including the mayor

3 MPs

14 representatives of the Muslim community

4 representatives of the Christian community

2 representatives of the business community

1 Why do you think these community leaders thought it was important to communicate with residents?
2 Are these leaders elected or non-elected?
3 What difference do you think it made to residents?
4 How do such actions affect community cohesion?

What do community leaders do?

Community leaders come in all shapes and sizes. They may be elected or may have become leaders by getting involved and taking on the role because they are accepted by others. Many represent religious groups and others represent business interests. These are some of things they might do:

- Encourage organisations and individuals to express their views
- Represent local concerns and perspectives
- Maintain a link between the users and providers of services
- Encourage the community to organise services for themselves
- Work with other community leaders in the voluntary, community and business sectors
- Offer vision and direction to local groups
- Encourage agreement between different interests and partners.

You will explore the effectiveness of community leaders.

Community groups

Community groups are as varied as their leaders. The Chamber of Commerce represents businesses in your area. There is often a Young Chamber too. They aim to help young people make contact with local businesses. There are groups representing most sectors of society, from parents to the elderly, from farmers to accountants. In many areas there are groups that want to protect or help the development of specific areas. They can have a strong voice when the council wants to change things.

Community groups can help to make people's lives different. Team London Bridge does all sorts of things to help people in the community. The picture shows young people performing at a concert at the Unicorn Theatre in London to showcase the range of activities that are funded by this organisation.

Leicestershire Chamber of Commerce – mission

'Owned by and run for local business as a powerful voice uniquely positioned at the heart of the local economy. The Chamber seeks to support and represent its members and the whole business community at local, regional and national level, adding value by helping them to succeed, grow and increase profitability.

In consultation with members, we aim to be an effective pressure group, engaging and influencing policy and decision makers as a mature, responsible and independent organisation. Working for what is believed to be best for the Leicestershire economy.'

Always positive?

Community groups can have a negative influence on communities if they want to protect their interests at the expense of others'. Most issues involve people with a range of points of view and it is essential that people work together if solutions to problems are to be found.

Action

1 Which community leaders do you know?
2 Find out about as many community groups in your area as you can. Can you beat 20?

Check your understanding

1 What sort of people are community leaders?
2 What groups might they represent?
3 How do they help communities?
4 What does a Chamber of Commerce aim to do?
5 How might a community group have a negative influence?

... another point of view?

'I'll join that community group because I know that it will look after my interests, whatever other people want.'
Do you agree with this statement? Give reasons for your opinion, showing you have considered another point of view.

Meeting community needs

Getting you thinking

Building better communities

'We aim to create strong, attractive and thriving communities and neighbourhoods. To do this we help people and local organisations to combat problems like community conflict, extremism, deprivation and disadvantage.'

The government aims to overcome discrimination by making communities more cohesive. People are less likely to behave badly towards each other if they get to know each other better. Often people are suspicious of people who they see as being different, but when they meet they find that they share more than they expect.

1 What are the government's objectives within this strategy?
2 Why do you think it wants to achieve these objectives?
3 Why do you think that people get on better when they get to know each other?
4 How would you go about achieving these objectives?

What can the government do?

Governments want the economy to thrive so everyone feels better off – and the government then gets re-elected. Some parts of the country face serious challenges because of unemployment, poor conditions, and a range of social and community problems. People who live in poor conditions suffer poor health and low educational achievement. This means that they find it hard to move out of poverty.

Very often it takes groups of organisations to help sort out the problems. The government's strategies for strengthening communities often try to achieve this.

Solihull aims to bridge the digital divide. This initiative is designed to bring broadband to the residents of a group of high-rise flats, whose residents include a mixture of long-term unemployed, low paid workers, single parent families with young children and those with disabilities. It also creates a wireless hotspot area that Solihull Metropolitan Council can use to help attract local businesses to a part of North Solihull undergoing major regeneration work.

The HAAYA 'MY Voice' project was funded by Hounslow Council's Preventing Violent Extremism Fund. The Hounslow Asian and African Youth Association is run by local young people and has considerable street credibility.

A steering group consists of a Metropolitan Police Officer (from the Muslim Contact Group, Scotland Yard), the Principal Community Cohesion Officer from the London Borough of Hounslow, local community leaders from Hounslow Jamia Mosque, a representative from Hounslow Homes, local Muslim business owners, and Muslim young people.

The key element of the project was to engage with 24 young Muslims, male and female, who would be empowered to deal with extremist ideologies. The young people would then cascade their learning and become role models, and engage with Muslims and wider society. The aim of the project was to promote an alternative view to the extremist ideas which were being expressed by vulnerable young Muslims in Hounslow.

You will explore the work of the government and other organisations in meeting community needs.

Helping community organisations

When trying to achieve community cohesion, it is important to engage with existing community groups. These groups often find it difficult to make ends meet so helping them has a double effect. Not only can they work more effectively, but they are likely to want to join government initiatives.

Organisations working together

Some organisations work together to make a difference. In Birmingham, an interfaith group has worked through Greenpeace to turn the oil from Balti restaurants into biofuels.

It is just one example of how such organisations can work together.

Faith organisations promoting community cohesion get £4.3m

The Communities Minister has offered grants totalling more than £4.3m to 343 organisations to promote a common sense of citizenship. Twenty-five organisations in Derbyshire, Leicestershire, Northamptonshire and Nottinghamshire are included.

Ministers have set out the challenge to all living in a multicultural Britain of learning to celebrate our shared heritage while doing more to understand our individual differences.

The announcement follows bids from more than 1,200 organisations to the Faith Communities Capacity Building Fund. This is the second round of a £13.8m fund to help organisations promote community cohesion and shared citizenship at a local community level.

Source: Government Office for the East Midlands

What does it take?

There is no fixed formula for meeting community needs. In some areas, community groups manage very well on their own because they have enough resources and enthusiasm to make their activities work. In other areas, which are often those with high levels of deprivation, more help is needed. The government then needs to target its support carefully in order to achieve its objectives.

If there are specific objectives that affect the whole country – such as meeting environmental targets – there may be a need for more general support.

Check your understanding

1 Why do governments want to promote community cohesion?
2 How do they go about it?
3 Why are community groups important?
4 When should the government help?

... another point of view?

'Communities should be able to make progress on their own.'

Do you agree with this statement? Give reasons for your opinion, showing you have considered another point of view.

Are we really equal?

Getting you thinking

He was bullied

My son was bullied at primary school and secondary school. The bullying was all about him being gay, although he never came out in school. As a result, he is now on medication, possibly for the rest of his life. The only thing he (and those who bullied him) learnt in school about gay people was they were gassed in the Holocaust. Surely, as a nation, we can do better than this? What's wrong with children knowing that sometimes people of the same sex fall in love with one another? What's wrong with explaining to children that this is OK, that they are committing no crime, and that it isn't a reason to call them names or bully them until they are ill?

Source: The Telegraph comments, 19 September 2008

Nineteen-year-old wins age discrimination case

Leanne Wilkinson claimed she had been unfairly dismissed from her job at Springwell Engineering in Newcastle, having been told she was too young for the job and they needed an older person with more experience.

The employment tribunal ruled in her favour, finding that evidence relied on by the company did not show Wilkinson lacked in performance, and judged she had been discriminated against on the grounds of age.

What does the law say?

Laws are in place to protect people from all sorts of discrimination – of age, race, gender and sexual orientation, as you discovered in Unit 1 (page 23). More and more aspects of difference have been added over the years as we have become aware of the effect of discrimination on different groups of people. Despite the fact that laws are in place, however, people still discriminate, as court records show.

When cases come to court, there can be arguments that someone is too old to do the job or one person has less experience that another. It is not always easy to work out fact from opinion.

Laws to protect people

Equal Pay Act	1970
Sex Discrimination Act	1975
Race Relations Act	1976
Disability Discrimination Act	1995
The Employment Equality (Sexual Orientation) Regulations	2003
Employment Equality (Religion or Belief) Regulations	2003
Employment Equality (Age) Regulations	2006

You will investigate whether discrimination on the grounds of age, race, gender or sexual orientation has ended.

What's happened to women's pay?

The gap between women and men's pay is shrinking but:

Full-time hourly pay for men	£14.98
Full-time hourly pay for women	£12.40
Full-time gender pay gap	17.2%

Part-time hourly pay for men	£13.10
Part-time hourly pay for women	£9.65
Part-time gender pay gap	35.6%

There are few women in the highest paid groups and many in low paid groups.

The gender pay gap would lose an average woman working full-time a grand total of £330,000 during her working life.

Race discrimination claim costs boutique chain £5,000

A sales assistant who claimed she was fired from a fashion boutique owned by Sadie Frost because of the colour of her skin was awarded more than £5,000 compensation.

What colour? What gender?

Mrs M, an assistant accountant, claimed that she was unfairly dismissed because of being a woman of Indian origin. During her five months of employment she was told by a colleague that the three company directors, who were also of Indian origin, did not approve of Asian women working for the company.

1 How have each of these people been discriminated against?
2 What laws have been broken?
3 How has the pay gap between men and women changed?
4 What do the figures on women's pay hide?

How do we compare?

The EU has its own laws preventing discrimination and member countries are expected to incorporate them into their own law.

In general, the UK meets the EU requirements but the UK still has a large gender pay gap by European standards. It is a third higher than the EU average, and twice that of Ireland. Of the larger member states, only Germany has a bigger gap.

Check your understanding

1 What types of discrimination are against the law?
2 What evidence is there that pay is becoming more equal?
3 What evidence is there that other forms of discrimination still exist?
4 Find out what is going on in your local community to reduce discrimination. Does your school have any policies to prevent students discriminating against each other?
5 How can discrimination be reduced?

... another point of view?

'The laws against discrimination should prevent it happening.'

Do you agree with this statement? Give reasons for your opinion, showing you have considered another point of view.

Your Citizenship Action: what's the choice?

Young people in Devizes discuss community issues

1 What issues do you think the young people in the picture might be discussing?

2 Think about your community – what needs changing?

3 What do you care about?

4 How do you think you can make a difference?

Your Citizenship Action

Citizenship is all about joining in and having an effect. Your Citizenship Action gives you the chance to have a go. There are lots of ways of participating as you will have found out already. There are also lots of questions to ask before you decide what you are going to do.

The objectives of your Action

Your Action must promote community cohesion or equal opportunity, or discourage discrimination in your school or local community.

Your Action must come under one of the following themes:

- gender
- race, ethnicity and culture
- age
- disability.

You have learnt a lot about these issues throughout the course, so think back to all you have learnt about discrimination and community issues, and consider how they affect where you are.

Before you begin, you must do some research to find out what the community thinks. Your Action must be based on evidence that there is an issue in the community, and the ways people think the issue can be overcome.

What's your issue?

When you've worked out the issues, there are two questions to ask.

1 Does the Action either
  • promote community cohesion
  • promote equal opportunity
  • discourage discrimination
  in your school or local community?

2 How are we going to make a difference?

There are all sorts of ways of making a difference. It's all about making your voice heard – or helping others to do so. School might be the right place to start.

• If you want other students to care about your particular issue, you might want to put on an event to help them understand.

• There may be others who care about the issue too. Get them together and form a pressure group.

• If the school rules ignore issues of gender, age, race, ethnicity and culture, or disability, you might want to negotiate a change.

• Perhaps Year 7s would enjoy an event that trains them to deal with issues of discrimination.

  There might be issues outside school – perhaps there are language difficulties in the community or access problems in some locations.

  How will your Action help the community to be more united?

• A website that informs people of the issue could also take their votes.

• A consultation in the local area could provide evidence for your Action.

• A debate would allow people to put across their side of the argument.

A voice in the community – young people in Stoke-on-Trent voting for their representatives. They are working against age discrimination

How are you going to make a difference?

Presenting a case to others about a concern

• Is your school accessible to people with disabilities? If not, discuss this with the senior leaders.

Conducting a consultation, vote or election

• Organise a grandparents' party to find out about their issues.

Organising a meeting, event or forum to raise awareness and debate issues

• Organise an event for new students and their parents to celebrate diversity in school.

Creating, reviewing or revisiting an organisation's policy

• Review, revisit or revise the school's policy on equal opportunities in sport.

Contributing to local community policies

• Meet your local councillor or youth council representatives to discuss a policy that concerns you.

Communicating views publicly via a website or display

• Organise a display to promote inter-generational respect.

Setting up an action group or network

• Organise a class link to another school in the UK or overseas to develop a better understanding of cultural diversity.

Making the choice

What's the issue?

Your Citizenship Action is an important part of the course. You need to collect evidence and keep a record of what happened at every stage as it is very important you show what you and everyone else did. You will also need to work out how well the Action went.

You may already be involved in suitable activities but, if not, you'll need to choose what to do. There are many possibilities for you to consider.

- Can you work with other young people to discuss community issues such as graffiti and vandalism, or services that you would like to see in your area?
- Could you create a display about people's rights and responsibilities as members of a community?

- Could you discuss issues of community cohesion with your local councillor?
- Does your school have a radio station? If not, could you start one up to promote involvement in local issues?
- Could you organise an 'origins and links' wall for students to idenfity their links around the world?
- Could you organise a consultation about an issue in school or the community?

Your Action could be based on any of these ideas or many others. Remember that being involved in something that really interests you always makes the task easier. For example, does the local environment concern you? Are you worried about crime in your area? Or do you want more facilities for young people in the area?

Working in a team

For your Citizenship Action you have to work as part of a team. The team may be made up of your school friends. It is important to think about the contribution each person makes to the Action. Make sure that everyone has a role in the Action as it makes it much easier to identify each person's contribution if you can explain their responsibilities.

A group of young people work on a community environment project

1 Make a list of the contributions you think people will have to make to plan and carry out this Action.
2 Why do you think it is a good Citizenship Action?
3 Which part of the course does it relate to? See pages 40–1.

What's the evidence?

While choosing your issue you carried out research into issues affecting school and the local community. Did you use a questionnaire or collect evidence from local papers or websites? If so, include them. Were there leaflets or information about it on the web? If you used web-based information, make sure it is relevant! Examiners don't want to wade through masses of material that isn't to the point. There are no marks for weight!

You need to be able show to the examiner that you thought about your choice and came to a conclusion. You don't have to write lots – just answer the question and add the evidence of what you did.

If you shared out roles, produce some evidence of how you went about it. Perhaps your teacher would sign a witness statement.

How does it link to Citizenship?

Work out which part of the course your issue fits into. Look carefully at the unit and work out exactly where it fits. Write four sentences to explain the connections.

Carrying out your Practical Citizenship Action

Take action

Sit down with a blank sheet of paper and think about what Citizenship Action you are going to choose.
1 Start by writing down all your ideas.
2 List all the advantages and disadvantages of each idea.
3 Put them in order from best to worst.
4 Is the one at the top the one you really want to carry out? If so, go ahead. If not, have another look at the list.

Check point

Before you make a final decision, check with your teacher that your Action is suitable for the course requirements.

You will need to show evidence of the contribution you and the others in your group made to the Citizenship Action, so it's a good idea to think about this right from the start.

Planning your Citizenship Action

The steps to success

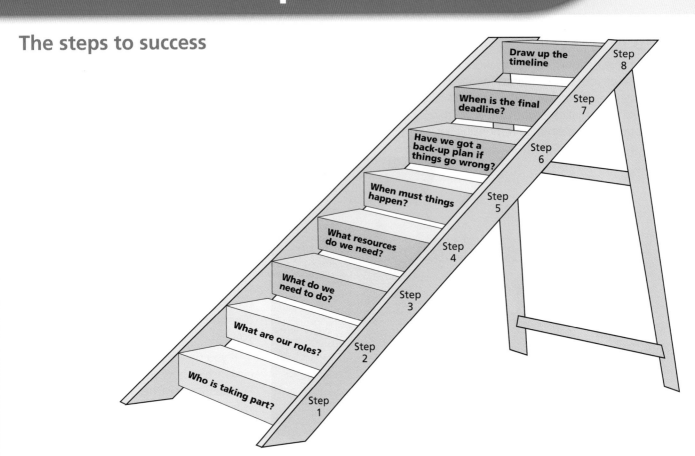

Step 1: Who is taking part?
Step 2: What are our roles?
Step 3: What do we need to do?
Step 4: What resources do we need?
Step 5: When must things happen?
Step 6: Have we got a back-up plan if things go wrong?
Step 7: When is the final deadline?
Step 8: Draw up the timeline

Planning

Planning means setting out what must be done and making sure that everyone knows their responsibilities. By following the steps above, you will be on the right track. You will need to gather evidence and be able to explain the links to Citizenship, so you need to build this into your plan. The following pages will help you with the stages of organising your Action and gathering the evidence you need.

Your targets

When you write up the planning stage you will need to:
- state the aim of your Practical Citizenship Action
- explain why it is important to promote community cohesion, promote equal opportunity and discourage discrimination
- explain how your Action will help to do this and provide evidence to support your answer
- describe the outcome of your research and explain how this has influenced your planning
- describe what your group plans to do and describe your own part in the plan

- describe how you overcame any problems at this stage and explain how you could have improved the planning phase of your work.

Keep this list in mind when you make your plans so that by the time you write up the planning stage, you will have gathered all the information together.

What will you need to do?

Brainstorm all the things that need to be done.
- Can you easily divide these things into groups?
- Who has the skills needed for each activity?
- Should people work in pairs or on their own?

Then, when you have made these decisions, draw up a list to explain exactly what everyone has to do. Make sure you keep the list safe. You will need it to check whether everything has been done, and to put in your records. You will need to complete a planning chart like the one below.

Team Member	Overall Role	Planned Action	Start Date	Completion Date

Plan the timeline

Look carefully at your plan and draw up your timeline, putting the name of the person responsible beside each task. This will give you markers to check whether everything is on track. It will also give everyone target dates for getting things done.

Remember that gathering information can take time, so make it a priority.

Example: planning your Citizenship Action

Take action

When you have decided on your Action, get together with the rest of the team and work out how you are going to go about planning and putting your idea into action.

Check point

Gather evidence to show:
- your research
- how you decided on your Action. Was it democratic?
- how your Action will make a difference
- what you and the rest of your group did
- problems that occurred and how you overcame them
- the links to Citizenship.

October 1

Start research into what your school or community needs.

October 14

Choose your activity. Keep a record of how you decided.

Draw up plan. Set deadlines for each stage. Work out links with Citizenship. Work out what you will need for your Action and set about organising it – will you need posters, presentations, websites, witness statements or videos of your Action?

Work out how your Action will affect the issue – keep a record.

How will you measure the impact of your Action?

October 21

Review materials and resources – are they convincing? Do you need anything else?

Make sure you have a record of letters, etc.

November 28

Review what happened.

Where there any problems? How did you overcome them?

Have you got enough evidence? Do you need to find out more about the impact of your Action?

Work out whether it has affected your views.

November 14

Launch the Action.

Keep a record of what happened – photographs of your involvement, of the posters, the presentations, people's comments – has the event changed their minds? – record/video them?

October 28

Let people know what you are doing – posters, school newsletter, school or community website, local community leaders.

Keep copies of the evidence.

Researching people's views – questionnaires

1 Why might you want to find out what people think?
2 Why do you need to be careful when planning the questions?
3 Why do you need to be careful when asking the questions?
4 How do you decide who to ask?

Why a questionnaire?

When planning your Citizenship Action you need to know what people in school or the local community think is important. You should also find out how they think you should go about your Action. You will then need the evidence from your research to justify your choice of issue and Action. You should think carefully about this research as the better your evidence, the better your evaluation is likely to be. You will be using your teamwork skills in this part of the Action, as you need to work with others to carry out this research.

A questionnaire is likely to be the best way to gather your evidence because it provides you with answers that you can compare.

Drawing up a questionnaire

- Before you begin, make sure you know exactly what you want to find out.
- Make the questions very clear, especially if people will fill in the questionnaire on their own.
- Make the questions quick. People won't spend long on the questionnaire.

- Avoid leading questions (they often start with 'Don't you think that … ?') as they give you the answer you want to hear but not necessarily what people really think.
- Consider whether the order of the questions is important. If so, work out which should come 1st, 2nd, 3rd …
- Consider whether you need to know:
  - how old people are
  - what gender they are
  - how much they earn
  - whether they are healthy.

  These are sensitive questions so ask them carefully.
- Think about whether you want short, sharp answers. If so, use closed questions (they often have 'yes', 'no' or 'don't know' as the answer).
- Think about whether you want more thoughtful answers. If so, use open questions as these will enable you to find out about people's opinions and why they hold them.
- Avoid obvious questions. No one will answer 'Yes' to 'Would you be cruel to animals?'

Working out the results

When you have used your questionnaire to carry out a survey, you need to work out what the answers mean.

Closed questions are easy. You simply have to add up the total number of each different response. Draw up a tally sheet showing the possible answers for each question. Count up how many people gave each answer and put the number in the box.

Question 1: How often do you go swimming?

Once a week or more	Once every two weeks	Once a month	Less often
IIII	III	IIII	II

The line drawn across 4 makes it 5. This makes counting easy.

Open questions ask people for their opinions and ideas. You therefore need to read the answers carefully in order to decide how to divide them up. Many people come up with fairly standard views so you can put them together into groups. You can then work out how many you have in each group and note any ideas that stand out from the others.

You should also jot down some good examples of what people thought as these will help with your report. Sometimes people offer very strange ideas. These can be noted in order to show the range of answers.

Displaying your results

In order to show other people your findings, you need to make them as clear as possible. Graphs and charts, including bar charts and pie charts, are good ways of showing data. If you put the results into a spreadsheet, you can choose a wide variety of different ways to show your evidence. Be careful to choose the one that best suits your data.

Check point

Try your questionnaire out on someone similar to the people you are planning to ask, to test whether it works. If some questions don't work, change them. Using duff questions is a waste of time!

Take action

Do you need to find out what people think? If so, set about writing a questionnaire. Think carefully about the guidelines provided here. You might start with closed questions and have an open question or two at the end. Make sure you are not asking leading questions. This can be quite hard when you really believe in something.

Key Terms

closed questions: ask for short factual answers

open questions: ask for a point of view or longer answers

Participation in action

1. How are these students (left, and on the next page) showing their Citizenship skills?
2. What do you think they had to do to plan their activity?
3. What sort of evidence do you think they collected?
4. How does their Action affect the community?

How can you affect your issue through action?

The number of young people who vote is declining. The students in the pictures are helping children at the local primary school to understand how voting and democracy works. Not only are they helping these young people but they are also hoping to stop the fall in the number who vote. An early start is always helpful!

When people participate in decision making in their community, they are more likely to have a sense of belonging which helps community cohesion.

Once you have set up your Action you need to be able to explain how it will make a difference.

Gather evidence of your Action and how you made a contribution

There are all sorts of ways in which you can submit your supporting evidence. It doesn't just have to be in writing. Here are some suggestions:

- PowerPoint slides
- videos
- CD-Roms
- letters
- photographs
- banners
- web pages
- audio or written records of presentation work
- questionnaires
- agendas or minutes of meetings.

Different types of evidence

A video that showed the extent of your Action would be fine. An audio recording of a meeting or a presentation about carrying out your Action would also give a clear picture of how you were working.

If you use PowerPoint or some other presentation software to explain or persuade people of your point of view, that will make a good piece of evidence.

If you create a website to let people know your plans or to persuade them about your issue, this will be helpful evidence as it shows just what you were trying to do and how you went about it.

If you investigate what people want or think, you may use a questionnaire. This, together with the results, would make a good piece of evidence as it would show the way you worked and what you found out.

You might produce a leaflet to explain, persuade or justify what you are planning. This would also be a useful piece of supporting evidence, as it would give people a good picture of the activity.

Agendas or minutes of meetings will show what you and others did.

Your teacher can give you a witness statement to prove that you have carried out the Action.

Gathering all the information as you go along will help you to put it all together. It's very easy to forget exactly what happened and when!

Take action

Work out how you are going to affect the issue through the action you are taking. The local aspects may be easy. You may need to decide how you are making a bigger impact. Think about the effect you've had on the people involved – and how you might have changed their attitudes or behaviour.

Work out how you are going to gather the evidence. Make sure you keep it safe!

Check point

Get organised! The evidence is important so build it into every part of your Action.

You should describe how each piece of evidence helped you do the activity. For example, an agenda of a meeting helped you plan a particular stage of your activity, or a questionnaire helped you get information about your activity. It is also important that you show how the evidence you have gathered can be used to support arguments and make judgements.

The impact of your Action

How has your Action contributed to your issue?

A Citizenship Action always aims to make a difference, so your records should show exactly what you did and why. To evaluate your Action, you will be expected to describe the impact of your Action on community cohesion, equal opportunity or discrimination, using the following prompts:

- Explain why you chose this particular Action.
- Explain how suitable your plan was. Did you achieve your aim?
- Evaluate the success of your Action. Support this with evidence of the feedback you got from others.
- Describe what went well.
- Explain how you might do things differently if you repeated this exercise.
- Describe the next steps that could be taken by you or others in following up your Action and increasing its impact.

Your responses to these prompts will depend on the sort of activity you took part in. For example:

- If your group was involved in creating a website to promote a positive image of old people, what was the result? You might carry out a 'before and after' survey to work out whether you have had an impact on the views of other students.
- If your group organised an after school club to encourage girls to participate in sport, what was the result? Did the range of sports activities change? Was there a change in participation?

What's the evidence?

Look carefully at each of the prompts for your evaluation. What evidence do you have to back up your evaluation? If you have run an event that aimed to promote the needs of disabled people, what evidence do you have of changing people's minds? This was part of your planning so this is where you need to make sure it is included.

The next steps

Once people start out on a mission, they often want to carry on. Part of your evaluation involves thinking about this.

'Describe the next steps that could be taken by you or others in following up your project and increasing its impact.'

You will need to work with your team, and perhaps some of the people you have tried to influence, to find out what the next steps might be.

- Do you want to do the same thing next year to influence another year group?
- Do you want to work with a different year group?
- How about talking to different community groups?
- Is there a related issue that you would like to influence?

Has your Action affected your views?

I'm even more committed!

When you came up with the idea for your issue, you probably thought it was worthwhile. You will have done some research to show why your Action was important. The evidence you produced may have increased your conviction that things need to be done.

I've changed my mind!

Citizenship is all about points of view.

If you wanted the council to enclose a basketball court or set up a skate park, you might have listened to the arguments about how the council spends its money. Perhaps other people have pointed out that spending money to meet your plans would mean spending less on old people, or reducing the hours the library is open. Did you decide which was more important?

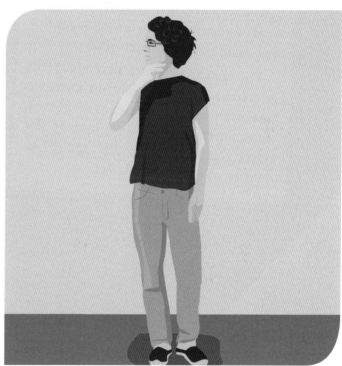

Recording it all

You can write up your Action in stages. There is quite a lot to think about so this is probably the best way. Your teacher will let you know how the writing should be planned. The most important things are:

- knowing how your Action fitted into Citizenship
- knowing whether you had an impact
- that you have collected the evidence for each stage and know what the evidence shows
- considering what you might do next.

Once these issues are clear, the writing up should be straightforward. Remember that your Action is worth 20 per cent of the whole GCSE, so you can get lots of marks for doing things rather than just taking an exam.

How judges make the law

Getting you thinking

Changing the law on divorce

Karen Parlour, the former wife of the Premiership footballer Ray Parlour has won her claim in the divorce courts. The judge agreed with her claim to more than a third of his future income in a legal landmark that could change the face of divorce law.

The appeal has set a new precedent in divorce law. Previously, maintenance was awarded on the basis of a spouse's 'reasonable needs', rather than on the equal share principle that applies to division of matrimonial assets.

Is duress an excuse?

Two men, Howe and Bannister, had been found guilty of murder. They had joined others in torturing a man who was then strangled to death by one of the others. They did it again but this time Howe and Bannister strangled the victim to death. They claimed that they had been threatened with violence by someone else and therefore acted under duress. The House of Lords dismissed their appeals against conviction and therefore duress could no longer be used as a defence.

1 Which case is criminal and which is civil?

2 How has the law been changed by each case?

3 Who is responsible for the change in the law in each case?

How are laws made?

Laws are made in the Houses of Parliament, as you learnt earlier in the course (see pages 70–1). Judges have power over laws as well. The decisions that they make set **precedents** – they determine what happens in future.

The two examples in 'Getting you thinking' show how both civil and criminal law can be changed by judges' decisions. Any decisions made affect all lower courts – so a decision in the House of Lords affects all the courts.
This type of law is known as **case law**.

There are some advantages to this system:

- Judges have clear cases to follow.
- Case law is developed in real situations.
- The law can develop but when members of the House of Lords feel that change is leading to uncertainty it can reinforce the rule.

... but there are also disadvantages:

- Once a rule has been laid down it is binding even if the decision is thought to be wrong.
- There is so much law that no one can learn all of it so cases might be overlooked.
- The law is slow to develop because the legal system is slow and expensive.

You will understand how the decisions that judges make affect the law in the future.

1. What does the law say about assisting suicide?

2. How has the House of Lords treated this law?

3. What is the Director of Public Prosecutions' attitude to people who have helped others to commit suicide?

4. What do you think the public thinks about the subject?

5. Why do you think the government hasn't done anything to change the law?

Assisted suicide is outlawed in the UK, with the 1961 Suicide Act making it illegal to 'aid, abet, counsel or procure the suicide of another'. Helping somebody to die carries a prison sentence of up to 14 years.

The Director of Public Prosecutions decides whether to go ahead with prosecutions. There have been no prosecutions of relatives of the 100 Britons who have gone abroad to end their lives at clinics run by the Swiss organisation Dignitas.

The Director of Public Prosecutions set an important precedent by refusing to prosecute the parents of Daniel James for helping him to commit suicide in Switzerland after a rugby accident that left him paralysed.

It is for Parliament to write a new law on assisted suicide, but in the meantime there is no clarity on what constitutes aiding or abetting.

The House of Lords rejected Dianne Pretty's appeal to guarantee that her husband would not be prosecuted if he assisted her to end her life. She was paralysed by motor neurone disease.

Action

Check whether judges have made any recent changes to the law in each case.

Check your understanding

1. What is civil law?
2. What is criminal law?
3. What is meant by case law?
4. What is meant by precedent?
5. How does public opinion sometimes affect decisions about changing the law?

... another point of view?

'We have elected the government so they should make the law.'

Do you agree with this statement? Give reasons for your opinion, showing you have considered another point of view.

Key Terms

case law: law that is created by the decisions of judges

precedent: a decision about a law that guides future cases

Supporting victims of crime

Getting you thinking

After the crime

The two men followed the young man off the bus. They held him at knife point to steal the expensive jacket that his mother had given him for Christmas. The young man had the presence of mind to put his iPod and phone into a trouser pocket when he saw the two thieves approach him.

The crime may sound routine, but it had a dreadful effect on the young man. He was so convinced that the thieves would target him again that he wouldn't leave the house. The robbery took place so close to the young man's house that he became convinced that they would return. The victim's mother was filled with anger, blaming herself for buying the jacket for her son, and blaming him for wearing it on the street.

The Victim Support volunteer tried to persuade the young man that the thieves were just opportunistic but to begin with he wouldn't believe this. The volunteer kept in touch with the victim for a few weeks, visiting him twice in his home, trying to persuade him that the robbery was not personal, and that he would be safe to go back out. He even suggested that they walk him round the corner to the shops, to show him that he was safe.

Because of the volunteer's experience and knowledge of crime, criminals and criminal behaviour, he was eventually able to persuade the victim to leave the house again.

1 What happened to the young man?
2 Why did he need help?
3 What is a volunteer?
4 How did the volunteer help?
5 Why was he good at the job?

What is Victim Support?

Victims of crime can be very distressed and in need of help. Victim Support is a government-funded voluntary organisation. It has branches across the country, which are run by staff, but the support work depends on volunteers. They will:

- talk to you in confidence
- give you information about police and court procedures
- help you when dealing with other organisations
- give you information about compensation and insurance
- offer links to other sources of help.

As the support workers are volunteers, they need training – which the central organisation provides.

Victim Support offers free help to anyone who has been affected by a crime – even if it hasn't been reported to the police.

You will discover how the victims of crime can be helped.

Our volunteers

We train volunteers to give emotional support, information and practical help to people who have suffered the effects of all kinds of crime – from burglary to the murder of a relative.

Our volunteers normally visit people at home and help by allowing them to talk through their feelings about the crime. Volunteers also give information about any practical and personal issues, and help victims find their own ways to overcome the effects of the crime. If you are interested in this kind of work, you need to be available for at least two hours a week, although your actual hours can be flexible and can include weekends and evenings.

Source: Victim Support website

Helping witnesses

Many witnesses are worried about going to court even if they are not the victims of the crime. Courts can seem very scary. Victim Support offers help to witnesses, families and friends at every criminal court in the country.

Although the Witness Service can't discuss the evidence, it can offer:

- someone to talk to in confidence
- a chance to see the court beforehand and learn about court procedures
- a quiet place to wait
- someone to go with you into the courtroom when giving evidence
- practical help, with forms for example
- access to people who can answer specific questions about the case
- a chance to talk about the case when it has ended and to get more help or information.

Check your understanding

1 Why might someone need help when they have been the victim of a crime?
2 Who can help?
3 Who are the helpers?
4 What help can they offer?
5 Who else can they help other than the victim?
6 What sort of help do they offer to these other people?
7 Why is this sort of help important?

Action

1 Visit your local court to watch how it works.
2 Look at crimes that have been committed in your local area and work out the sort of help victims might need.

Does prison work?

Getting you thinking

Children in prison are 18 times more prone to commit suicide than children of the same age in the community.

Prison Reform Trust

How many?

There are currently over 80,000 men, women and children in prison in England and Wales. The prison population has been rising steadily since 1993 when it was 42,000. There is a higher percentage of people in prison here than in any other country in Western Europe.

Costs and benefits?

Prisons cost £2.2bn a year. With re-offending rates still at about 60 per cent, and over 75 per cent for young offenders, prison is an expensive failure, which has no impact on crime levels or the fear of crime.

Why does it fail?

It damages family relationships and the chances of successful reintegration back into the community. These are two of the most important factors in reducing re-offending. The size of the prison population means that few prisoners get enough education or constructive activity.

Source: Howard League for Penal Reform

What is prison for?

Is prison for:

- punishment – keeping offenders locked up?
- prevention – keeping offenders off the streets?
- rehabilitation – helping offenders deal with the outside world?
- revenge – enabling victims to get their own back?

People hold different views about this but most would agree that at the end of the prison sentence, offenders should be able to fit into society again. If they can't, they will probably re-offend.

Effects of prison

People who have been in prison are much more likely to go back. This is even more true of young people. Prison makes it more difficult to function in the outside world because:

- it breaks contacts with families and friends
- a prison record makes it harder to get a job
- education in prison is often not adequate
- people get out of the work habit
- people lose the skill of organising themselves.

Many people who are in prison are addicted to drink or drugs and, when they come out, re-offend to pay for the habit.

What works?

People who receive community penalties are less likely to re-offend than those given short periods in prison. Within two years of conviction, 39 per cent of people given community penalties are likely to have re-offended compared with 75 per cent of those given prison sentences of six months or less. The probation service supports people who have been given community penalties.

You will investigate the effect of penalties on the reduction of crime.

Intensive Fostering Programme

Working with a carer

Instead of being sent to a young offenders' institution, young people live with a specially trained foster carer for up to 12 months as part of their Supervision Order.

They are expected to cooperate with the conditions of the Order and to comply with the targets set out in their individual programmes.

The programme helps young people to build on skills and knowledge they already have, and to develop new skills and knowledge that will help them to avoid getting into further trouble.

Intensive foster care is not an easy option and young people may find it difficult at times. However, there is a team of people around to help young people in the programme to talk about any issues they have a problem with.

A young offenders' institution

1 How many people in the UK are in prison?
2 How does this compare with the rest of Western Europe?
3 What other penalties can a court impose on an offender? See page 75 for help.
4 What percentages of adults and children re-offend after they have been in prison or a young offenders' institution?

5 Why do so many people re-offend?
6 What is the Intensive Fostering Programme?
7 Explain why this programme is likely to be more or less successful than prison.

Cutting crime in Chirkdale Park

Chirkdale Park in Liverpool was a crime hot spot. A programme was devised to sort out the problems. It included ASBOs for key individuals, and street-based activities for young people. As a result, antisocial behaviour halved in one area and incidents reached an all time low in Chirkdale Park.

Making amends to the community

Offenders sentenced to unpaid work as part of a community order carry out tasks which benefit local people and their neighbourhoods.

They work on developing a children's nature trail in a neighbourhood centre, and improving the Leeds and Liverpool canal and its surroundings. A clean-up squad of young offenders dredged the canal to remove shopping trolleys and bikes.

Offenders carry out their community orders in the area where they committed their crime. This ensures they are punished and also understand their impact on local people.

Source: Community Justice Centre, North Liverpool

Check your understanding

1 How does the number of people in prison in the UK compare with other European countries?
2 What are the effects of sending people to prison?
3 Why are people likely to find it difficult to fit into the community on leaving prison?
4 Why do people say that prison works?
5 Draw up a list of the advantages and disadvantages of sending people to prison. On balance, what is your opinion?

... another point of view?

'We should lock up criminals and throw away the key.'

Do you agree with this statement? Give reasons for your opinion, showing you have considered another point of view.

Who's involved in civil law?

Getting you thinking

Arsenal must pay £2.2m for Spanish teen star

Arsenal must pay the £2.2m bill for taking Fran Merida away from Barcelona's youth ranks after the Spanish club won a civil court ruling against the player yesterday.

Fran Merida, a star of Barcelona's youth squad, was signed by Arsenal. He walked out of Barcelona's stadium, Camp Nou, aged 15 and then signed for Arsenal once he passed his 16th birthday.

In Spain, a footballer under 16 can't sign a professional contract. Cesc Fabregas's success at Arsenal has led to a steady stream of youngsters signing for the Premier League.

Barcelona sued Merida in the Spanish civil court for the costs of his development and his future value. The damages were calculated at £2.2m. Arsenal picked up the bill.

1 Why did Barcelona sue Fran Merida?
2 Why was this a civil issue rather than a criminal case? (See pages 72–3.)
3 Why was Barcelona awarded damages?
4 What did the damages cover?

How does civil law work?

Most civil cases are dealt with in the county court. More complex cases go to the High Court, which also deals with disputes involving large contracts and large claims for damages (usually above £50,000). Most civil cases are held before a judge.

The claimant is the person who starts the case.

⬇

The defendant is the person the claimant takes action against.

⬇

The defendant will be found either 'liable' or 'not liable'.

⬇

If found liable, the defendant is considered to be in the wrong and will usually have to pay damages. This is usually a sum of money which acts as compensation.

You will investigate the roles of people and courts in civil law.

What does the High Court do?

The High Court is divided into three sections, which deal with different aspects of civil law.

- The Queen's Bench Division deals with disputes relating to contracts, general commercial matters, and breaches of duty such as negligence, nuisance or defamation.
- The Chancery Division deals with disputes relating to land, wills, companies and insolvency.
- The Family Division deals with matrimonial matters, including divorce and the welfare of children.

What do lawyers do?

When people go to court they often have lawyers to represent them. Lawyers give advice to people about their disagreements in court. It is the lawyer's job to talk to the judge and jurors for the people who come to court. Each lawyer represents only one person in court. So, if many people are involved in a disagreement, there might be more than one lawyer in court. Lawyers usually sit next to the person they represent in the court.

Do I need a lawyer?

You don't have to use a lawyer – you can represent yourself. If the case is complicated, however, you probably do need a lawyer. If the case is simple and the evidence is very clear, you may not. Courts can be intimidating places, though, because they are very formal and have rules and practices that most people do not understand.

Who makes the judgement?

Most civil cases do not have a jury. Judges hears the cases on their own. They decide who is right and who is wrong by looking at the facts and applying the relevant law. They then give a reasoned judgment. They encourage the claimant and defendant to cooperate with each other and help the parties to settle the case. There is usually a jury in libel and slander cases.

Judges in civil courts no longer wear wigs (see page 77) in order to make the court seem less formal and remote from people.

Yes

- Lawyers know the law and understand the way the court works.
- Lawyers know what to do when the other side doesn't play fair.
- Lawyers know about the judges, and how they like to run their courtrooms.
- Lawyers have gone through trials many times.

No

- You won't win just because you have a lawyer.
- Lawyers can be very expensive.
- Lawyers don't always do the right thing. They can make mistakes.

Check your understanding

1 What is civil law?
2 What is a claimant?
3 What is a defendant?
4 What are damages and why are they paid?
5 What do lawyers do? Why would you use a lawyer?
6 Who makes the judgement in civil cases?

… another point of view?

'A jury should always make the decision about people's guilt.'

Do you agree with this statement? Give reasons for your opinion, showing you have considered another point of view.

Why break the law?

Getting you thinking

For animal rights

Members of a gang involved in campaigning for animal rights were warned today they would be jailed for up to 12 years. They had admitted blackmail against the owners of a farm breeding guinea pigs for medical research. The owners had faced a six-year campaign of terror ending in the theft of an elderly relative's dead body.

Why speed?

Mr B was driving his wife to hospital to have a baby. He was doing 45 miles per hour in a 30mph limit.

Mr J who had only recently passed his test was doing 90 miles per hour on the motorway.

Miss P was driving on a busy motorway with someone right on her tail. She was doing 90 miles per hour but couldn't get out of the way. When she slowed down, the car behind just got closer. She was frightened.

Woman of 78 caught shoplifting

Rachel Jones was in court last week on a charge of shoplifting. She'd been caught with a packet of chicken thighs in her handbag. She said she couldn't afford to buy any more food that week as she'd had to pay the electricity bill so that her supply wouldn't be cut off.

Against globalisation

Germany was trying to recover from the worst violence for six years yesterday after thousands of masked anti-globalisation protesters went on the rampage, pelting police with firebombs and stones, and torching cars in clashes that injured over 900 people.

Police said that 433 officers were injured, 33 of them seriously, in the violence that erupted after a peaceful anti-globalisation demonstration. They wanted their voices to be heard at the summit of G8 leaders who met to discuss global problems.

1 What were the motives for breaking the law in each case?

2 If the people involved in these cases were taken to court, would you expect them to be found guilty or not guilty? Explain your answers.

3 How do you think the animal rights and anti-globalisation protestors justify their actions?

4 Rank the speeding drivers in order of their guilt. Explain your answer.

5 How would you deal with the old lady who had stolen the chicken?

6 How would you compare her crime with that of shoplifters who want to sell the items they steal?

7 Are there any other occasions when you think people ought to be given different punishments for the same crime? Explain why.

You will develop an understanding of why people break the law and consider why we should uphold the law.

Why do people break the law?

In 'Getting you thinking', you found a variety of reasons for breaking the law. Many people would have sympathy with the man who was taking his wife to hospital and the old lady who was hungry. We have probably all been a passenger in a car on the motorway when an inconsiderate driver wants to get past but you just can't get out of the way. It's quite frightening!

When cases come to court, magistrates have some discretion, especially when there are mitigating circumstances. The old lady would probably be treated more sensitively than someone who just wanted to sell the items they had stolen.

Protestors often break the law and justify it by saying that it was the only way to get attention. Whether you think they are right will depend on your point of view. When taken to court, they are usually found guilty of criminal damage or other appropriate offences.

Many of the rights we accept today have been brought about by protest – because people wanted to change things. Have a look at pages 84–5 and consider what it took for women to achieve the vote.

Action

Have there been any protests recently? Did the protestors break the law? What is your opinion of their actions? Explain why.

Check your understanding

1 Why do people break the law?
2 Are there circumstances that make someone's actions more acceptable?
3 Sometimes people want to change the law. Is it acceptable to break the law under such circumstances?
4 How do people who are protesting affect the human rights of others?
5 How does an individual decide whether such actions are acceptable?

... another point of view?

'There is no excuse for breaking the law.'

Do you agree with this statement? Give reasons for your opinion, showing you have considered another point of view.

Whose human rights?

Anti-globalisation and other pressure groups are usually protesting about people's human rights but may limit others' rights in the process. Such actions are against the law and, although they get media attention, the protesters may lose the sympathy of the public. Protestors at Stansted Airport objected to the expansion of air travel but prevented people travelling for work or pleasure. Whether they are damaging property or preventing people going about their business, protestors are interfering with human rights.

Protestors close Stansted airport. Fifty flights were cancelled

Getting elected

Getting you thinking

1 What made Jo decide to become an MP?
2 How did Jo decide which political party to join?
3 Why does Jo think people should have their say?
4 What issues do politicians deal with?
5 What could happen if you don't bother to vote?

'Politics has an impact on every aspect of our lives. From protecting our environment, to the quality of your education or how much you get paid for your Saturday job: all of these things are affected by politicians. I decided to stand for election because I wanted to change things, and not just complain about what I didn't like.

I first became interested in politics when I took part in a Parliamentary debate at my secondary school. We took the parts of the government and opposition parties, and throughout the day we debated various issues such as education, health and defence. It was fast and furious. It brought politics to life for me. The issues that I felt particularly strongly about were education and trying to change the way the electoral system works. I joined the Lib Dems when I was a student, mainly because of these two issues. Over time I became interested in other issues such as civil liberties, the environment and the way businesses work with the community.

For a long time I was determined to take up a career in business and keep politics as an interest for my spare time. But when I was first persuaded to stand for Parliament, I began to realise that politics was my real passion. I decided to follow my ambition to represent my home seat in Parliament. Lots of young people don't seem to be interested in politics. But it's all about everyday life, so it's important to vote and play a part. If you don't, you can't really complain about what happens. Becoming an MP means I can really have my say.'

Jo Swinson, MP for East Dunbartonshire

Getting selected

Jo had to be selected by her **constituency** party before standing for Parliament. The main parties all have approved lists of candidates, although the Labour party allows constituencies to choose people too. The first move, therefore, is to be approved for the list. Once Jo was on the list, she had to go through a selection process as there are often several people who would like to represent the constituency. This involves being interviewed by, and presenting to, the selection committee. Once selected, a candidate has to be nominated. Ten people who can vote in the constituency must sign the nomination paper. The rules are the same for local elections but the Welsh **Assembly** and the Scottish Parliament use **proportional representation**, which means the rules are different. All candidates must put down a deposit of £500, which they get back if they get more than 5 per cent of the vote. The aim is to prevent people standing if they are very unlikely to be elected.

Becoming a Member of Parliament

There are 646 **Members of Parliament** (MPs). They have all been elected to represent a part of the country known as a constituency. Most MPs are chosen by one of the political parties to be its candidate at an election. If the MP wins the election, he or she then becomes the MP who represents everyone in that area.

A few people stand as independents and therefore do not go through the party system. This was the case with a doctor, Richard Taylor, who was furious that the local hospital was to be closed; he stood as an independent and won the seat.

You will discover how an MP gets elected to the House of Commons in order to understand how the electoral system works.

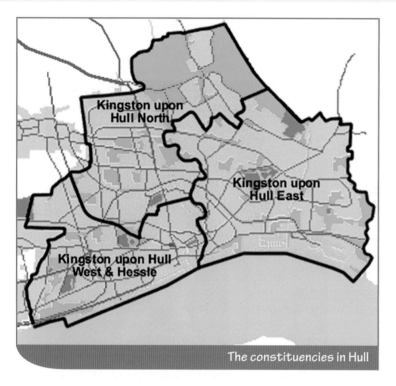

The constituencies in Hull

Fighting an election

You have all seen posters everywhere at election time. The campaign starts the minute a **general election** is declared, if not before. The current government tries to choose the best moment to 'go to the country', which is another way of saying 'call an election'.

Jo Swinson campaigning

To attract voters, the political parties and candidates will:

- send out leaflets telling people what they have done in the past and plan to do in future
- go canvassing
- attract press coverage
- hold public meetings.

Action

1 Who is your local MP? Which political party do they belong to?
2 How many candidates were there at the last election in your constituency? Which parties did they represent? How many votes did each of them win?

Check your understanding

1 How many MPs are there in the House of Commons?
2 What is the name for the area represented by an MP?
3 Do all candidates represent one of the main political parties? Explain your answer.
4 How do candidates try to attract voters?

... another point of view?

'An MP can only represent a constituency if they belong to one of the main political parties.'

Do you agree with this statement? Give reasons for your opinion, showing you have considered another point of view.

Key Terms

assembly: a body of people elected to decide on some areas of spending in a region

canvassing: when people try to persuade others to vote for their party in an election

constituency: the area represented by an MP

general election: an election for a new government. In the UK, these take place at least every five years

Member of Parliament: a person who has been elected to represent a constituency in Parliament

proportional representation: an electoral system in which the number of seats a party wins is roughly proportional to its national share of the vote

What does an MP do?

Getting you thinking

'Entering the House of Commons for the first time was really exciting. I'd worked so hard throughout the election, so winning my seat was great.

As an MP, I hope to make a difference in two ways. Firstly, I can help the 105,000 people who live in my constituency. They raise questions and ask me to help sort out their problems at my regular surgeries. They also contact me by letter, telephone or email. I take a keen interest in local issues and get involved in supporting community initiatives.

Secondly, in the House of Commons, we all debate new laws and changes to existing ones. The detailed work on new laws is carried out in committees and not all in the chamber of the House of Commons, which you tend to see on television. There are also committees that check up on the work of government departments such as education and health.

I think being an MP is the best job in the world because I can really have an effect on the future of the country.'

1. Why was Jo so excited when she entered the House of Commons for the first time?
2. What might you think if you had become an MP and entered the House of Commons for the first time?
3. What did Jo expect to do once she had become an MP?
4. If you had just become an MP, what would you like to change?

Jo Swinson enters the Houses of Parliament for her first day in office

Taking your seat

For a new MP, taking your seat in the **House of Commons** is an exciting event. After what might be years of wanting and waiting to be elected, joining the body that runs the country is a big moment.

MPs debate new laws and policies in the House of Commons. Sometimes debates become furious and the **Speaker** has to act very firmly to keep things in order. On occasion, an MP can be temporarily thrown out of the House of Commons if things get out of hand.

Starting work

MPs have a range of responsibilities.

Their first responsibility is to the people who elected them. There is often a lot of mail from the constituency, which must be dealt with. MPs hold frequent 'surgeries' in their constituency to listen to people's ideas and worries. They take part in debates in the House of Commons and will usually vote with their political party, although they sometimes they follow their conscience.

An MP who has a post in a government department works on government policy and new laws. Some MPs sit on a committee that keeps a check on the activities of the government departments.

You will discover what Members of Parliament do.

The Speaker is an MP, who is chosen by the rest of the MPs to organise business and keep order.

Backbench MPs who don't have jobs in the government or opposition sit on benches at the back.

The government benches: the **Prime Minister** sits at the front surrounded by the **Cabinet**.

The opposition benches: the Leader of the **Opposition** sits at the front, surrounded by the **Shadow Cabinet**.

MPs who don't belong to the main party or largest opposition party also sit on the opposition bench.

Into power

When a political party wins a general election, it forms a government. The leader usually becomes the Prime Minister. His or her first task is to choose the members of the Cabinet. This is the inner circle of people who run the government departments. These departments include:

- the Treasury, which runs the finances of the country
- the Home Office, which is responsible for protecting the public
- the Foreign and Commonwealth Affairs Office, which is responsible for the UK's interests abroad.

Other departments cover:

- health
- defence
- justice
- children, schools and families
- culture, media and sport
- business and enterprise
- environment, food and rural affairs
- transport
- international development.

Wales, Scotland and Northern Ireland also have their own departments. The people who lead these departments are known as **Secretaries of State**. They have assistants who are called **Ministers of State**. There is also a range of other jobs for non-Cabinet MPs in the departments.

After the election, MPs wait for a call from the Prime Minister's office, in the hope of getting a job in the government. Getting your first job in a government department is a step towards becoming a Minister.

Check your understanding

1 What is the responsibility of every MP?
2 What does a Secretary of State do?
3 What do government departments do?
4 Who is in the Cabinet?
5 What is the role of the Cabinet?

... another point of view?

'MPs should always vote with the party they belong to.'

Do you agree with this statement? Give reasons for your opinion, showing you have considered another point of view.

Key Terms

Cabinet: a group of MPs who head major government departments. It meets weekly to make decisions about how government policy will be carried out

House of Commons: the more powerful of the two parts of the British Parliament. Its members are elected by the public

Minister of State: an assistant to a Secretary of State

Opposition: political parties who are not in power

Prime Minister: the leader of the majority party in the House of Commons and the leader of the government

Secretary of State: an MP who is in charge of a government department such as health or defence

Shadow Cabinet: MPs from the main opposition party who 'shadow' MPs who head major government departments

Speaker: the MP elected to act as chairman for debates in the House of Commons

Making votes count

Getting you thinking

In England and Wales

'Young Labour has listened to the excellent campaigns organised by the British Youth Council, UK Youth Parliament, the Votes at 16 Coalition and other youth organisations – Young Labour was keen to spearhead votes at 16 within the Labour Party.'

Olivia Bailey, Vice Chair of Young Labour

In Scotland:

You can go to war for your country, legally have sex, get married or be held responsible for a crime.

Now the Scottish Government has called for the voting age to be lowered to 16 and demanded the powers from Westminster to implement the change in Scotland.

In Jersey:

You can vote in the elections when you are 16 and 17.

1 What are the successes of the Votes at 16 Campaign?
2 What changes does the Scottish Government want in its powers?
3 What else can you do at 16 that indicates that you should be able to vote?
4 Draw up a list of pros and cons of people being able to vote at 16.

How democratic?

Democracy originated in the Athens of Ancient Greece, where all citizens voted on every issue. This was less democratic than it sounds because only a small proportion of the population were classed as 'citizens'. Women and slaves, for example, were excluded.

In the UK, we elect MPs to represent us, because the country is too large for everyone to have their say on all occasions.

Threats to democracy?

In the 2005 General Election, only 60 per cent of the electorate voted. The Labour Party won 55 per cent of the seats in the House of Commons with only 35 per cent of the votes. Some say that this means the United Kingdom is no longer a very democratic country, and ask whether we should change the system or make it easier for people to vote.

You will develop an understanding of how well different voting systems work.

Making your vote count

'**First past the post**' is the system used for general elections in the UK. People have one vote in one constituency and the candidate with the most votes in each constituency becomes the MP for that area. If you added all the votes in the country together, sometimes the winning party does not have the most votes. In each constituency, the candidate with the most votes wins, whether the majority is small or large. If the party that wins the most seats has lots of small majorities, the total vote count may be smaller than that of the opposition.

When all the constituencies in the country are taken together, the proportion of the votes each party won might not be the same as the proportion of seats each party has in the government. This also makes it hard for small parties to win any seats.

Proportional representation

Proportional representation (PR) means that every vote counts. Northern Ireland uses the single transferable vote system (STV) of PR. The constituencies are larger, so each one elects five or six people. Voters put all the candidates in order of preference, putting 1 against their favourite candidate, 2 against their second favourite, and so on. Candidates with the most votes overall win their seats in government.

The Welsh Assembly, the Scottish Parliament and the London Assembly all use a mixture of 'first past the post' and proportional representation. This means that everyone has an elected representative but it can lead to tension between the two groups of elected members. Sometimes one area can have more than its fair share of representatives and this also leads to tension.

Because PR represents people more fairly, it can lead to many small parties in Parliament. This can make it very difficult to make decisions.

One issue: one vote

In a referendum, you vote on a particular issue, so people really feel that they can have an effect. This might encourage more people to vote because they can pick and choose the policies they agree with. It is, however, very difficult for a government to plan ahead if referenda are held on every topic.

Persuading people to vote

Whatever the system used, it is important that the majority of people vote if the country is to be democratic. Here are some possible ways of increasing participation.

Would people vote if they could vote:

- **by post?**
- **before election day?**
- **on Sunday?**
- **online?**
- **at the supermarket?**

Check your understanding

1 Why might low voter turnout be a bad thing for democracy?
2 What does 'first past the post' mean? How does it affect small parties?
3 Why might proportional representation be a fairer system than 'first past the post'?
4 What are the pros and cons of the two systems?
5 Comment on the different ways of helping to increase participation in elections. Do you think they would be successful? Are there any disadvantages? Give reasons.
6 Plan your own campaign to attract young voters and present it to the class.

... another point of view?

'Voting at 16 would make the UK more democratic.'

Do you agree with this statement? Give reasons for your opinion, showing you have considered another point of view.

Key Terms

first past the post: an electoral system where voters have one vote per constituency and the candidate with the most votes wins

One nation or four?

Getting you thinking

A new nation?
Scottish Nationalists have campaigned for a long time to cut the ties with England and Wales and become an independent country.

Yes
- Scotland would be much wealthier and better prepared than many other independent nations around the world
- Revenue from oil and other energy industries could be invested to provide a secure fund to support future generations
- Much of ther political and civil framework needed to run the country is already in place, and the people are highly educated

No
- Without subsidy from the rest of the UK, it is claimed that there would be a tax deficit of up to £11bn
- Promises to cut taxes while increasing spending on pensions and higher education would put the country in the red
- If the bonds that unite Britain were severed, all the countries of the union would suffer economically and culturally

0

1 Why do Scottish Nationalists want to be independent?
2 Why do you think England does not want Scotland to break away?
3 What do you think about it?
4 Do you think that electing people to represent you locally is more democratic than if they are in an assembly or parliament further away? Explain you answer.

Separate or together?

The Scottish Parliament and Welsh Assembly were both set up following referenda. There had been lengthy campaigns for **devolution** in both countries. People wanted devolution because it shifted some power and authority from London to their own capital cities. Scotland voted strongly for its Parliament, which has the ability to raise taxes and pass laws. There are constant debates about how much power the Parliament should have. As you found out in 'Getting you thinking', the Scottish Nationalists want complete independence.

You will find out about the changing relationships between the countries of the UK.

The Powers of the Scottish Parliament

Agriculture, fisheries and forestry
Economic development
Education
Environment
Food standards
Health
Home affairs
Law – courts, police, fire services
Local government
Sport and the Arts
Transport
Training
Tourism
Research and statistics
Social work

The Welsh voted by a narrow margin of 0.6 per cent for their assembly. The Welsh Assembly can spend the UK government's allocation of money to Wales, but it cannot set taxes and make laws because it is not a parliament.

Since the formation of Northern Ireland in 1921, there have been many attempts to create some form of government there. The current assembly has powers to control education, health and local government, but the assembly has often been suspended because of disagreement among Irish politicians.

There are calls for regional assemblies in the rest of the UK too. Many people in regions such as Cornwall feel that their part of the country is distinctive and has different needs from the rest of the UK. People in the North East, however, rejected the idea when a referendum was held. The cost of running a regional assembly was one factor in their decision.

A source of tension?

The UK Parliament allocates funds to the Scottish Parliament and Welsh Assembly. The amount given is based on the objective of a fair distribution across all countries. It is difficult to do this because of the variations within the countries – and the population changes that take place.

The powers held by the different parliaments and assemblies can lead to tensions. In Scotland, for example, students receive more support for higher education than they do in England. The elderly also receive more help with care than they do in England.

As Scottish and Welsh MPs sit in the House of Commons, they can make decisions about such issues in England. English MPs cannot, however, do the same for Scotland or Wales. A pressure group called the Campaign for an English Parliament has been established to promote a parliament in which only English MPs could vote on English affairs.

Check your understanding

1 What's the difference in the amount of power held by the Scottish Parliament and the Welsh Assembly?
2 Why do some people want to have regional governments?
3 Why do some Scots want independence?

... another point of view?

'Devolution means that better decisions are made for a region because they are made locally.'

Do you agree with this statement? Give reasons for your opinion, showing you have considered another point of view.

Key Terms

devolution: the transfer of power from central to regional government

Media influence

Sarah's Law

When eight-year-old Sarah Payne was abducted and murdered, the *News of the World* campaigned for the law to be changed. It wanted lists of known paedophiles to be published so everyone knew where they lived – and actually published its own list.

The campaign led to vigilantism and people were persecuted because they were suspected of being offenders. A paediatrician, a doctor who looks after children, was even chased by protestors who didn't know the difference between the two words.

The *News of the World* closed down its campaign but still claimed the credit when eight years later, the government introduced a six-month pilot scheme in four parts of the country.

It's victory for Sarah

A government minister said:

'This would not have happened without the campaign of the paper. It's a very good beginning and I welcome it.'

The pilot

Concerned parents and carers can seek from their local police details of the background of friends, neighbours and relatives who have unsupervised access to their children. But they must sign a legal agreement not to misuse any information they receive.

1 What effect do you think this campaign had on sales of the *News of the World?*

2 What immediate effect did the campaign have?

3 What was the long-term effect?

4 Why do you think the government decided to pilot the scheme rather than make it law for everyone?

5 If the pilot becomes law, what effect do you think it will have on voters?

What's the message?

Newspapers have one key motive – to make a profit for the owners. Making a profit means selling more papers. Selling more papers means advertisers want to buy space because they will reach more potential customers.

In times when newspaper sales are falling because people get their news from other sorts of media, competition is fierce. The editor of the *News of the World* was well aware that the Sarah's Law campaign would attract customers.

Customers are not innocent players because they tend to buy more papers when the headlines are dramatic.

The government has responded to this campaign but has not met its demands. Instead of creating a public list of offenders, the government gives information to individuals in confidence. Voters may be tempted to support a party that it thinks listens to public opinion – but the ideas often have to be moderated if they are to work in practice.

You will find out how the media influences government policy.

Fox hunting

The Campaign for the Protection of Hunted Animals and the League Against Cruel Sports joined forces to campaign against fox hunting. Both pressure groups had been campaigning for years because they wanted the law to change.

Should the media be controlled?

There are controls on the press as you discovered on pages 102–3 but people often don't think they are strong enough. The courts have become tougher on people's privacy recently. Britney Spears turned this to her advantage when she left rehab.

Although the media does not always present the whole truth, the freedom to communicate is important for democracy. In countries where the government controls media messages, people's human rights are often at risk.

Check your understanding

1 What is the first motive of a newspaper?
2 How can this affect the stories it highlights?
3 What is a pressure group?
4 What is the objective of a pressure group?
5 Why is the media powerful?

... another point of view?

'The freedom to communicate is more important than having a biased media.'

Do you agree with this statement? Give reasons for your opinion, showing you have considered another point of view.

The Mirror says

So it was only ever about ripping animals apart in the name of sport. And most British people don't agree with that. So we rely on our MPs to stop it.

Fox slaughter banned at last

North West League Against Cruel Sports

'Every Saturday during the hunting season we will be out monitoring the activities of one of our local hunts. We do this so that we can gain evidence of the cruelty which is involved in hunting and we use this evidence to inform the press, television and radio, who can bring these cruelties to a wider audience.'

1 What did the League Against Cruel Sports wish to achieve?
2 How did it go about it?
3 Why did it think it was in the right?
4 What role did the media play?
5 Why do you think the government decided to ban fox hunting?

Britney bans leaks

Britney Spears has obtained an emergency injunction from the High Court in London to stop information about her time in treatment being released.

A number of British tabloid newspapers printed stories claiming to be from 'sources close to Spears' describing her time in rehab.

Your Citizenship Enquiry: the research

The theme

Your enquiry is based on a theme which OCR provides each year. To help you get going, you will be given a source book with lots of evidence about the theme. Each year, there will be a different theme which has been chosen because it is topical. You will find lots of material in the newspapers and on the newspaper websites. During your Citizenship course, you should keep your eyes and ears open because the theme will probably be in the news.

Each year's theme will be based on material about:

- citizenship, identity and community cohesion in the UK
- the legal and justice system
- democracy and voting.

You will be given the source book and the Key Question, which relates to the material in the source book. Your teacher will give you guidance on the research. When you have time to carry out your research, you will be given the Task. This will ask you to discuss a particular point of view on the theme.

DNA records of innocent to be kept

Mass arrests have no place in a democratic country

Law 'urgently' needed to protect witnesses

Should Scottish MPs vote in UK parliament?

School bans student for wearing Sikh bangle

Protestors break the law

Your research

There are all sorts of sources of information about Citizenship issues. You might look to some of the following:

Pressure groups

Political parties

Religious organisations

Government – both national and local

Support organisations such as the Citizens Advice Bureau

What sort of information might be useful?

Surveys

Surveys can be very helpful because they can tell you what is going on or what people think. Have a look at pages 182–3 to make sure your questionnaire really works.

You don't always have to carry out the survey yourself. There are many professional organisations that carry out research for pressure groups and interest groups. The evidence they produce is often more powerful than any survey carried out by a small group because they use a bigger sample of people.

Interviews

If you want to find out about people's points of view, you might want to interview people. The questions in the assessment ask you to think about different points of view on an issue. You might be able to find some opinions on the internet but asking people yourself gives you the opportunity to find out the details of why they hold their point of view. It is a good idea to record or take notes in the interview so you can use the information later.

Internet blogs

If you are looking for different points of view, blogs can be useful. Be careful that you know something about the source because some sources of information are more valid than others. Make sure you record why they hold a point of view not just the view itself.

Leaflets and campaign material

Governments produce lots of information to support their policies and offer advice to the general public. Political parties offer manifestos and other information about their policies. Pressure groups often offer persuasive material to support their points of view. It is important to remember to think about other points of view when reading this material as you will be asked to offer different perspectives in the Task.

What have I learnt?

Your Citizenship course will have offered all sorts of material and ideas, which will help you to answer the question in the Task. You will need to use Citizenship concepts and knowledge in your answers. You will also use the vocabulary that is explained in the Key Terms boxes throughout this book.

Make sure you understand the relevant material thoroughly and can use it to explain the ideas involved in the Task.

Check point

Work out your programme of research. Remember that you need evidence of different points of view, so select your sources to meet this need.

When you look at the information in the source book, think about the sorts of questions that might come up.

Think about how what has been going on in the news relates to the information. Although the Task will have been set well before the assessment, you can show your expertise by bringing in relevant, up-to-the-minute examples of your views – and those of others.

Take action

When you have collected your evidence, look at it carefully as you want the most useful material to take into the assessment session. If you have too much, you will just get lost and confused. It is important to select relevant material before you set about the controlled assessment.

You can use four pieces of research to complete your controlled assessment. This might include the results of a survey, the report of an interview, some notes from the internet and a leaflet or two showing different points of view.

Your Citizenship Enquiry: the Task

Carrying out the Task

When you have completed your research on the Theme and Key Question, the time will come to write it up. This is independent work so you won't be able to talk to your friends!

You will be given three viewpoints and you must choose to write about one of them.

If the Theme was 'Should people have the right to protest freely about issues they believe in?', you might be given the following viewpoints:

- **Viewpoint 1**

  People should be able to break the law if they want to protest about an issue.

  The law should be changed to allow such protests.

- **Viewpoint 2**

  People can protest in some areas provided that they do not break the law.

  The law should remain as it is.

- **Viewpoint 3**

  People should only be allowed to protest if they have permission from the police.

  The law should be changed to require permission.

Brian Haw has been protesting about war. He was ordered to limit the area of his protest in Parliament Square to 3 metres

Using the source material

The source material will have given you ideas about all these viewpoints, so think carefully about how you can use the evidence to support your argument. You have plenty of time to write your answer and you may do it at more than one sitting. This means that you have time to work out which arguments and evidence you can use to support your point of view.

Should people be able to protest peacefully?

Using your research

In your source material you might have newspaper articles about animal rights protestors breaking the law to draw attention to their cause. You might want to consider how this affects other people's human rights. Which argument does this support?

You might have come across an article about people being prevented from protesting or police action to limit the effect of a protest. These can be used effectively to support your point of view.

Perhaps you have carried out a survey to gather people's points of view on the issue. You might have found a survey carried out by others – but do think about who has carried it out. A survey by one newspaper might have a very different answer from another newspaper because of its readership.

If you have looked at a pressure group that has strong views on the issue, it will probably offer an opinion. Make sure that the evidence gives reasons for the views that are expressed. A statement of the views alone will not give you support for the argument – which is essential if you are going to get good marks!

Take action

Your evidence is clearly very important when you write up your Enquiry. Gather it all together before the scheduled time for assessment and work out which items you think will be most helpful to support an argument. Look carefully at the source book and try to make a match with the issues but also be aware of new and additional material that will add weight to an argument.

Your answer must:

- **show that you can use and understand the key terms from the source book**
  In your write-up, the examiner will be looking for use of the key terms. If you are using them properly, it shows that you have a sound understanding of the ideas and concepts that you are using to support your point of view. Don't just write from the heart. Use your head as well!

- **explain why you support your chosen viewpoint**
  A statement that you agree with a point of view is not enough. You need to use the Citizenship ideas and key terms to explain why. Make a list of the reasons why you agree with a viewpoint.

- **use your evidence to support your explanation**
  For each of your reasons, look carefully at the evidence you have gathered in your research and in the source book. What have you got that supports each reason? Use it to help to explain each of your reasons. You can attach your evidence rather than writing it all out – but you must explain the connection.

- **evaluate the alternative viewpoints and explain why you do not agree with them**
  Work out why you do not agree with the other points of view. Use your evidence again to show why you disagree – just as you did to support your own point of view.

- **evaluate existing UK law on the issue or how the political system works**
  This issue asks you to think about the law. Other issues might ask you to think about how the political system works. Work out what is currently going on and think about the advantages and disadvantages of the current system. What works and what doesn't work?

- **advocate the changes you may wish to make to UK law on this issue or the political system, or explain why you think the law should remain as it is**
  Once you have come to your conclusions and provided the evidence, you need to explain how you think things should change or stay the same. Explaining is important. Don't just state the change you think should happen or that there should be no change. What effect would your decision have?

- **communicate well by writing clearly and legibly and by using suitable punctuation and grammar**
  You have plenty of time to do this piece of work so there is time to check that you have written it well. There are marks for good communication. Make the most of them!

Index

William Collins' dream of knowledge for all began with the publication of his first book in 1819. A self-educated mill worker, he not only enriched millions of lives, but also founded a flourishing publishing house. Today, staying true to this spirit, Collins books are packed with inspiration, innovation and practical expertise. They place you at the centre of a world of possibility and give you exactly what you need to explore it.

Collins. Do more.

Published by Collins
An imprint of HarperCollinsPublishers
77–85 Fulham Palace Road
Hammersmith
London
W6 8JB

Browse the complete Collins catalogue at
www.collinseducation.com

© HarperCollinsPublishers Limited 2009
ISBN-13 978-0-00-732439-2

Jenny Wales asserts her moral right to be identified as the author of this work.

British Library Cataloguing in Publication Data
A Catalogue record for this publication is available from the British Library

Cover design: Angela English
Cover image: istock Photo
Internal design: Thomson
Picture research: Suzanne Williams
Illustrations: Yane Christensen, Sylvie Poggio Artists; Aetos Ltd, Jerry Fowler
Printed and bound by: Graficas Estella

Acknowledgements

The publishers would like to thank the following for permission to reproduce photographs. The page number is followed, where necessary, by t (top), c (centre), b (bottom), l (left), or r (right):

p4 (l) Tim Page/Still Pictures; p4 (c) Dominic Lipinski/PA Wire/PA Photos; p4 (r) Empics/PA Photos; p5 (l) Neil McAllister/Alamy; p5 (c) George Doyle/Stockbyte/Getty Images; p5 (r) Jenny Wales; p6 Alex Bartell/Science Photo Library; p7 istockphoto; p8 (l) Lucinda Marland/Janine Wiedel Photolibrary/Alamy; p8 (tc) Hartmut Schwarzbach/argus/Still Pictures; p8 (bc) Ton Koene/Picture Contact/Alamy; p8 (tr) Joerg Boethling/Still Pictures; p8 (br) Steven Clevenger/Corbis; p9 (l) Tim Page/Still Pictures; p9 (r) Sipa Press/Rex Features; p10 (b) John Walmsley; p12 Digital Vision/Getty Images; p13 (t) Justin Kase zonez/Alamy; p13 (b) Dave Bowman/Alamy; p14 (tl) Kevin Peterson/Photodisc/Getty Images; p14 (tc) Kevin Peterson/Photodisc/Getty Images; p14 (tr) Barbara Penoyar/Photodisc/Getty Images; p14 (bl) Kevin Peterson/Photodisc/Getty Images; p14 (br) Kevin Peterson/Photodisc/Getty Images; p16 (tc) Peter Titmuss/Alamy; p16 (cl) Stuart Rimmer/Alamy; p16 (cr) Neil McAllister/Alamy; p16 (bl) Neil McAllister/Alamy; p16 (br) David Hoffman Photo Library/Alamy; p18 Harriet Cummings/Alamy; p20 Empics/PA Photos; p21 Malcolm Case-Green/Alamy; p22 (tl) Alex Segre/Alamy; p22 (tc) Neil McAllister/Alamy; p22 (tr) Martin Jenkinson/Alamy; p22 (c) Colorblind/Stone/Getty Images; p22 (b) Dominic Lipinski/PA Wire/PA Photos; p24 James Brey/istockphoto; p26 The SMASH Youth Project; p27 courtesy of Costain.com and Katesgrove Primary School; p28 (t) Friedrich Stark/Das Fotoarchiv/Still Pictures; p28 (b) Fairtrade; p29 George Doyle/Stockbyte/Getty Images; p30 (tl) Glyn Thomas/Alamy; p30 (tr) Sally and Richard Greenhill/Alamy; p30 (c) Motors/Alamy; p30 (b) Melanie Stetson Freeman/The Christian Science Monitor/Getty Images; p32 (l) Melanie Stetson Freeman/The Christian Science Monitor/Getty Images; p32 (tr) Slim Aarons/Getty Images; p32 (br) Richard Gardner/Rex Features; p33 Simon Hadley/

Alamy; p34 (l) Steve Williams/Rex Features; p35 (t) Sipa Press/Rex Features; p35 (b) Top Photo Group/Rex Features; p36 (t) Shout/Rex Features; p36 (b) Alex Segre/Alamy; p38 (l) fine art/Alamy; p38 (r) Rex Features; p39 (t) Issouf Sarogo/AFP/Getty Images; p39 (b) PumpAid; p40 (t) People & Planet; p40 (b) People & Planet; p42 Tim Sloan/AFP/Getty Images; p43 East Sussex County Council; p46 Jenny Wales; p47 (b) David Hoffman/Photofusion; p48 People & Planet; p50 Manchester Evening News; p51 (t) Tim Ockenden/PA Photos; p51 (b) Tim Ockenden/PA Photos; p52 People & Planet; p53 Derby College Students' Union; p54 (l) Rex Features; p54 (c) PA Photos; p54 (r) Magnum Photos; p55 (l) Aldbourne Youth Council /www.4children.org.uk; p55 (c) Denis Farrell/AP/PA Photos; p55 (r) United Nations Photo Library; p56 (tr) nagelestock.com/Alamy; p56 (tl) Rex Features; p56 (br) Rex Features; p58 (cl) Steven Clevenger/Corbis; p58 (cr) Corbis; p58 (tr) Dr Heinz Linke/istockphoto; p58 (b) Shout/Rex Features; p59 (l) Maggie Murray/Photofusion Picture Library/Alamy; p59 (r) Scope West Sussex; p60 (tl) Adina Tovy/Robert Harding Picture Library Ltd/Alamy; p60 (cl) Neil Holmes/Holmes Garden Photos/Alamy; p60 (tr) Sally and Richard Greenhill/Alamy; p60 (bl) Paul Doyle/Alamy; p60 (br) Guy Somerset/Alamy; p61 Telegraph & Argus Bradford; p63 (r) Graham Oliver/Alamy; p65 (tl) David Montford/Photofusion; p65 (bl) Getty Images; p65 (c) Magnum Photos; p65 (r) Ulrike Preuss/Photofusion; p66 (tl) Tim Pannell/Corbis/Alamy; p66 (tc) TravelStockCollection/Homer Sykes/Alamy; p66 (tr) David Hoffman Photo Library/Alamy; p66 (cr) Paul M Thompson/Alamy; p66 (br) Fotex Medien Agentur GMBH/Rex Features; p66 (bc) Yavuz Arslan/Black Star/Alamy; p66 (c) Alexandra Carlile/Elvele Images Ltd/Alamy; p66 (bl) Stefan M. Prager/Redferns; p68 Sally & Richard Greenhill; p70 (l) Lawrence Wiles/Alamy; p70 (c) Richard Gardner/Rex Features; p70 (tr) Loop Delay/WestEnd61/Rex Features; p70 (br) Ron Levine/Digital Vision/Getty Images; p71 Rex Features; p72 (tl) Nikos Vinieratos/Rex Features; p72 (tr) Chris Jackson/Getty Images; 72 (br) Gareth Cattermole/Getty Images; p76 Rex Features; p78 Chris Pearsall/Alamy; p80 (l) Vikram Raghuvanshi/istockphoto; p80 (c) Anna Milkova/istockphoto; p80 (r) Umbar Shakir/istockphoto; p81 Citizens Advice Bureau; p82 International Criminal Court-CPI; p83 Sipa Press/Rex Features; p84 (t) George Cruikshank/photo by Spencer Arnold/Hulton; Archive/Getty Images; p84 (bl) PA Photos; p84 (br) Votes at 16 coalition; p85 Library of Congress; p86 (t) Vano Shlamov/AFP/Getty Images; p86 (b) Desmond Kwande/AFP/Getty Images; p87 (t) Sipa Press/Rex Features; p87 (b) Denis Farrell/AP/PA Photos; p88 (bl) David Hartley/Rex Features; p88 (tl) Jenny Matthews/Alamy; p88 (tc) Buzz Pictures/Alamy; p88 (tr) Purestock/Alamy; p88 (br) Daniel Sambraus/STOCK4B/Getty Images; p89 Aldbourne Youth Council /www.4children.org.uk; p90 Shout/Alamy; p91 (l) Peter Marshall/Alamy; p91 (r) Ulrike Preuss/Photofusion; p92 No2ID; p94 UK Youth Parliament; p95 Amnesty International; p96 Stuart Atkins/Rex Features; p97 Mark Bourdillon/Alamy; p98 (l) Alisdair Macdonald/Rex Features; p98 (r) E. M. Welch/Rex Features; p99 Scope West Sussex; p100 (tl) Helene Rogers/Alamy; p100 (tc) Mark Boulton/Alamy; p100 (tr) Tom Grill/Photographer's Choice/Getty Images; p100 (bl) Chris Ratcliffe/Rex Features; p100 (bc) Rex Argent/Alamy; p100 (br) Comstock Select/Corbis; p101 courtesy of number10.gov.uk; p102 (l) George Pimentel/WireImage/Getty Images; p102 (c) Rex Features; p102 (r) Tim Rooke/Rex Features; p104 Norbert Michalke/imagebroker/Alamy; p106 AFP/Getty Images; p107 (t) AFP/Getty Images; p107 (b) Bettmann/Corbis; p108 AFP/Getty Images; p110 (t) Stewart Golf; p110 (b) istockphoto; p111 Mychele Daniau/AFP/Getty Images; p112 (l) Veronica Garbutt/Rex Features; p112 (r) Mark Read/Camfed; p114 Sri Lanka/Beatrice Progida/October 2006-118; p116 United Nations Photo Library; p117 (tl) Marie Frechon/United Nations Photo Library; p117 (tr) R LeMoyne/United Nations Photo Library; p117 (br) drawing by a former child soldier of the armed group National Liberation Forces, Burundi, 2006 used by permission of Coalition to Stop the use of Child Soldiers; p126 (l) Neil Cooper/Alamy; p126 (c) Nilsson-Maki, Kjell/Cartoonstock; p126 (r) Paul Glendell/Alamy; p127 (l) Jeff Blackler/Rex Features; p127 (c) Paula Solloway/Photofusion Picture Library/Alamy; p127 (r) Harmut Schwarzbach/Still Pictures; p128 Mike Abrahams/Alamy; p129 Daniel Berehulak/Getty Images; p130 Which?; p132 istockphoto; p134 Confederation of British Industry; p135 Unite the Union; p137 (l) David Frazier/Corbis/Alamy; p137 (r) Jamie Dupliss/istockphoto; p138 uk retail/Alan King/Alamy; p139 Horizon International Images Limited/Alamy; p140 (t) National Motor Museum/Motoring Picture Library/Alamy; p141 Ulrike Preuss/Photofusion; p142 Ray Tang/Rex Features; p143 Tetra Images/Getty Images; p144 (bl) Phototake Inc/Alamy; p144 (tr) BP; p144 (br) Arriva; p145 (l) Paul Glendell/Alamy; p145 (r) MJ Kim/Getty Images; p146 (tl) Grantly Lynch/UK Stock Images Ltd/Alamy; p146 (tc) Jeff Blackler/Rex Features; p146 (tr) John Birdsall/PA Photos; p146 (cr) Jeff Blackler/Rex Features; p146 (br) Peter L Hard/Alamy; p146 (cl) Joe Fox/Alamy; p146 (c) Paula Solloway/Photofusion Picture Library/Alamy; p146 (bb) Tim Boyle/Getty Images; p147 (t) David J. Green/Alamy; p147 (b) Nikola Gruev/Wikimedia; p148 Harmut Schwarzbach/Still Pictures; p149 Kim Naylor/Divine Chocolate; p150 Nilsson-Maki, Kjell/Cartoonstock; p151 Kubes Tomas/isifa

Image Service s.r.o/Alamy; p152 Saul Loeb/AFP/Getty Images; p153 Neil Cooper/Alamy; p162 (l) Mauro Carraro/Rex Features; p162 (c) David Taylor/Alamy; p162 (r) Big Green Challenge; p163 (l) Roger Cracknell 05/London/Alamy; p163 (c) Michel Spingler/AP/PA Photos; p163 (r) David Williams/The Photolibrary Wales/Alamy; p164 (tl) Mauro Carraro/Rex Features; p164 (bl) Joe Gough/istockphoto; p164 (r) Paul Francis/Alamy; p165 Drayton Manor High School; p168 (t) The Word, www.respect-theword.com; p168 (c) Len Copland; p168 (b) RADIO SALAAM SHALOM "Muslims and Jews Talking Together"; p170 Rex Features; p171 (l) Team London Bridge; p171 (r) Leicestershire Chamber of Commerce; p172 (t) David Taylor/Alamy; p172 (b) Times Newspapers Ltd/Rex Features; p173 Big Green Challenge; p174 North News & Pictures; p176 Wiltshire County Council Development Service for Young People; p177 Stoke-on-Trent City Council; p178 Christa Stadtler/Photofusion; p179 Paula Solloway/Alamy; p189 Tim Graham/Alamy; p190 S.P. Rayner/istockphoto; p191 (l) Brad Killer/istockphoto; p191 (r) Andy Lauwers/Rex Features; p193 (l) Angela Hampton Picture Library/Alamy; p193 (r) Adrian Sherratt/Alamy; p194 Phil Cole/Getty Images; p196 (t) Dori O'Connell/istockphoto; p196 (b) Michel Spingler/AP/PA Photos; p197 Chris Radburn//PA Photos; p198 Jo Swinson MP; p199 (l) Hull City Council; p199 (r) Jo Swinson MP; p200 Paul Hackett; p201 Empics/PA Photos; p202 National Youth Agency; p204 David Williams/The Photolibrary Wales/Alamy; p207 (t) Peter Jordan//PA Photos; p207 (b) Jackson Lee/Starmax/EMPICS Entertainment/PA Photos; p208 John Walmsley; p210 (t) Angela Hampton Picture Library/Alamy; p210 (b) Johnny Grieg Portraits/Alamy; p211 Roger Cracknell 05/London/Alamy.

The publishers gratefully acknowledge the following for permission to reproduce copyright material. Every effort has been made to trace copyright holders, but in some cases this has proved impossible. The publishers would be happy to hear from any copyright holder that has not been acknowledged.

Thanks to:
Crown copyright material is reproduced with the permission of the Controller of HMSO and the Queen's Printer for Scotland: p. 6, 10, 15, 17, 57, 60, 62, 101, 136, 137, 167, 173;
Oxford University Press for the use of statistics from the Human Development Report 2007/8: p. 38;
Population Reference Bureau for use of HIV/AIDS statistics: p. 116.